Christology and Ethics

Edited by

F. LeRon Shults and Brent Waters

WILLIAM B. EERDMANS PUBLISHING COMPANY

GRAND RAPIDS, MICHIGAN / CAMBRIDGE, U.K.

© 2010 Wm. B. Eerdmans Publishing Co.

Published 2010 by
Wm. B. Eerdmans Publishing Co.
2140 Oak Industrial Drive N.E., Grand Rapids, Michigan 49505 /
P.O. Box 163, Cambridge CB3 9PU U.K.

Printed and bound in Great Britain by
Marston Book Services Limited, Didcot

16 15 14 13 12 11 10   7 6 5 4 3 2 1

Library of Congress Cataloging-in-Publication Data

Christology and ethics / edited by F. LeRon Shults and Brent Waters.
   p.   cm.
   Includes index.
   ISBN 978-0-8028-4509-2 (pbk.: alk. paper)
   1. Christian ethics — Congresses. 2. Jesus Christ — Person and offices —
Congresses. I. Shults, F. LeRon. II. Waters, Brent.

 BJ1189.C52 2010
 241 — dc22

                                              2009048016

www.eerdmans.com

Contents

Contents

Acknowledgments

This book grew out of a conference sponsored by the Stead Center for Ethics and Values, and held on the campus of Garrett-Evangelical Theological Seminary, March 3-4, 2007. In addition to thanking the contributors to this volume, who also served as conference lecturers, we would like to thank President Philip Amerson and Dean Lallene Rector of the seminary for their generous support and extravagant hospitality. We are also greatly indebted and grateful to Erik Wiebe who served as conference coordinator. Quite literally the conference would not have occurred and this book would not have been written without his tireless efforts.

F. LeRon Shults
Brent Waters

Prologue

F. LeRon Shults

What is the relation between faithful teaching about the reality of Christ and teaching faithfulness to the way of Christ? How is christological doctrine related to theological judgments about normative human agency? The title of this collection of essays — Christology *and* Ethics — points to our shared concern that the *relation* between these disciplines within Christian theology requires renewed attention and creative reformulation. All of the authors hold in common a desire to overcome disciplinary xenophobia and develop fresh ways of tending to these perennial questions.

The emergence of this new interdisciplinary space has been made possible by developments in biblical studies and historical theology, as well as by shifts in philosophical categories and cultural interpretation. To varying degrees, the following chapters appropriate and reinforce these developments and shifts. The epilogue will tease out some of the material and methodological differences and similarities among the proposals, but this prologue focuses on briefly introducing some of the factors that contributed to the bifurcation of Christology and ethics and some of the developments that have helped shape a new conceptual (and practical and liturgical) space within which they can now be brought together in new ways.

First, we can identify developments within the field of Christology itself. In the early modern period, especially in Protestant Scholastic theology, Christology "proper" increasingly became focused on the *person* of Christ — in distinction from soteriology, which discussed the *work* of Christ. This abstraction of the treatment of the identity of Jesus Christ from the agency of Jesus Christ in the thematic organization of doctrinal formulation contributed to the abstraction of "Christology" (especially the doctrine of the incarnation) from concrete questions of Christian moral discernment.

Soteriology itself was often articulated primarily in terms of the salvation of individual souls based on a past event (the death of Christ) that enacted retributive justice ensuring a future beatific state (for the elect). Discussions about the concrete forms of Christian life in community in the present were typically delayed to later sections on the "application" of Christ's work by the Spirit. This early modern dichotomizing tendency played itself out in other distinctions, which became increasingly hardened: justification vs. sanctification, faith vs. works, doctrine vs. piety. The separation of themes like Pneumatology, ecclesiology, sacramentology, and eschatology from Christology contributed to the sense that theological "ethics" as a discipline is subordinate — logically, chronologically, and even ontologically.

While few theologians today would aim to erase the *distinction* between these aspects of Christian thought and life, a growing number are concerned that the way in which they have been *separated* has had a deleterious effect on both our understanding of and our participation in the way of Jesus. Feminist and liberation theologians in particular have been critical of the abstraction of Christology from ethics in early modern (as well as much ancient and medieval) theology. They have pointed out how such dichotomizing can be (and has been) used to reinforce political forces of subordination, and have called for articulations of Christian faith that account for the experience of those who have been oppressed on the basis of race, class, or gender.

Second, we can identify tendencies prevalent with the tradition of theological ethics itself that have also contributed to its distanciation from Christology. For example, the individualistic focus of soteriology was mirrored by the ethical focus among Scholastics on the vices and virtues of individuals. Here too the concrete and dynamic concerns of ecclesial and political relations were too often subordinated to questions about the states or powers of individual souls. Several of the essays in this book attempt to overcome this separation by paying special attention to the social and embodied dimensions of human life, integrating discussions about the incarnation, atonement, Trinity, and eschatology with analyses of the conditions for and evaluation of human moral agency in community.

Moreover, some of the most popular options in theological ethics have been framed in such a way that complicates their relation to Christology. For example, some forms of divine command theory based theological ethics primarily on the legal prohibitions and injunctions of the absolute will of God. The role of Christology in such a case is only derivative; the death of Jesus satisfies divine justice or the life of Jesus fulfils God's commands, but the significance of Christology is dependent on a prior law or command. Similarly, many versions of natural law ethics could be expounded without immediate reference to the life, death, and resurrection of Jesus. In such cases, theological ethics was based primarily on the structures of creation rather than the dynamics of redemption.

Although most proponents of these theories *also* tried to buttress them with reference to Christology, the latter did not play a primarily generative role in much theological ethics. Several of the essays in this book explicitly address these challenges by exegetical attention to biblical themes that have often been bracketed from or marginalized in both Christology and ethics, such as resurrection, Trinity, communion, and eschatology. Our proposals are not intended to be exhaustive but to promote further exploration of the interconnection between our disciplines and broader theological concerns. More attention will need to be paid to the links between Christology, ethics, and other doctrinal loci (such as Pneumatology) as well as other resources for moral reflection.

This brings us to a third set of developments that have impacted the conceptual space within which Christology and ethics interact. Here I have in mind the broader discourse in philosophy, culture, and science on the categories by which we make sense of and respond to human moral agency. The last two chapters deal extensively with some of these scientific and philosophical developments, so I will limit myself here to a shift in late modern discourse about "goodness," a theme that clearly crosses over the concerns of theological ethics and Christian articulation of the manifestation of God in the life, death, and resurrection of Jesus Christ. The idea of "the Good" has been a regulative principle for ethics or moral reasoning in Western philosophy at least since Plato's *Republic,* and Christology aims to explicate the way in which Jesus mediates the goodness (love, righteousness, etc.) of God.

In late modern discourse, however, general concepts of *goodness* (or the Good) have come under suspicion. This is not only because of the nominalist resistance to generic or abstract universals such as "goodness" but also because of the social critique of the contextual embeddedness of all human moral judgments. Moreover, ethical dialogue is increasingly focused on the role that the moral valuation of finite *goods* plays in the organization and orientation of human life. Every moral decision involves adjudicating the distribution of some goods — material or otherwise. Morality and justice are understood increasingly as political categories, as concepts that shape and are shaped by the concrete ways in which power is used in human communities.

While this may seem to be a challenge to Christology, insofar as it wishes to resist moral relativism, it is also an opportunity to retrieve the politically liberating power of Jesus' own way of acting in relation to his neighbors. In fact, as several of the chapters will argue, Christian ethics does not need or should not want a "generic" or universal moral standard that is abstracted from Christ's way of acting in the world. The practical concrete struggle over acquiring and securing particular "goods," which creates conflict and debates in ethics, is a common theme in Jesus' teaching about the truly good life within the reign of divine peace. This is why the authors of this book applaud holistic models that attend to differentiated wholes rather than separated parts (or substances). This plays itself out in approaches to Christology (and soteriology) that embrace the *totus Christus* (the whole life of Christ) and approaches to ethics that insist on the embodied and social mediation of personal agency.

This shared interest in the generative value of intrinsically relational and dynamic categories helps to explain some of the recurrent themes in these essays. For example, we desire to explore and develop models of integrating Christology and ethics that are especially attentive to contextuality, embedded both within practical concerns for ecclesiological transformation and within conceptual concerns for incorporating broader relational Christian intuitions.

Some of the authors are inspired primarily by a desire to respond to more internal pressures for reform, such as insights from biblical exegesis and the recovery of traditional resources. Others are motivated to engage more external pressures, including philosophical, scientific, and cultural shifts in late modernity. What we all share is the conviction that these challenging developments also provide fresh opportunities for the ongoing task of linking the study of Jesus Christ and theological reflection on normative human agency.

1. The Incarnation and the Christian Moral Life

Brent Waters

The incarnation of the Word of God is the formative moment of the Christian moral life. In this act God completes the reconciliation with creation and its human creatures that was initiated in the covenant with Israel. In and through Jesus Christ there is both a divine judgment upon the sin that separates humans from their Creator, and a pardon that reinstates their fellowship; a simultaneous negation and affirmation of the human condition. Consequently, to speak of Christian ethics is unavoidably and properly to speak about Christology in general and the incarnation in particular.

Yet it must be emphasized that it is not only the birth and life of Jesus that bears the weight of Christian moral deliberation. Jesus is not merely an exemplary figure whose life and teachings should be emulated, but the one who through his death, resurrection, and exaltation is the savior of the world. The Word made flesh is also the end or *telos* of the creation that was created in and through Christ. The doctrinal claims of Christology, especially in respect to the incarnation, provide the proper vocabulary of Christian moral discourse. This is not to discount the life and ministry of Jesus, but to recognize that their revelatory and didactic power presupposes broader theological convictions and dogmatic confessions. Or in liturgical terms, the incarnation is not confined to the seasons of Christmas and Epiphany, but permeates the entire calendar from Advent through Ordinary Time.

To illustrate this relationship between Christology and Christian ethics, this chapter examines and explicates (1) the crucifixion, resurrection, and exaltation of Jesus Christ as the culmination of the incarnation; (2) the corresponding virtues of charity, hope, and obedience which these events inculcate; and (3) how the church's worship, sacraments, and ministry form and enact these virtues. Given the broad range of these topics the following inquiry is necessarily terse, even cursory, but it serves to indicate what is at stake in the relationship between Christology and Ethics, and to plot terrain for further exploration.

Crucifixion, Resurrection, and Exaltation

The crucifixion, resurrection, and exaltation of Jesus Christ mark the tripartite culmination of the incarnation. Together they establish the reconciliation between Creator and creation. Although these are not discrete events that can stand on their own — for none in isolation from the others has the power to save and reconcile — each may be examined separately in order to highlight a pertinent characteristic for the purpose of this inquiry.

In the crucifixion there is *suffering*. This is apparent in Jesus' pain and misery, but more extensively he is broken by bearing the weight of the sins of the world. Jesus, the Word made flesh, suffers the judgment of God against the sinful creatures among whom he has dwelt. In this respect, Jesus not only suffers with humans but also suffers on their behalf. Moreover, although Jesus bears the sins of the world, his death also amplifies the divine judgment against the sinful acts that result in his execution: the flesh which the Word became destroys the means of its own reconciliation with God. What remains unresolved at Golgotha is how this judgment will be rendered.

The gospel, of course, does not end with Good Friday, so the verdict is not announced until Easter Sunday. In the resurrection of Jesus Christ it is not only Jesus' life and ministry that is *vindicated*, but also the created order in which the Word of God is incarnate. In raising Jesus from the dead the goodness of creation is reaffirmed, and the promise of its full redemption and reconciliation with its Creator is vouchsafed. Following Oliver O'Donovan, in the resurrection God has not allowed the human creature to "uncreate" what God has created.[1] The flesh which the Word became is not rejected and abandoned by God.

---

1. See Oliver O'Donovan, *Resurrection and Moral Order: An Outline for Evangelical Ethics* (Grand Rapids: Eerdmans, 1986), pp. 13-15.

This steadfast refusal to abandon creation sets the stage for the *joy* of Christ's exaltation. The one who died for the sins of the world, and who in being raised from the dead vindicates its created order, is also the exalted one who governs creation and its creatures. It is Christ's rule that now governs the people, nations, and affairs of the world, even when that rule is not acknowledged. It is, however, a rule unlike any earthly governance, for it is predicated upon the supremacy of grace and forgiveness which temporal judgment and retribution have been ordered to serve. In conquering death Christ is made the reconciler who governs the vindicated creation as such. Consequently, the flesh which the Word became remains, through the power of the Holy Spirit, a suitable dwelling.

Although the characteristics of suffering, vindication, and joy have been noted sequentially, it is important to emphasize that they cannot be separated, for together they constitute the singular, but tripartite, culmination of the incarnation. No single characteristic can stand on its own, and if one is emphasized in isolation from or to the detriment of the other two the Christian moral life is distorted. This distortion may be illustrated by observing three instances.

When suffering, for instance, is emphasized to the virtual exclusion of a vindicated creation and the joy of Christ's exalted rule, there is a tendency to assign human suffering a redemptive significance it cannot bear. Lingering too long at Golgotha reduces Jesus to an admirable but tragic figure. Consequently, if Jesus' death is to have any redemptive purchase, then disciples of every generation must replicate his sacrifice in their own suffering. This premise turns suffering into the goal of discipleship rather than a possible, or in some cases probable, consequence. The disciple of Jesus Christ must partake of his suffering by joining him on his cross. This quest to suffer, however, fails to recognize that it is not Jesus' suffering that is redemptive. Rather, his suffering results from his obedience to God that cannot be borne by any creature but only by the incarnate Word. Followers of Jesus Christ are not called to suffer, but suffering may be a consequence of their obedient discipleship. In failing to give Easter Sunday and Ascension Day their due, the resulting moral vision is consigned to an endless repetition of Good Friday in which the world is never vindicated and is devoid of joy.

A similar distortion occurs if one remains fixed at the empty tomb. Christians rightfully celebrate the resurrection of Jesus Christ as the vindication of created order. Yet to remain fixated on this act is also to reduce Jesus to a heroic figure who has earned God's favor through his wise teaching and wondrous deeds, a figure not unlike Hercules of Greek mythology. Herein lies a subtle trap: if Jesus can earn God's favor then so also can his disciples. They too can become heroes. Consequently, God's vindication is corrupted into self-vindication. Easter is merely an object lesson demonstrating the power of the will to will the Good. Such a stance, however, fails to acknowledge that much of the suffering leading to Good Friday is a result of all failed attempts at self-justification, and also a failure to recognize that the rule of the ascended Christ is one of grace and not works. In elevating the vindication of the resurrection to the detriment of the suffering of the crucifixion and the joy of the exaltation, a Christian tries to become, following Karl Barth, her own savior.[2]

In focusing too narrowly on the rule of the exalted Christ, there is a tendency to equate inclusion or association with what is good or right. To acknowledge Christ's rule is to place oneself on the right side of history; to affiliate with the victors rather than the vanquished. Consequently, whatever is presumably said or done for the sake of Christ's rule is by definition what is good or right, a stance that is contradicted by history and present practice. How may this contradiction be explained? It is a result of distorting joy into moral superiority. Such presumed and unwarranted superiority is insufficiently self-critical because of its deficient eschatology, for the joy of Christ's exaltation is largely anticipatory. It fails to recognize that the rule of the exalted Christ is an interim regime for the present time between the times.

In short, it confuses the ascension with the *parousia,* and in doing so fails to acknowledge that although suffering *will be* redeemed in Christ, that is not presently the case, and it fails to comprehend that a vindicated creation is *not* synonymous with its full and complete redemption. The end of suffering, the end of creation's redemption, can only occur with the end of Christ's rule. For the end of reconciliation with God is eternal fellowship with the triune God in which the political metaphors of the kingdom of God and Christ the King are discarded because they are no longer needed. Consequently, whatever moral judgments and acts are made in this interim rule of Christ, they

---

2. See Karl Barth, *Church Dogmatics,* IV/1, ed. G. W. Bromiley and T. F. Torrance, trans. G. W. Bromiley (Edinburgh: T. & T. Clark, 1975), pp. 769-70.

are always tentative, penultimate, subject to critical appraisal and reform, and predicated upon grace, forgiveness, and reconciliation.

Charity, Hope, and Obedience

For the purpose of this chapter, it is proposed that the characteristics of suffering, vindication, and joy promote the corresponding virtues of charity, hope, and obedience.[3] "Virtue" refers not only to practices that form the character and shape the deeds of individuals, but also serve as metaphors that shape a moral vision in respect to broader issues of social and political ordering in light of the crucifixion, resurrection, and exaltation of Jesus Christ. These virtues are interwoven, presupposing and reinforcing each other, but again each one may be examined separately.

In his crucifixion Jesus surrenders his life for the sake of others. In this respect, it is the supreme act of *charity*, for the charitable life is a life lived for others. This is the central message of the incarnation, in which God freely gives himself for the sake of creation and its creatures. It is important to note, however, that this act is based on need and not desert. The Word becomes flesh not because humans deserve a reconciler, but because they need one. Charity, therefore, is primarily a response to the needs of others. A Christian, then, is called to live a life that is oriented toward satisfying these needs. On rare occasions this calling may require sacrificing one's life for the sake of others, but more routinely it entails acts, deeds, and participation in social structures and political institutions in which priority is given to providing what is needed and not necessarily what is deserved.

In his resurrection, the life of Jesus — and therefore as the Word made flesh — creation's order — is vindicated. In this respect this act

---

3. The reason why *faith* is not included as one of the virtues examined is that, given the narrow scope of this inquiry, faith serves as an overarching virtue or quality that links other virtues together with the common object of Christian belief. The God revealed in Jesus Christ and upon whom Christians place their faith is the same God who inspires and commands charity, hope, and obedience. Admittedly charity could also serve, following St. Paul (1 Corinthians 13), such an overarching role. Again, given the limited scope of this inquiry, charity is construed narrowly as an orientation toward the other, but presupposes a larger, Pauline concept of love of God and neighbor as the operative principle of the Christian moral life.

embodies the virtue of *hope,* for the hopeful life is one that entrusts its destiny to God. The incarnation — and therefore the lives of creatures with whom the Word has dwelt and dwells — does not end with a life-less corpse. Rather, it ends in eternal life and fellowship with the triune God. The virtue of hope requires humans to renounce any attempt at mastering their fate, as exemplified in a desperate striving to construct immortal lineages, histories, empires, or, in a fit of technologically in-spired hubris, personal immortality. Christians instead entrust their destiny to that which was promised on Easter Sunday. Consequently, hope is the affirmation that it is God, not death, who speaks the final and eternal word of human life and lives.

In his exaltation, Jesus Christ assumes the authority to govern the world, inspiring in his disciples a response of joy. In this respect, to honor the rule of Christ requires the virtue of *obedience,* for the joyful life is also an obedient life. To obey the commands of Jesus Christ is a re-sponse of joyful gratitude for the gift of divine grace. Practically the rule of Christ is exercised by granting a limited authority to ecclesial, social, and political offices that are authorized to perform certain functions, issue commands, and render judgments.[4] It must be emphasized, how-ever, that such authority is *always limited,* for it is granted and exercised under the sovereignty of Christ's rule, and never in its own right.

It should be stressed again that the virtues of charity, hope, and obedience cannot be isolated from each other, for together they em-body the suffering, vindication, and joy that characterize the tripartite culmination of the incarnation. None of these virtues is self-sufficient, and emphasizing one at the expense of the others distorts the Chris-tian moral life. This distortion may again be illustrated by noting three instances.

When charity is sequestered away from hope and obedience, it may be corrupted into self-aggrandizement. A life lived for others is turned around and becomes a life lived for oneself, for the giving of oneself becomes an end itself rather than a means. Giving is effectively disfigured into receiving, for meeting the needs of others becomes the way of meeting one's own need to give. The giver draws attention to herself rather than the beneficiary, and more importantly diverts atten-tion away from the one in whose name the charitable act is performed. What this stance fails to recognize is that the charitable act should not

---

4. See Romans 13.

draw attention to the giver but to the one who commands that the gift be given. The charitable life, in short, is one that bears witness to Jesus Christ whose life was given to and for the sake of others. The needs of others are thereby satisfied in the hope of Christ's destiny, and in obedience to Christ's rule. When the virtue of charity is not tempered by the virtues of hope and obedience, a life for others becomes a life of self-justification. Somewhat like the suffering examined in the previous section, ends and means are transposed: suffering is sought for its own sake; one gives in order to receive. What remains unacknowledged is that Jesus' crucifixion is not only an act of charity, but also an act of hope and obedience.

When the virtue of hope is disentangled from the virtues of charity and obedience it may mutate into the vice of indifference. When one becomes fixated on a vindicated creation that is destined for a full redemption that lies beyond temporal and finite existence, worldly concerns are diminished. In its most extreme form such indifference is exhibited in a nihilism in which the moral categories of good and evil are rendered irrelevant. More prevalent, however, is an outlook that effectively replaces Jesus Christ as the proper object of hope with a projected desire of one's own making. Hope is not placed in a judge, savior, and reconciler that awaits creation and its creatures at the end of time, but in one's own timely efforts to achieve salvation and reconciliation on one's own terms, and in ways that try to evade divine judgment against those very efforts. This amounts to little more than a strategy to avoid suffering and undercut the authority of Christ's rule.

Charity is not so much an act to satisfy the needs of others as a calculated gesture of benevolence to protect the giver from potential suffering that may result from social unrest, and obedience is reduced to an expedient ploy to comply with commands and expectations that are seen to be based on raw power rather than lawful authority. A morality based predominantly upon hope is ineffectual, for it cannot recognize the origin and end of genuine hope, and therefore cannot align itself properly with the destiny of a vindicated creation. What remains unacknowledged is that the resurrection is the result of suffering and charity, and the prerequisite of joyful obedience.

When the virtue of obedience is emphasized to the diminishment of the virtues of charity and hope, it can be reduced to a slavish devotion to powers and principalities claiming a loyalty that is properly reserved to God alone. In short, obedience is distorted into idolatry. As was mentioned above, under the rule of Christ social and political structures have been granted a limited authority to govern creation in the time between the times. Consequently, Christians should joyfully respect, honor, and obey lawful commands that promote peace and justice. Yet as was also stressed, under the rule of Christ all earthly authority is *limited*. Consequently, Christians must also withhold their obedience from commands that clearly contradict or contravene the commands of Jesus Christ.

Moreover, in order to see the virtue of obedience as a joyful response to the exaltation of Jesus Christ, we must also say something about authority and obedience as the prerequisites of freedom. Every command to which obedience is owed contains a prohibition that in turn enables permission; a no to this in order to allow a yes to that. This is necessarily so because, in O'Donovan's words: "Authority is the objective correlate of freedom."[5] In the absence of sufficient constraint humans remain enslaved to the "incapacity to obey."[6] One must refrain from the ways of singleness, for example, in order to be free to be a spouse, and the ways of marriage must be renounced for one to remain free to be single. The desire for vengeance must be denied so we are free to seek lives of peace, justice, and reconciliation. The exaltation of Jesus Christ not only entails obedience, but also participation in the rule of charity and hope.

Worship, Sacrament, and Ministry

If the virtues of charity, hope, and obedience are derived from the crucifixion, resurrection, and exaltation as the tripartite culmination of the incarnation, then concretely how are they formed and enacted within the Christian moral life? To answer this question we must turn our attention to the church. Following Barth, one cannot encounter Jesus Christ in the absence of the church, for the church is Christ's body on earth and in that body Christ is encountered directly.[7] The church, as the body of Christ, is not an abstract concept, but a living community that through its acts and deeds bears witness to its Lord and sav-

---

5. O'Donovan, *Resurrection and Moral Order,* p. 122.
6. O'Donovan, *Resurrection and Moral Order,* p. 23.
7. See Barth, *Church Dogmatics,* IV/1, pp. 759-60.

ior. Consequently, worship, the sacraments, and ministry may be examined as tangible arenas of where and how the Christian moral life is formed and enacted.

It is within *worship* that the pattern and trajectory of the Christian moral life are formed. Every act of worship presupposes, represents, and reaffirms the crucifixion, resurrection, and exaltation of Jesus Christ as the reconciler and incarnate Word of God. In Advent believers expect the impending death, victory, and rule of Christ, and on Ascension Day they look back upon the birth and resurrection of Jesus in anticipation of his return. Every act of worship necessarily and unavoidably embodies and proclaims the crucifixion, resurrection, and exaltation as the culmination of the incarnation, and therefore necessarily and unavoidably incorporates and emphasizes the attendant characteristics of suffering, vindication, and joy in its formation of the Christian moral vision. In short, one may also say that the Christian moral life is one of suffering, vindication, and joy.

It is important to note, however, that worship is not the foundational principle of Christian ethics, because the church cannot possess its own ethic which properly originates in and belongs to the Lord that it worships. Rather, following Bernd Wannenwetsch, worship reminds the church of its mode of being in which its ethics is lodged. Worship is a form of life which acknowledges that the "future of the world cannot be secured by morality, nor can immorality destroy it." Worship therefore forms Christian judgments, deeds, and acts.[8] Moreover, worship is the public space in which the rule of Christ is recognized, acknowledged, and celebrated without qualification, and as such also bears witness to Christ's judgment, forgiveness, and reconciliation of the world in which the church is at present sojourning. In this respect, we may also say that in embracing the suffering, vindication, and joy entailed in the crucifixion, resurrection, and exaltation of Jesus Christ, worship provides the content and context of the corresponding virtues of charity, hope, and obedience.

The considerations of content and context are seen with greater clarity by focusing attention upon the *sacraments*. Baptism is the rite of initiation into the church of Jesus Christ. In and through this sacrament individuals are incorporated into the church, for in and through

---

8. See Bernd Wannenwetsch, *Political Worship: Ethics for Christian Citizens* (Oxford and New York: Oxford University Press, 2004), pp. 1-14.

baptism they share in Christ's death and resurrection. The church, as Christ's body on earth, is comprised exclusively of the baptized, and as such bears witness to its head as its Lord. Although the lordship of Jesus Christ has been confirmed in his crucifixion, resurrection, and ascension, his status as the Lord of creation is not yet fully and universally acknowledged. Christ's reign in its full reality remains an eschatological hope in this time before the culmination of creation's redemption in the fullness of time. Consequently, there is an anticipatory element of baptism through which the church proclaims its hope in Christ's reign.

This anticipatory element bears much of the weight of baptism's inherent *witness*. In the absence of Jesus Christ baptism would have no meaning, for, in fellowship with the Father and Holy Spirit, it is Christ who authorizes the church to baptize in his name. The act of baptism, therefore, bears witness to the one who commands the church to baptize. This witness, however, is not directed solely toward the church, for its Lord is also the lord of creation. The sacrament invariably discloses the anticipation of the full reality of Christ's reign in the fullness of time. Baptism and the life of the baptized in the church bear witness not only to the gracious salvation of individuals, but also to the redemption of the world.

This witness has two principal aspects. On the one hand, it is a witness to the church. As the sacramental rite of initiation, baptism reminds the church that it is the body of Christ, and that the life of the baptized is one of obedience to its head. The witness of baptism, however, is also one of hope and charity, for the life of the baptized is never self-referential, but points expectantly to the rule of Christ and his *parousia*. On the other hand, baptism is a witness to the world. As the sacrament that shares in the death and resurrection of the world's redeemer, the act of baptism and the moral life of the baptized remind the world that it is temporal, and its affairs are penultimate rather than ultimate. In bearing witness to the lord of creation, the church expresses its love for the world by refusing any idolatrous claims it might offer. Baptism and the life of the baptized remind the world that its destiny is not in its own hands.

If baptism is the sacrament of initiation into the church, then we may also say that the Eucharist is the integrative sacrament that forms the pattern and trajectory of the Christian moral life. The principal features of this formation may be identified in a rudimentary fashion by focusing on two aspects of the Eucharist. First, the Eucharist is an act of remembrance. When Christians gather at the Lord's Table they remember that on the night that Jesus was given over to death he shared a meal with his disciples; they remember Jesus' act of charity, hope, and obedience, and they recite together that Christ has died. In that death there is both a judgment pronounced against the sin that has disfigured the created order and the promise of a salvific grace that vindicates it.

Consequently, to be admitted to the Lord's Table the baptized must continue to confess their sins, repent, accept forgiveness, and amend their lives in accordance with God's commands. Moreover, the Eucharist is a communal act that takes place in the public space created wherever the church gathers to worship. Those assembled, however, are not merely a collection of individuals who share common interests, but are gathered as the indivisible body of Christ. It is only those who through baptism have shared in Christ's death and are therefore incorporated into his body that are permitted and welcomed to the Lord's Table. As such, when the church remembers its Lord it cannot help but also remember the faithful who have preceded them and anticipate those who will succeed them. In the Eucharist Christians affirm that they are part of a body that has a past and future; the act of remembrance is also inescapably an act of expectancy.

Second, the Eucharist is, then, an act of anticipation. When Christians gather at the altar they recite together that Christ will come again, anticipating that day in the fullness of time when they will sit at table with their Lord. In the meantime, they place their hope in this promise of eschatological fellowship which in turn requires a response of charity and obedience. The Eucharist provides a foretaste, albeit imperfectly, of that anticipated banquet. This eschatological trajectory reorients both the common elements used in, and the adherents participating and enfolded into, the sacrament. The bread and wine serve as reminders that daily material needs are not negated but rather sustained by the Lord of creation, and that the body of Christ is also temporal and finite, and likewise must be sustained by the church's Lord.

In this respect, the sacrament is as much a sensual as a spiritual communion. The act itself resembles an ordinary meal, but it is the *Lord's* Supper, and as such is unlike any other meal. It is, for instance, an inhospitable meal, reserved exclusively for the baptized. Unlike the family or household table, the Lord's Table is not the place to entertain and extend hospitality to strangers; as an eschatological banquet it anticipates that day when there are no strangers to exclude, for all have been made one in Christ.[9] Moreover, those who gather at the Lord's Table do not do so as spouses, parents, children, workers, professionals, rulers, subjects, citizens, or any other social or political role, but as sisters and brothers in Christ, for the Eucharist looks forward to that day when all temporal institutions, distinctions, and offices have found their completion, and thereby their transformation in Christ.

Taken together, the sacraments provide the context in which the virtues of charity, hope, and obedience are formed, and in turn the content of their practice and enactment. Christians die and are raised with Christ, and in obedient response to this hope they are called to live charitable lives. Together, baptism and Eucharist require Christians to acknowledge that they remember Jesus who points toward the rule of his exaltation, and serve a living Lord who directs the attention of his disciples back to his life, ministry, and death. The Christian is incorporated into a history of anticipation, and anticipates a destiny that is inexplicable in the absence of its historical antecedents. Together, the sacraments form an orientation that simultaneously conserves the history and anticipates the future of Jesus Christ. The Christian is called to both remember and anticipate faithfully. Charity, hope, and obedience, then, are simultaneously conservative and proleptic virtues.

Given the sacramental context and content of these virtues, we may further say that the trajectory of the Christian moral life is one embodying and repeating a pattern of confession, repentance, forgiveness, and amendment of life. Christians confess and repent the sins they commit, which in God's mercy and grace are forgiven, and they in turn amend their lives in order not to commit the sins again.[10] In respect to ethics this entails admitting wrongs that have been committed, seeking forgiveness of and reconciliation with those who have been wronged, and changing conduct in ways that prevent the wrongs from being repeated. On an interpersonal level, this pattern is repeated frequently. I may, for instance, say something hurtful to a friend, offer an apology which is accepted, and continue on with the friendship.

Admittedly, the pattern becomes more complex when a more se-

---

9. Attempts to make the Eucharist more inclusive, inviting, or hospitable to those who have not professed faith in Jesus Christ and been initiated into the church through baptism disregard the eschatological trajectory of the sacrament, effectively turning the Lord's Supper into a church brunch or happy hour.

10. Such amended reordering of life is admittedly not always successful, prompting subsequent rounds of confession, repentance, forgiveness, and amendment of life.

vere wrong is committed. In the case of neglect or abuse for instance, forgiveness may be achieved after a long and painful period, but the ensuing reconciliation may rightfully require discontinuing the relationship. Larger civil and ecclesial communities also repeat this pattern. Injustices stemming from discrimination, for example, may be committed against individuals or groups. Once these injustices are admitted, repentance, forgiveness, and reconciliation are expressed through some type of restitution or compensation for the aggrieved, and practices, policies, or laws are enacted to prevent such discrimination being repeated in the future. The actual performance of this pattern is admittedly rarely ideal. What these clumsy examples illustrate is the simultaneously conserving and proleptic orientations of the Christian moral life. In hope we must always look back in order to confess and repent as acts of obedient charity, and we must also in hope look forward to forgive and reconcile as acts of charitable obedience.

If the virtues of charity, hope, and obedience are formed in worship and the sacraments, and if the ensuing pattern of the Christian moral life is one of confession, repentance, forgiveness, and amendment of life, then we must also say something about the *ministry* of the church. The ministry of the church *is* the ministry of the baptized, for it is the baptized who bear witness to Jesus Christ. Witness alone, however, does not suffice. It must be grounded in ecclesial offices and vocational callings, otherwise it lacks the authority of Christ's rule over the church and creation. The body of Christ is not an ephemeral fellowship of believers, but a community that endures over time in the time between the times. The church is not a community that indulges utopian fantasies, but orders its life under the rule of Christ in anticipation of his *parousia*. Consequently the church requires, for example, institutional structures and offices that both support and judge the validity of the witness of the baptized. In the absence of such ecclesial structures and offices, this witness degenerates into little more than individual or corporate opinion that is both disobedient and ineffectual. The church does not speak, either to itself or to the world, its own mind, but the commands of its Lord. In short, the church may only speak and act by what it has been authorized to say and to do by Jesus Christ, and all unauthorized speech and deeds diminish the efficacy of its witness.[11]

---

11. This is a notoriously difficult process, involving such issues as what criteria should be employed in discerning what Jesus Christ has authorized the church to say

Practically, the witness of the baptized is embodied in and through the church's ministry. It is virtually impossible to conceive a church that professed to have no ministry. The performance may in practice prove to be faithful or unfaithful, effectual or ineffectual, confident or fearful, but if the church foreswore ministry altogether it would cease to be the church. It would also be perverse to imagine the church's ministry performed by the un-baptized. The church's ministry is not comprised of discrete tasks that can be outsourced or accomplished by mercenaries. Rather, the church's ministry embodies the witness of baptism, for ministry is literally the work of the baptized: the work that Jesus Christ authorizes those who share his death and resurrection to perform in the church and in the world.

In the absence of baptism the church has no ministry, for its work would be neither formative of Christ's body nor governed by his rule. If ministry may be said to be the work of the baptized, then we may also speak of the dual nature of the church's ministry that corresponds with the twin aspects of the witness of baptism. There is first and foremost a ministry of and to the church. Through the sacraments and proclamation of the gospel the body of Christ is encountered by the incarnate Word, and is renewed and empowered by the Holy Spirit to be comprised of charitable, hopeful, and obedient disciples of Jesus Christ. The various ministerial offices enable the proclamation of God's judgment and grace, and the corresponding responses of confession, repentance, forgiveness, and amendment of life. In this respect, worship is properly the centerpiece of the church's ministry.

There is secondly a ministry of the church to the world. This ministry is primarily one of evangelization, for Christ calls the church to fulfill its commission by going into the world "to make disciples of all nations."[12] The church is thereby a gathering rather than gathered community, for its commission is not complete; the nations of the world have not yet been gathered entirely into Christ's kingdom.[13] Whenever the church gathers for worship, for example, it should not presume that those present constitute a full and complete fellowship.

---

and to do at a particular point in time, how such discernment should be pursued, and how conflict within the church is resolved. Given the limited scope of this chapter, these issues are not addressed, but it is assumed that in principle they are resolvable.

12. Matthew 28:19.

13. See Oliver O'Donovan, *The Desire of the Nations* (Grand Rapids: Eerdmans, 2005), pp. 175-76.

Rather, the church at worship is anticipatory, looking forward to that day when every knee shall bow and every tongue confess that Jesus is Lord.[14] In its ministry to the world God's judgment and grace are proclaimed, and those who hear are invited to confess their sin, repent, accept forgiveness, amend their lives, and through baptism be welcomed into the church's fellowship. Although worship properly forms the life of the baptized within the body of Christ, it is also the springboard of the church's ministry to the world.

It is important to emphasize that the ministry of and in the church, and its ministry in and to the world, are *not* parallel tracks. Both are performed in the name of Jesus Christ as the Lord of the church and creation, and both share a common origin and source of authority. Although actual practice is functionally discrete given the differing contexts, they are both nonetheless ministries of and by the church, and thereby formed by its worship and sacraments. This functional and contextual differentiation entails inevitable tensions, but they are debilitating only when one pole is excluded or emphasized over the other. Historically this is seen, for instance, when the church seeks to preserve its purity by avoiding the world as a source of contagion, or when individuals dismiss the church as irrelevant for living a moral life based on Christian principles. Effectively the former has no world to evangelize while the latter has no need to. Consequently, both have divorced themselves from the church's formative features of worship and sacrament, for its eschatological orientation cannot authorize either the denial of the church's evangelical commission, or a churchless Christianity. In either case the life of the baptized is trivialized into a statement of personal preference for the church over the world or vice versa. Instead, the baptized are drawn deeply and simultaneously into the church and the world.

All baptized Christians are called to ministry in and for the church, and in and to the world. For some this entails a calling to ordination, specialized service, or institutional governance. The ordained are entrusted primarily with overseeing worship, the administration of the sacraments, and the provision of pastoral care through appropriate ecclesiastical offices such as priest and bishop. It is through the authority of these offices that the church is ordered and governed under the rule of Christ, and it is often through these offices that the church

14. Philippians 2:9-11.

is represented formally to the broader civil community which, whether acknowledged or not, is also under the rule of Christ. Consequently, these offices may be said to look simultaneously "inwardly" toward the life of the church, and "outwardly" toward the world. In this respect the functions of ordained ministry are not confined exclusively to the ecclesial sphere. A bishop, for instance, may offer pastoral counsel to a diocese as well as to a magistrate. Other baptized Christians may not be called to ordination but are called to perform specialized tasks under the authority and at the direction of the church, such as monastics devoted to lives of prayer and service for both the church and the world. Still other Christians are called to assume responsibilities that enable the church's governance and ministry, such as serving on congregational committees, denominational governing bodies and commissions, and boards of trustees of church-related schools.

There is, then, a distinction between these ministries — between the ordained and laity — but it is a functional difference that implies no inherent or natural hierarchy, for it is only together that the church exercises its ministry under the authority of Jesus Christ, for the church's ministry *is* the ministry of the baptized. To use St. Paul's imagery,[15] the body of Christ is comprised of various parts, and its ministry is thereby performed by the variety of gifts these parts bring with them. In this respect the ministry of the laity is of equal importance to that of the ordained, because it too is exercised in obedience to and under the authority of Christ's rule. In saying this, however, it must be emphasized that this ministry is not confined to those instances that enable and maintain the church's institutional structures and activities. As important as serving on ecclesiastical boards and committees might be, the laity are also engaged in ministry in pursuing their secular callings and vocations. It is as a business executive, laborer, professional, civil servant, elected official, parent, spouse, and the like that Christians also bear witness to their baptism, and therefore minister in the name of the one in whom they are baptized. There are, in short, no part-time ministers in the church, because there are no part-time disciples of Jesus Christ.

May we not say, then, that in worship and the sacraments the virtues of charity, hope, and obedience are enacted, embodied, and habituated in the lives of believers? And may we not also say that the formation of these virtues promotes a pattern of the Christian moral life as one of

---

15. 1 Corinthians 12.

confession, repentance, forgiveness, and amendment of life? And may we not further say that this pattern is not confined to the ecclesial sphere but is followed by all Christians in engaging the world through the various callings and vocations that bear witness to their baptism, and is thereby the ministry of the baptized? The rule of Christ in this time between the times is not confined to the church, but is extended over a creation whose order has been vindicated by Christ. It is through the various callings and vocations of Christians, both ordained and secular, that the singular ministry of the baptized engages, evangelizes, and orders the world in the name and under the authority of Jesus Christ.

Applying the pattern of confession, repentance, forgiveness, and amendment of life to questions of social and political ordering is a difficult and often perplexing task. Under the rule of Christ, how exactly are individual and corporate lives of charity, hope, and obedience best formed, promoted, sustained, and reformed as needed? What concrete and practical acts, deeds, policies, and laws need to be undertaken, enacted, and administered? In respect to economic exchange, for example, are the virtues of charity, hope, and obedience best promoted by free markets or by centralized planning and control? What form of political governance do these virtues suggest: anarchy, democracy, oligarchy, monarchy? Moreover, even if some rough consensus on broad principles of social and political ordering that best embody the rule of Christ could be achieved, that does not relieve the burden of the practical necessity of making judgments in regard to their implementation.

For instance, what kinds of taxes should be collected, and how should this revenue be allocated? Are the needs of the poor best met through grants and aid or private investment? What is the proper balance between the punishment of criminal conduct and reincorporating criminals back into the civil community? What are the limits of coercive force that should be employed by government in preserving the peace of civil community, and protecting its citizens? Most perplexing of all, when social structures and political institutions fail to govern properly under the rule of Christ, how is the life of civil community amended in a fitting manner? How do the members of a civil community, for instance, confess past sins of injustice? How does the community repent of these sins? How is forgiveness given and received between the offenders and offended? How is genuine reconciliation between these parties achieved so that the ensuing reforms are based on the more stable foundation of free consent rather than grudging compliance?

Forgiveness and the Ordering of Civil Community

I will not attempt to answer any of these questions in a detailed manner. More modestly the remainder of this chapter examines, in broad outline, the idea of forgiveness in light of the task of ordering civil community in a manner that is obedient to Jesus Christ. Forgiveness has been selected because of its admittedly problematic nature in respect to issues of social and political ordering. Within the relatively narrow range of interpersonal relationships forgiveness is an explicable and necessary act. Friends and family members who occasionally wrong one another must offer and receive forgiveness if those relationships are to be maintained. The refusal to offer and receive forgiveness may effectively end a friendship, or severely erode familial bonds.

It is in respect to broader social and political associations that forgiveness is conceptually challenging.[16] How does (or can) a group forgive individual members who have wronged it, and conversely, how do (or can) individuals forgive a group that has wronged them? In particular, how does (or should) a government forgive citizens who have committed crimes, and how does (or should) a private association, such as a bank, forgive a delinquent loan? And conversely, how do (or should) citizens who have been wrongly imprisoned forgive their government, and how do (or should) consumers forgive a bank for predatory lending practices? Assuming that such acts of forgiveness are possible, how are they authorized and enacted within the political, public, and private associations within the civil community? More broadly, is forgiveness necessary, or does it have any practical purchase regarding the good ordering of these civil associations?

Arendt argues that forgiveness is a necessary component for a governing political community.[17] Her account begins with the observation that human beings cannot undo what they have done in the past. All human action results in unanticipated consequences that may inspire a sense of guilt, remorse, and responsibility. In short, humans suffer the results of their deeds and acts, ironically leading them to be less free within the very realm of freedom (the *polis*) that they created

16. For an overview of various issues see P. E. Digeser, *Political Forgiveness* (Ithaca, NY: Cornell University Press, 2001).

17. Unless otherwise noted, the following discussion of Arendt's understanding of forgiveness is drawn from Hannah Arendt, *The Human Condition* (Chicago: University of Chicago Press, 1998), chaps. 32-34.

through their own free action. Political association, which for Arendt is the highest form of human activity or work, is apparently stymied by the necessity of undoing prior acts and deeds that cannot be undone. She proposes a twofold solution to this dilemma: forgiveness is the remedy for the irreversibility of deeds and acts, and the remedy for the unanticipated consequences of such acts and deeds is the ability to make and keep promises. Humans are unable to undo what they have done, but they have the capacity to ameliorate the ill effects of the irreversible and unpredictable nature of what they do and fail to do.

Consequently, *forgiving* and *promising* are necessary and inseparable political concepts and practices. An inability to forgive and keep promises would prevent any meaningful human action, especially political action, because individuals and associations would be frozen by the unintended consequences of their acts. Forgiveness and promise-keeping are thereby predicated upon the central reality of plurality: political community is not a static whole, but a dynamic amalgamation of different individuals and associations pursuing their respective and changing interests. Moreover the central practices of forgiving and promising enable the political community to embrace and affirm a wide range of differences, contradicting the more constricting Platonic political principles of rule, domination, and control. Promise-keeping, however, remains an unpredictable enterprise, because the nature of future agents and their deeds and circumstances cannot be known with exact precision; a promise is based on trust instead of certainty. When unwarranted certainty is attributed to promises they lose their binding power, losing in turn their capacity to serve as an antidote to domination and control. Civil community is thereby bound together by its promises, or in legal terms its contracts, and it is due to these mutual pledges that uncoerced corporate action is possible. The uncertain nature of promise-keeping is the price that must be paid to maintain freedom.

The uncertainty of promise-keeping is the reason why it is intrinsically linked with forgiveness, and why together they provide the lynchpin of a good social and political order. Arendt contends that Jesus discovered the central role that forgiveness should play in human affairs. The religious foundation of his teaching, however, is irrelevant, because its secularized version lies at the heart of the Western political tradition. In this respect, forgiveness may be based upon mutual respect instead of love, promoting a kind of civil friendship. Most importantly, such respect is not predicated upon admiration or esteem, but upon a fundamental equality that is shared among friends. This equality is already latent in Jesus' teaching. Friends or neighbors do not forgive each other because God has first forgiven them. Rather, individuals have a duty to forgive friends and neighbors who have wronged them. It is in the dutiful act of forgiving and being forgiven that political relationships are renewed, and in their renewal the possibility of new, and potentially better, acts and relationships are created; the act of forgiving is the prerequisite for keeping promises and making new ones.[18] Although forgiving and promising cannot undo the wrong that has been done, they can ameliorate its paralyzing aftermath. The uncertainty of forgiving and promising is substituted for the certainty of vengeance, thereby breaking the escalating cycle of seeking revenge in response to wrongs that have been committed. Consequently, forgiveness can, should, and must play a central role in political ordering, for it is the only action that frees humans from a destructive fate.[19]

It should not be assumed that Arendt is offering an idealistic or naïve solution to an intractable problem. She is aware that there are other alternatives, often entailing force or capitulation, for breaking the cycle of vengeance. She readily admits, for instance, that the fundamental "alternative to forgiveness, but by no means its opposite, is punishment, and both have in common that they attempt to put an end to something that without interference could go on endlessly."[20] Indeed, forgiveness is unintelligible in the absence of punishment, for what cannot be punished cannot be forgiven, a necessary condition that creates the vexing dilemma of so-called "radical evil" that can be neither punished nor forgiven sufficiently. Arendt's preference for forgiveness as an alternative to punishment is that it represents a partial attempt to undo the wrong that has been done, thereby creating a greater range of renewing and novel possibilities for political action.[21] When a judgment is rendered that an individual (or individuals comprising a group) has wronged other individuals or groups, assigning a fitting punishment is the appropriate response of the political community.

---

18. In this respect, forgiving and promising are linked with Arendt's concept of "natality"; see *The Human Condition,* chaps. 1-2.

19. See Hannah Arendt, *The Promise of Politics* (New York: Schocken Books, 2005), pp. 58-59.

20. Arendt, *The Human Condition,* p. 241.

21. See Hannah Arendt, *Essays in Understanding, 1930-1954* (New York: Schocken Books, 1994), p. 308.

This cannot be a wooden judicial process, however, for it would then preclude the possibility of forgiveness as the preferred method of breaking the cycle of vengeance. Judgment and punishment would effectively be corrupted into a crude political instrument of exacting a "final revenge" for those who are in a position to assert their will over their adversaries. Rather, Arendt envisions a more dynamic and fluid relationship between judgment and forgiveness in which punishment is one, but not the only method for attempting, albeit imperfectly, to undo a wrong that has been done. "Every judgment is open to forgiveness, every act of judging can change into an act of forgiving; to judge and to forgive are but two sides of the same coin."[22] These two sides, however, follow different rules. Law demands, for instance, that only acts, not persons, matter. In contrast, forgiveness is focused exclusively on persons. Somebody, not something, is forgiven; the thief is forgiven but not the act of thievery. Such forgiveness both disrupts and rejuvenates political ordering, for justice demands equality, while mercy is predicated on inequality, therefore requiring a relation of inevitable tension among judgment, punishment, and forgiveness that when properly maintained resists being reduced to any standardized formulae. Without invoking the name of the bishop of Hippo, Arendt affirms the Augustinian principle that it is the sin and not the sinner that should be despised, and therefore it is the latter and not the former that can be judged, punished, and forgiven.

To summarize, Arendt contends that forgiveness and promise-keeping are required to liberate political action from the inertia of the irreversibility of past deeds and the unpredictability of present acts. Together, forgiving and promising also break the cycle of vengeance, renewing the political community and creating new possibilities for subsequent action, thereby providing an antidote to the Platonic principles of rule, domination, and control. The practical application of this scheme requires public structures that enable a more fluid relationship among judgment, punishment, and forgiveness.

There is much to commend in Arendt's account of the role that forgiveness (and promise-making and -keeping as its conjoined twin) should play in social and political ordering. The attempt to create political structures that enable a more fluid and dynamic relation among

---

22. Hannah Arendt, *Reflections on Literature and Culture* (Stanford, CA: Stanford University Press, 2007), p. 254.

judgment, punishment, and forgiveness is a welcome departure from the late modern emphasis on politics as little more than raw power. Politics, as she insists, is primarily a practice of governance stemming from discourse about the common good, and only secondarily an exercise in asserting coercive force. Without denying the necessity of judgment and punishment for the good of civil community, she nonetheless tempers an automatic and predictable recourse to coercion by emphasizing forgiveness as an alternative, yet unpredictable, means of breaking cycles of vengeful violence,[23] and thereby creating new possibilities for political action. In creating a space for these possibilities, a political association may come to embody and enact more fully such civil virtues as civic friendship and compassion.[24] In this respect, there are striking similarities between Arendt's account of political ordering and the Christian moral life as a pattern of confession, repentance, forgiveness, and amendment of life developed in this chapter.

Despite these resemblances, however, Arendt's scheme cannot deliver what she proposes because she places a moral weight upon forgiveness that is too heavy to be borne. Two instances may serve to expose this weakness. First, Arendt places too much emphasis on forgiveness, too little on judgment, and ignores confession and repentance altogether. Consequently, judgment, punishment, and forgiveness become isolated and free-floating acts that collide in a haphazard manner. These collisions stem from Arendt's mistaken assumption that judgment and forgiveness are discrete acts. A judgment is made that a particular act has wronged an individual or group and deserves to be punished. Arendt argues that rather than assigning punishment, forgiveness may serve as a substitute, enacted, for example, as a commutation or pardon. Yet in the absence of any discussion of the necessity of confession and repentance (or their equivalents) on the part of the individual who committed the wrong, forgiveness simply diminishes or negates justice. If a criminal, for instance, is pardoned, for whatever good or plausible reason that may be invoked, for a crime that he never admits committing, much less expressing remorse, then his presumably subsequent promise to refrain from criminal behavior is vacuous. How does he amend his life in reaction to an act that

---

23. The contrast becomes more distinct in Arendt's various inquiries into the differing political implications of emphasizing natality as opposed to mortality.

24. See her discussion of compassion and pity in Hannah Arendt, *On Revolution* (New York: Viking Press, 1965), chap. 2.

he neither confesses nor repents? In this instance forgiveness is an empty and capricious gesture that ignores what justice demands, and necessarily so given the chasm Arendt has dug between her equality of justice and the inequality of mercy.

Judgment and punishment, however, are inseparable, because, as O'Donovan contends, punishment *is* enacted judgment, and not a separate act following judgment.[25] Judgment and punishment are one and the same, and cannot be separated without subsequently diminishing or distorting both. Since punishment is enacted judgment there can be no substitution; otherwise judgment would have no substantive content. Rather, forgiveness is a subsequent act in response to punishment, and subsequent promises or amendment of life. If forgiveness is to have any substantive content, then it must be predicated upon a preceding process of judgment, confession, and repentance. Consequently, it is the act of judgment, not forgiveness, that creates the space for new possibilities of political action and promises. Or in O'Donovan's words: "Judgment . . . both *pronounces retrospectively on,* and *clears space prospectively for,* actions that are performed within a community."[26]

Second, Arendt does not adequately address the issue of ameliorating or attempting to undo wrongs that were committed in the distant past but still exert rippling effects upon present action. The problem in this instance is that the dead can neither forgive nor be forgiven. Moreover, the problem is exacerbated when the wrongs at issue have been committed by and against groups rather than individuals. Suppose, for example, that generations of a religious or ethnic group have suffered discrimination or persecution by the larger civil community. A consensus has emerged that such discrimination or persecution is wrong and should be rectified. Accomplishing this goal would presumably entail making and keeping promises that would amend the life of the civil community, and Arendt would presumably contend that these promises would be predicated upon the religious or ethnic group forgiving the civil community, and the civil community in turn receiving their forgiveness.[27]

It is difficult to imagine, however, how wrongs that originated in

25. See Oliver O'Donovan, *The Ways of Judgment: The Bampton Lectures, 2003* (Grand Rapids: Eerdmans, 2005), pp. 107-8.

26. O'Donovan, *The Ways of Judgment,* p. 9 (emphasis original).

27. Arendt's discussions of forgiveness as a political act suggest that such acts are always reciprocal rather than unilateral.

the distant past can be forgiven within Arendt's scheme. In respect to the wronged group, who has the authority to speak on behalf of both its living and dead members — to in effect say to the civil community that its past deeds are forgiven? More importantly, Arendt contends that forgiveness stems from mercy. Yet how can the persecuted be merciful to their persecutors? Is not mercy always the prerogative of the strong and not the weak? Enacting such mercy would presumably require a reversal of roles. A civil community would need to pronounce a judgment upon itself for the wrong of discrimination or persecution committed over time, and assign a fitting punishment such as reparation.[28] Following Arendt, would not the wronged group then be required to exercise its duty to forgive, out of mercy, the debt it is owed by the civil community that has confessed, repented, and promised to amend its life? More problematic, political leaders in virtue of their office seemingly have the authority to apologize for past wrongs that have been committed by the civil community.

This presumed authority, however, assumes a continuity of governance and stability over time that may not exist. Is a newly formed republic dedicated to greater inclusion and human rights, for instance, culpable for discriminatory policies or persecution that originated in and was perpetuated by preceding autocratic or tyrannical regimes? It is difficult to address these issues on Arendt's terms given her failure to discuss, in any sustained manner, the role of representative authority — that is, who is authorized to speak and act on behalf of the civil community and the groups comprising it in ways that extend both backward and forward in time. Or in Arendtian terms: Who has the authority to forgive the wrongs of the past and make promises for the future? It is a curious omission given the weight she places on forgiving and promising as the preferred way of breaking the cycle of vengeance that is often the driving force behind religious and ethnic strife. In the absence of a normative account of representative authority, the best Arendt can offer are promises based on forgetfulness rather than forgiveness. The wrongs of the past are not undone but ignored in order to move on. Consequently, forgiving and promising are not the result of either the equality of justice or the inequality of mercy, but expedient amnesia and force of political will.

28. Or such a judgment could be rendered and punishment assigned by an occupying force or international tribunal.

Both of Arendt's problems — the unwarranted emphasis upon forgiveness as an alternative to judgment, and inability to forgive wrongs committed in the distant past — stem from her mistaken assertion that Jesus' teaching on forgiveness can be stripped from its religious foundation. She attempts to surgically remove Jesus' teaching and transplant it into a Kantian host emphasizing the centrality of the will. The goal is that the political will to forgive, and therefore promise, serves as an effective antidote to the poisonous principles of rule, domination, and control. The surgery fails to achieve its objective, however, because too much confidence is placed in the good will and wisdom of the *polis* to provide the authority of its self-governance. The transplanted forgiveness does not negate the necessity of rule but cloaks it in the will to forgive, thereby masking but not eliminating the will to dominate and control. In short, the political will to forgive cannot replace the divine command to forgive.

The strength and purchase of Jesus' instruction is not the pedagogy employed, but the Christological status of the instructor. Jesus' teaching on forgiveness is not only wise counsel, but a command given by the Word made flesh. In the crucifixion, resurrection, and exaltation of Jesus Christ as the incarnate Word, judgment, punishment, and forgiveness have already been representatively enacted in both a retrospective and prospective direction. Consequently, Jesus' teaching on forgiveness contains both imperative and teleological elements that are lost in Arendt's transplantation into a Kantian political body. Some effects of this loss can be seen by focusing on the exaltation. The exaltation of Christ initiates a new rule for the ordering of creation in this time between the times. Such a rule is retrospective in that it is based on the vindication of created order, and prospective in its expectation of the *parousia*. In respect to political ordering, the civil community exercises judgment, punishment, and forgiveness not because it possesses the necessary will and power to do so, but because it has been authorized by Christ to perform these functions in obedience to his rule to which it is subject.

What Arendt fails to recognize is that rule *per se* needs no antidote, for it does not lead inevitably to domination and control. Rather, the rule of Christ is oriented toward forgiveness and mercy, the very qualities Arendt champions in her political philosophy, and in the absence of this rule they cannot be genuinely enacted. Judgment does not merely create a space for new possibilities for political action, but creates a space in which the civil community may better amend and align its life to the rule and *telos* of Christ. In this respect, the *polis* provides a fitting image, but it is the City of God rather than the City of Man that should seize the imagination in determining the proper relationship among judgment, punishment, and forgiveness.

We may now briefly revisit Arendt's two problems and suggest some ways that restoring the Christological foundation of forgiveness might solve them. First, as discussed above, Arendt is mistaken in arguing that forgiveness may be a substitute for punishment, because the latter is an enacted judgment. Forgiving the person who has wronged another, however, may mark a prospectively redemptive response to the singular act of judgment and punishment. Although no human acts of judgment, punishment, and forgiveness are redemptive in their own right, neither can their anticipatory qualities be ignored given the salvific *telos* of Christ's rule.[29] These acts both anticipate and are tempered by God's final acts of judgment, punishment, and forgiveness, but God's redemptive economy is also at work in the penultimate affairs of civil community.

Consequently, the tension between the equality of justice and the inequality of mercy is eased given the teleological trajectory of political ordering. Forgiveness is not only an act of mercy but also one that restores the broken bonds of civil fellowship in anticipation of their full restoration in the *parousia*. Judgment and punishment are not thereby negated but properly tempered by forgiveness. Consequently, forgiving is not a capricious act that ignores or overrules the demands of justice. Rather, civil community may forgive because it confesses that it too is in need of forgiveness and amendment of life. The equality of justice is accompanied by the equality of sin, and therefore the universal need of mercy.

Second, Arendt's principal difficulty in attempting to undo wrongs committed in the distant past stem from her failure to address the category of representative authority. No person or office is in a position to speak for or to the dead who presumably can neither forgive nor be forgiven. In his crucifixion, resurrection, and exaltation Jesus Christ has assumed a representative authority, both retrospectively and prospectively. Past, present, and future generations are subject to the rule of Christ, and therefore also subject to his judgment, punishment,

---

29. See O'Donovan, *The Ways of Judgment*, pp. 87-100.

and forgiveness, which are at least partially exercised through civil community in obedience to Christ. Consequently, forgiveness is not a duty to be merciful, but the acknowledgment of the need for frequent confession, repentance, and amendment of life.

The purpose of forgiveness, therefore, is not to undo (or forget) what was done in the past, but to restore, forge together, and reorient broken social and political associations toward their proper *telos* in Christ where, in the fullness of time, the past is redeemed. This reorientation helps to alleviate the need to create the artificial and awkward situation in which the wronged group must be merciful to the civil community and its antecedent regimes that committed the wrong in order to enact the duty to forgive, as well as negating the problematic nature of political governance and stability over time. Admittedly, this reorientation does not in itself suggest concrete ways that civil community can forgive and be forgiven for wrongs committed in the distant past, but it at least provides a starting point for developing a moral and political principle upon which fitting legislation, policies, and practices can be derived.

2. "Where Christ Is": Christology and Ethics

John Webster

What follows is a moral theological gloss on some aspects of the Christology of Colossians. Three preliminary comments will serve as orientation. First, behind the argument lies a twofold affirmation: that moral reasoning is biblical reasoning (for the moral life is within the domain of the Word of God), and that biblical reasoning does well not to stray too far from exegesis, because exegesis is a hearing of the Word, and "the unfolding of [God's] words gives light; it imparts understanding to the simple" (Ps. 119:130).

Part of the discipline of dogmatic and moral theology is coming to terms — often after some struggle against our own sophistication — with the fact that this is so: that we will not get very far unless moral reason is disciplined by the divine self-declaration encountered through the prophets and apostles, and that, as we do so govern moral reason, we are granted illumination. Exegesis — indeed, the theological enterprise in its entirety, including moral theology, is calling upon God: "I cry to thee, save me, that I may observe thy testimonies. I rise before dawn and cry for help; I hope in thy words" (Ps. 119:146-47). Patiently pursued, as a work in which theological reason is quickened by the Spirit, exegesis is an act of *hope* in God's words.

As it engages in exegesis the church is entitled to expect divine instruction, and so — in the case of moral theology — may with good cause count upon being directed to a conclusive word about its perplexities, and not simply to further dilemmas. Moral knowledge, and therefore intelligent moral action, is *possible* because the divine Word in Holy Scripture is law, that is, a truthful command in which God extends his rational government of the church by instructing it about his purposes and about the ways in which he guides ruined creatures into moral fellowship with himself. Scriptural instruction is of course no exception to the rule that creaturely moral knowledge is acquired over time, *learned*. But such knowledge is not simply the by-product of improvisation in moral practice; it is *taken to* the moral situation. It is "heavenly" doctrine, because both its substance and its source are the church's heavenly master (Col. 4:1), and it generates both "spiritual wisdom and understanding" (Col. 1:9) and fruitfulness in good works (Col. 1:10).

Second, accordingly, the gospel dispenses a double knowledge: first, of God and God's acts, and second of the will of God for creatures. "What may be known of God," remarks John Owen, "is his nature and existence, with the holy counsels of his will."[1] The matter of Christian theology encompasses dogmatics and morals, because the heart of the gospel of which theology seeks to provide a conceptual account is God's "beloved Son" (Col. 1:13), in whose "person and mediation . . . there is made unto us a representation of the glorious properties of the divine nature, and of the holy counsels of the will of God."[2] Theological apprehension of Christ and his dominion is at once metaphysical and moral — only moral because metaphysical, and because metaphysical necessarily moral. Of this, Colossians furnishes a compelling canonical example.

Third, therefore, what Colossians has to say about the moral life of believers cannot be restricted to the so-called *Haustafel* (Col. 3:18–4:1), but is an integral element of its entire presentation of Christ. A long tradition of scrupulous (and largely inconclusive) form-critical inquiry into the *Gattung* and *Vorlage* of the household code has heightened its isolation by analyzing it diachronically as traditional material originating elsewhere and subsequently implanted into the letter with little relation to the letter's theological impulses.[3]

Whatever conclusions may be reached concerning the literary and

---

1. J. Owen, *ΧΡΙΣΤΟΛΟΓΙΑ, or A Declaration of the Glorious Mystery of the Person of Christ* (1679), in *The Works of John Owen* (Edinburgh: Banner of Truth Trust, 1965), vol. 1, p. 65.

2. J. Owen, *ΧΡΙΣΤΟΛΟΓΙΑ*, p. 65.

3. For a thorough critical account of the history of interpretation, see J. Hering, *The Colossian and Ephesian Haustafeln in Theological Context: An Analysis of Their Origins, Relationship, and Message* (New York: Lang, 2007).

historical questions surrounding the *Haustafel,* there is surely an exegetical (and theological) misstep here, an inadequate conception of the scope and integrity of Colossians, whose paraenesis is not lightly Christianized Stoic commonplaces, but instruction that flows from a Christologically derived and shaped understanding of the redemption of moral nature and moral situation, and of its integral imperatives: "As therefore you received Christ Jesus the Lord, so live in him" (Col. 2:6).

With this in place, what may be said of the relation of Christology and Ethics in Colossians?

I

Jesus Christ "is before all things, and in him all things hold together" (Col. 1:17). Jesus Christ is the absolutely existent one and, by virtue of that absolute existence, the one in whom creaturely reality in its entirety coheres. Together, this αὐτός and its correlative ἐν αὐτῷ are the foundation of creaturely existence, as well as of its intelligible unity and its movement toward perfection. And so to invoke the name of Jesus Christ in a moral context is to indicate the one by whom τὰ πάντα are moved, the one in whom action has its ground and telos. Creaturely moral action is action in the economy of grace, the ordered disposition of reality in which in Jesus Christ God's goodness is limitlessly potent.

What more may be said of this one? First, he is "pre-eminent in everything" (Col. 1:18); he is "the head of all rule and authority" (2:10). He is determinative of created reality in a comprehensive way; his rule knows no restriction or competition; he has authority over all other authority because he is the author of all things — "whether thrones or dominions or principalities or authorities — all things were created through him and for him" (1:16). In another image, he is "the substance" (τὸ σῶμα, 2:17), the true ultimate reality by which all other realities are rendered provisional, non-final, to be left behind on the way to what is to come. All created dominion is relativized by the stunningly simple Christological confession: ὅς ἐστιν ἀρχή (1:18).

Second, all this is attributed to Jesus Christ by virtue of his antecedent deity. In order truthfully to grasp his history and the identity it enacts, he has to be confessed as "the image of the invisible God" (Col. 1:15), the coming into visibility of the one who entirely eludes creaturely imagining. He is the dwelling place of the utter plenitude of God, the one "in whom all the fullness of God was pleased to dwell" (1:19), God's perfect life present in matter and time. "In him the whole fullness of deity dwells bodily" (2:9): the divine πλήρωμα is now also — astoundingly — "somatic." And, once again, to grasp this "somatic" reality, we must talk of a divine movement and presence, the movement of the divine good pleasure, the presence, not simply of divine virtues but, as Bengel puts it, the very divine nature: "Deitas plenissima: non modo divinae virtutes, sed ipsa divina natura."[4] What takes place in Jesus Christ's history is not contingent but an eternal correlate of the Father's will to be manifest to creatures. "God's mystery" and "Christ" are identical (2:2): Jesus Christ is not simply the occasion in which that mystery is revealed, but its very content, both mode and matter.

Third, in and as this one God, Christ has effected the decisive alteration of the condition of creatures. This one, αὐτός, is within the plenitude of the divine being, and as such the reconciler.[5] That is, his eternal being in the godhead is directed toward creatures; in him there takes place a divine mission. "In him all the fullness of God was pleased to dwell"; and therefore through him God "reconciled to himself all things" (Col. 1:19-20). Jesus Christ's being is thus doubly defined: by ἐν αὐτῷ, in which his relation to God's inner plenitude of life is stated, and by δι' αὐτοῦ, through which attention is drawn to his "external" acts as reconciler. This external work, God's goodness in the economy, is an extrinsic but not a purely "closed" act, for its term is the remaking of creatures and of creaturely relation to God.

There is a real καὶ ὑμᾶς, "and you," which follows inexorably from the indwelling and the objective reconciliation: "And you, who once were estranged and hostile in mind, doing evil deeds, he has now reconciled in his body of flesh by his death" (Col. 1:21-22). What is described as reconciliation can otherwise be indicated: as deliverance from dominion (1:13); as redemption or forgiveness (1:14); as making alive (2:13); as the canceling of a bond (2:14); or as the disarming of hostile forces

---

4. J. A. Bengel, *Gnomon Novi Testamenti* (Edinburgh: Williams & Norgate, 1862), p. 739.

5. Hering's concern to underline the "benevolent" character of Christ's dominion (*The Colossian and Ephesian Haustafeln in Theological Context*, p. 65) and to disavow any idea of that dominion as pure power, imaged in hierarchical human relations, lends a distinct "economic" cast to his reading of the Christology and soteriology of Colossians; this in turn leads to some neglect of the rooting of redemption in the eternal being of the exalted Son.

(2:15). Its result is existence in a sphere of rule that *establishes* creatures after they have been overtaken by enmity with God; that sphere is "the kingdom of [God's] beloved Son" (1:13). Christian life and activity take place in the domain of God's *love,* that is, his perfect inner relations of Father, Son, and Spirit which is the eternal depth of his charity to lost creatures. This is the kingdom of the eternal Son of the Father's love, and therefore divinely good and secure.

Fourth, in this kingdom of the Son, reality is illuminated and true knowledge made possible. Christ's rule is intelligible and renders intelligible that over which he rules. In view of this kingdom, it makes sense for the apostle to pray that his readers should "increase in the knowledge of God" (Col. 1:10; see also 3:10), precisely because the divine office of the apostle in the church is "to make the word of God fully known" (1:25) on the basis of the fact that in Jesus Christ a revelation has taken place in which the hidden mystery is "now made manifest to his saints" (1:26). In Christ are "hidden all the treasures of wisdom and knowledge" (2:3): "hidden" because he is the agent of their manifestation, and "in him" because he is their content.

Fifth, Christ's kingdom is a moral commonwealth.[6] To exist within the domain of the Father's beloved Son, to know "the riches of the glory of the mystery" of "Christ in you" (Col. 1:27) is at the very same time to be drawn into transformation of life-activity. "Spiritual wisdom and understanding" is thus confirmed as "knowledge of his will" (1:9); or again, "increasing in the knowledge of God" entails "leading a life worthy of the Lord, fully pleasing to him, bearing fruit in every good work" (1:10). To grow in knowledge of this mystery is also to learn how to act in the wake of its manifestation. Reconciliation in Christ is, similarly, purposeful: the Son's work of reconciliation is "in order to present you holy and blameless and irreproachable before him" (1:22), an end that carries the *moral* entailments of "continuing in the faith, stable and steadfast" (1:23).

This coinherence of acknowledgment of Christ and manner of

---

6. In this connection, Hering's presentation of the coordination of the vertical (divine-human) axis and the horizontal (intrahuman) axis of what Colossians has to say of Christ's rule is substantially correct; see *The Colossian and Ephesian Haustafeln in Theological Context,* pp. 61-105. He argues that the key redemptive "movements" of Christ's dominion in his death and resurrection "become a part of the new and unfolding context of life for the hearers, who now partake in them as their identity is increasingly defined in terms of, and therefore intrinsically tied to, Christ" (p. 69).

life is, of course, basic both to the overall argument of Colossians and to its most characteristic pattern of moral appeal, which might be called Christological deduction, a pressing of the moral logic of *is:* "as . . . so" (2:6); "if . . . why?" (2:20); "if . . . then" (3:1); "seeing that . . ." (3:9), and most of all, the ubiquitous "therefore," οὖν (2:16; 3:5; 3:12).[7]

All this serves to indicate in an initial way that Jesus Christ presides over a *moral* economy; knowledge of him is in this sense practical. To apprehend his being is to feel the *forward* pressure of the "therefore" toward modes of action that are impressed by his own: "as the Lord has forgiven you, so you also must forgive" (Col. 3:13); "Let the peace of Christ rule in your hearts" (3:15); "you are serving the Lord Christ" (3:24). The Christology is *moral* Christology. Yet, there is no ethical nominalism here, in which invocation of Jesus Christ is simple ornamentation. To be summoned to life in this moral economy is to feel the *backward* pressure of the "therefore," its reference back to Christ as God's fullness.

It is ethically crucial that Jesus Christ is an ontological *perfectum,* a complete reality, *a se* and *in se,* not one somehow produced or extended in Christian moral history. If he were so produced, he would not be Lord of the moral life, and Christian action would not be undertaken in reference to a given order. One rule therefore for Christian moral determinacy is: "Him we proclaim" (Col. 1:28). Yet proclamation includes "warning" and "teaching" (1:28) and has as its end the creature's perfection in Christ. The moral life thus revolves around two affirmations in their necessary connection and their proper sequence: "in him the whole fullness of deity dwells bodily" (2:9), and "you have come to fullness of life in him" (2:10).

So far, the apostolic gospel in Colossians. We may now stand back a pace and restate the matter in a rather more formal idiom.

II

Jesus Christ determines the order of moral being and the order of moral knowing; he is the ontological and noetic foundation of good human conduct; ethical reflection is accordingly an expansion of his name as that name exalts itself in the field of creaturely activity.

7. On this, see W. Nauck, "Das οὖν-paräneticum," *Zeitschrift für die neutestamentliche Wissenschaft* 49 (1958): 134-35.

To explicate that name requires us to trace two movements from the central point of Jesus' history as the embodied fullness of God. The first is a movement backward, into the infinite depth of the eternal Son and his relations to the Father by whom he is generated and the Spirit whom with the Father he breathes. In tracing this movement, we come to see that Jesus Christ's name is spoken out of the unrestricted fullness of the triune life, that — in the more abstract idiom of trinitarian dogmatics — his history is a divine mission, a turning outward of the abundance of the divine processions, a divine act *ad extra* resting upon the triune life *ad intra*.

The second movement is a movement forward, the movement in which the eternal Word speaks of himself now, making himself present to creaturely knowledge, love, and obedience. The eternal Word, made flesh to redeem creatures, is also the Word spoken through the apostles as the consolation and direction of the gospel. To speak of Jesus Christ is to speak of this one: the Father's eternal Son in whom the Father's reconciling will has been accomplished and who through the Holy Spirit is now drawing creatures back into fellowship with the Father. Such expansions of the name of Jesus can only be assumed here, however; we press on to reflect upon the ontological and noetic corollaries.

A. Jesus Christ Determines the Order of Moral Being

That is, in an ethical context Christological statements function as reality-indications. From them we can build up a picture of the moral field, that is, a portrait of the identities of the divine and human agents in their encounter in the economy of God, and of how human beings ought to act in that economy. This is who God and his creatures are; this is where they meet; this is the character of their meeting. In an ethics that is Christologically determined, we are not dealing with an "indefinite" sphere of human action, but with one that is "fixed and limited," having a particular character.[8] Put slightly differently: from the

---

8. K. Barth, *The Christian Life* (*Church Dogmatics,* IV/4), trans. Geoffrey W. Bromiley (Grand Rapids: Eerdmans, 1981), p. 7; paragraph 74 in its entirety is an important example of the kind of moral ontology I am recommending; on the issues here, see further my *Barth's Ethics of Reconciliation* (Cambridge: Cambridge University Press, 1995). I remain agnostic about whether the task of theological identity description of moral agents is helped by a "theodramatic" conception of the Christian faith, as proposed in, for exam-

church's confession of Jesus Christ as the center of God's dealings with creatures, theology generates a metaphysics of morals, an account of moral natures, a moral ontology. As we have already seen from Colossians, the interpenetration of the moral and the ontological is basic to a Christian theological account of the conduct of *creatures*. To be a creature is to have a particular given nature, and to act in accordance with it. The principle here is enunciated by Turretin: "As the creature has itself in being with respect to God, so also it ought to have itself in working, for the mode of working follows the mode of being."[9]

The kind of *esse* which is proper to creatures takes place as *agere;* the kind of *agere* which is proper to creatures is action in accordance with being. The separation of *esse* and *agere* — in a modern context, by retraction of *esse* and expansion of *agere* as self-realization — makes it hard for us to understand what it means to act as a *creature,* one to whom a determinate nature is given to complete in fellowship with God who creates, redeems, and perfects that nature. To act well is to act in accordance with my nature and so to move toward perfection, that is, the entire realization of my nature. Christian moral ontology attempts to listen to the gospel's instruction concerning that nature and its history, and in so doing tries (a) to assist in the formation of moral reason and its acts of judgment, and (b) to display before the intellect, the affections, and the will those objects toward which God desires and enables creatures to move.

This being so, Christian ethics is a *contemplative* as much as a *practical* science, an orientation of redeemed reason to *being* as much as to *action.* We may explicate this by meeting an objection with the claim it invites. The objection is that to speak thus is radically to misperceive the object of Christian ethics, which is the unfolding moral history between God and creatures. Moral ontology resolves moral history into abstract moral nature. The objection is already articulated with some force in Barth's Münster ethics lectures from the late 1920s, where, eager to dispose of a conception of "the ethical question" as serene observation of possible conduct, he told his hearers:

---

ple, K. Vanhoozer, *The Drama of Doctrine: A Canonical-Linguistic Approach to Christian Doctrine* (Louisville: Westminster/John Knox Press, 2005); B. Quash, *Theology and the Drama of History* (Cambridge: Cambridge University Press, 2005); and (more lightly) M. Horton, *Lord and Servant: A Covenant Christology* (Louisville: Westminster/John Knox Press, 2005).

9. F. Turretin, *Institutes of Elenctic Theology,* vol. 1 (Phillipsburg, NJ: Presbyterian and Reformed, 1992), VI.iv.9 (p. 503).

We no longer have the time to wander in distant metaphysical regions in search of the good. We no longer have the time to try to *contemplate it as being.* This *being* somewhere above the "ought" is the infallible mark of an ethics that does not quite take the "what?" of the ethical question seriously, that gets its knowledge elsewhere from the actual ethos of the ethicist and his time and background, and that is really making no more than an appearance of asking.[10]

Something similar — albeit a good deal more sophisticated — can be found in Bonhoeffer's *Ethics* as he broods on the relation of reality and the good:

> The subject matter of a Christian ethic is God's reality revealed in Jesus Christ becoming real among God's creatures, *just as the subject matter of doctrinal theology is the truth of God's reality revealed in Christ. The place that in all other ethics is marked by the antithesis between ought and is, idea and realization, motive and work, is occupied in Christian ethics by the relation between reality and becoming real, between past and present, between history and even (faith) or, to replace the many concepts with the simple name of the thing itself, the relation between Jesus Christ and the Holy Spirit. The question of the good becomes the question of participating in God's reality revealed in Christ. God is no longer an examination of what exists, for instance my essence, my moral orientation, my actions, or of a state of affairs in the world. . . . Good is the real itself, that is, not the abstractly real that is separated from the reality of God, but the real that has its reality only in God.[11]

Perhaps the most probing recent reflection on this theme can be found in Hans Ulrich's *Wie Geschöpfe Leben.*[12] The book is, at heart, an appeal to take moral history seriously, and so to resist the reduction of the new creation to some "moral *Ur-Situation.*"[13] The object of ethical

---

10. K. Barth, *Ethics* (Edinburgh: T. & T. Clark, 1981), p. 68.

11. D. Bonhoeffer, *Ethics* (Minneapolis: Fortress Press, 1996), pp. 49-50.

12. H. Ulrich, *Wie Geschöpfe leben. Konturen evangelischer Ethik* (Münster: LIT Verlag, 2005); see my article "*Wie Geschöpfe leben:* Some Dogmatic Reflections," *Studies in Christian Ethics* 20 (2007): 275-87.

13. Ulrich, *Wie Geschöpfe leben,* p. 19.

reflection is the eschatological reality of life with God in the new creation, creaturely existence in the movement of God in Jesus Christ. As such, Christian ethics is not concerned with "the course of things"[14] or with some general *humanum,* but with "the praxis of historical life";[15] its matter is not a given state of affairs, a *principium,* but an *initium concretum,*[16] which is the conversion of life brought about by God's turn to creatures in Christ.

In their different ways, these are all appeals to reintegrate the ethical and the temporal, after the bifurcation of history and the good in "metaphysical" ethics, and to do so precisely on Christological grounds: naming Jesus Christ in an ethical context precludes flight into moral essentialism or extrinsicism. There are some dogmatic dimensions to the matter: Bonhoeffer and Ulrich (and even Barth in the ethics lectures) give only a slender role to the perfection of Christ, that is, to his fully realized identity anterior to creaturely moral history, and are much more interested in the ways in which "Jesus Christ" names God's temporal presence with creatures. These dogmatic matters are of some import, but here must be laid to one side. What can be said, however, is that the antithesis between moral ontology and moral history is specious. In Christian ethics to contemplate being is not simply to note a state of affairs, for that "state of affairs" is the living commanding Christ who out of the depths of eternal deity makes history by making himself present, drawing our scattered and incoherent moral histories before him in order to judge and heal and integrate them.

This presence of his is a determination — *the* determination — of our situation: not an offer of a set of possibilities but a decision about what creatures are, and the execution of that decision in time. To contemplate this determination — that, for example, we have been transferred into the kingdom of God's beloved Son (Col. 1:13) — is not merely to observe something anterior to our moral histories so much as to grasp what our historical identity is by virtue of the active presence of Christ. Put formally: moral ontology is concerned not only with moral *space* but also with moral *time;* or perhaps we might say that moral space is not a bounded sphere populated by a set of inert objects possessed of a certain nature, but "a space to become a dramatic historical

---

14. Ulrich, *Wie Geschöpfe leben,* p. 42.
15. Ulrich, *Wie Geschöpfe leben,* p. 48.
16. Ulrich, *Wie Geschöpfe leben,* p. 88.

agent."[17] Moral ontology concerns the creature's appointment to be a certain kind of being, the creature's being moved in order to engage in a certain movement. Yet that moral *movement* is imperfectly undertaken without apprehension of moral *nature*, without intelligence of who and where we are, and of by whom we are met.

Against this, it might still be objected that appeal to knowledge of moral nature may fail to acknowledge (may indeed inhibit) the necessity of continuing moral *learning*. If knowledge of the good is not something that is more or less complete prior to action but rather occurs *in* active obedience, then it is more appropriate to speak of practices of moral learning, of coming-to-know over the course of dealing with the particularities of moral history — in the case of Colossians, over the course of believers figuring out conduct within the Christian assembly and the household (Col. 3:12–4:1). Thus "doing everything in the name of the Lord Jesus" (3:17) is the place at which knowledge of Christ is acquired, not simply the occasion for its application. A corollary is that appeal to moral nature is limited in its power to illuminate particular ethical situations or to generate particular moral claims, since it can furnish only statements of a high level of generality.

By way of response, one might begin by noting that the theological and rhetorical structure of Colossians reflects the pattern: *agere sequitur esse*.[18] But the relation of *esse* and *agere* is not one of temporal succession: *sequitur* does not mean that being is first at rest and subsequently in act, for the order of *esse* and *agere* is not chronological but logical. *Esse* as much as *agere* refers to moral history.[19] However, the moral history performed in *agere* is to be understood as emerging and taking place within the economy of God's saving works in which the agent's being as creature, and therefore his or her creaturely acts, are

---

17. Quash, *Theology and the Drama of History*, p. 214.

18. This point is made explicit in J. Ernst's comment on Colossians 3:1-4, *Die Briefe an die Philipper, an Philemon, an die Kolosser, an die Epheser* (Regensburg: Pustet, 1974), p. 220.

19. Chrysostom's perception of this is one of the strengths of his homilies on Colossians (despite their incipient moralism). On Colossians 1:10, for example, he comments: "He that hath understood God's love to man (and he doth understand it if he have seen the Son delivered up) will have greater forwardness. And besides, we pray not for this alone that ye may know, but that ye may show forth your knowledge in works: for he that knows without doing, is even in the way to punishment" (*Homilies on Colossians* [NPNF 13], p. 295).

subject to transformation. In Christian moral metaphysics, "being" means: creaturely moral reality as the recipient of redemptive divine action and as summoned to redeemed creatureliness. Further, moral learning occurs as the result of the disclosure over time of the antecedent reality described in Colossians 1 and 2. It is deepening apprehension of and obedience to the gospel imperatives by constant reiteration of the indicatives known and confessed in Christian baptism: "he has delivered us"; "you . . . he has now reconciled"; "you were buried with him in baptism, in which you were also raised with him through faith in the working of God, who raised him from the dead."

Why must Christian ethics contemplate being? In order that our moral lives can be conducted away from idols toward reality. The metaphysical impulse in Christian theology is not a flight from history — far from it: it is an element in the ascesis imposed upon sinners by the gospel, part of the needful dispossession and reengagement with the truth in which the baptismal form of Christian existence is impressed upon the subjects of God's redemptive goodness. I cannot act well if I do not know who I am; I must *learn* who I am by having my gaze drawn to a set of realities that I must come to love even though I fear and hate them; my will must make friends with those realities, at the heart of which is Christ himself and Christ in himself. The role of theological metaphysics in ethics and elsewhere is thus to ensure that we do not for a moment let our attention slip from the αὐτός ἐστιν and the ἐν αὐτῷ by which creaturely being and action are constituted. Only reality obliges us; only truth can chasten and redirect the will.

What kind of reality-indications may be derived from the confession of Christ as he expounds himself to us in his apostolic witnesses?

(1) They are *counter-indications*. They indicate a decisive alteration in reality brought about by a new act of divine goodness, by which creatures are secured for their intended perfection. Created reality has become the subject of deliverance from one dominion to another (Col. 1:13); more comprehensively, it has been set in a reconciled relation to God. The counter-reality thus established is grounded in Jesus Christ's resurrection: he is "the first-born from the dead" (1:18); we have been raised "with him" (2:12; 3:1) and "made alive together with him" (2:13). This new disposition of creation calls the "old" reality into question in a drastic way; Christian conduct is a point at which God's "setting aside" or "disarming" of disordered reality (2:14, 15) is to be visible, precisely because it is given to believers to know themselves drawn into the

abolition and regeneration of reality in Christ: "If with Christ you died to the elemental spirits of the universe, why do you still live as if you belonged to the world?" (2:20). To continue to be oriented to that which God in Christ has set aside is untruthful, living "as if," failing to see the abolition of the "old nature" (selfhood and practices) and its replacement by a new reality of permanent regeneration (3:9-10).

From here, we may formulate an answer to what Bonhoeffer thought "the ultimate and decisive question: With what reality will we reckon in our life?"[20] We are to reckon (proximately) with the history of regeneration into whose movement we and our acts are caught up, and (ultimately) with what Colossians 3:1 calls τὰ ἄνω, the things that are above, where Christ is. Bonhoeffer perceived the first, but — held back, perhaps, by some emphases in Lutheran Christology, as well as by worries about spatial conceptions of God's relation to creatures — he had a less secure grasp of the second.

> [T]he reality of God has revealed itself and witnessed to itself in the middle of the real world. *In Jesus Christ the reality of God has entered into the reality of this world.* The place where the questions about the reality of God and about the reality of the world are answered at the same time is characterized solely by the name: Jesus Christ. God and the world are enclosed in this name.[21]

And so

> there is no real Christian existence outside the reality of the world and no real worldliness outside the reality of Jesus Christ. For the Christian there is nowhere to retreat from the world, neither externally nor into the inner life.[22]

But: Christ is *above;* only because that is so do we have moral history in the world.

(2) The gospel's counter-indications of reality are not transparent, for the alteration of reality that is indicated by the confession of Christ is actual in an indirect way, and, because it is thus in some measure hidden, it is subject to contest and misperception. The believer too

---

20. Bonhoeffer, *Ethics*, p. 49.
21. Bonhoeffer, *Ethics*, p. 54.
22. Bonhoeffer, *Ethics*, p. 61.

may fail to see or to see fully its constitutive character, and may continue in allegiances and modes of action stemming from an uncertain grasp of the believer's true condition. Thus the basic pattern of exhortation in Colossians: believers must live their lives in accordance with the divinely accomplished alteration of their condition, and refuse other perceptions of reality that present themselves with self-evident force. "See to it that no one makes a prey of you by philosophy and empty deceit, according to human tradition, according to the elemental spirits of the universe, and not according to Christ" (Col. 2:8). "Philosophy" and "deceit" offer an account of the creaturely condition that carries weight; the worldly asceticism they recommend is a matter of what is by general repute "wisdom" (2:23). Believers must therefore venture their acts with a measure of defiance, on the basis of the fact that, though they "have all the riches of assured understanding and the knowledge of God's mystery, of Christ" (2:2; cf. 1:26-27), they can expect no public consent.

The natural corollary of this situation is exposure to deceit, delusion by the self-evidences of "human precepts and doctrines" (Col. 2:22). In this situation, the apostle exhorts his hearers to nonconformity, to be unafraid of the prestige of false conceptions of reality, and to allow the authority of the reality manifest in Christ to free them from harassing illusion: "Let no one pass judgment on you" (2:16); "Let no one disqualify you" (2:18); "Why do you submit to regulations . . . ?" (2:20). In short: the Christian moral life, arising within a perception of the primacy of God's regenerative grace in Christ which the gospel announces, entails learning how to steady oneself by its reality, how to act in its wake, how to refuse the charms and threats of other reality-indications.

(3) The gospel's counter-indications of reality are the law of Christian conduct, in two senses. First, they *orient* the believer in moral space and time.[23] One of the functions of moral reason is the discernment of the order of reality and of our place in that order. Reality-indications — in this case, the instruction that redeemed reason receives from the gospel about Christ's kingdom as the moral situation of believers — uncover the intelligibility of our moral lives, displaying their form and so promoting intentional occupation of moral space and movement

---

23. See the treatment of *Orientierung* in I. U. Dalferth, *Die Wirklichkeit des Möglichen. Hermeneutische Religionsphilosophie* (Tübingen: Mohr Siebeck, 2003), pp. 34-46, 149-64.

through moral time. Reality-indications enable us to read the patterns and teleology of human life, to discern that moral identity and movement are more than random accumulations. Reality is law in the sense of determinate and intelligible shape.

Second, the gospel's reality-indications function imperatively: they serve to quicken action. Hence, for example, in the apostolic injunction: "Do not lie to one another, seeing that you have put off the old nature" (Col. 3:9), the present imperative ("Do not lie") draws its authority to command from the aorist ("you have put off the old nature").[24] To say "is" is to say "ought," to be obligated by reality.

B. Jesus Christ Determines the Order of Moral Knowing

Jesus Christ is communicatively present to those who have "heard and understood the grace of God in truth" (Col. 1:6). His exaltation and session do not entail his removal from relation to creatures, nor his withdrawal into some divine darkness; rather, as the exalted one he explicates himself, addressing himself to his community, and so constituting the world as the place of revelation. Christian moral existence and conduct take place within a sphere in which a decisive noetic alteration has taken place: within the domain of the Word of God. Because this Word has been and continues to be spoken and heard, believers are summoned to a course of life shaped by "the grace of God in truth." How can this ethical domain of the Word of God be more closely characterized?

(1) Most generally, Christian existence and conduct arise from hearing a *truthful* Word, a communicative act that is penetratingly direct, untainted by deception, that does not seek to delude or manipulate, that is cold, clear truth.[25] Because this Word is true, it is trustwor-

---

24. *Apekdysamenoi* is not to be read synchronously as part of the command, but as the reason for the command; Aletti notes that "putting off" (and "putting on" in v. 10) "sont plus que de simples modalités d'exécution de ces imperatives, ils en determinent l'effectivité, et ont une function causale: c'est *parce que* les croyants se sont dépouillés du vieil homme et ont revêtu l'homme nouveau, qu'ils peuvent rejeter les vices qui constituaient leur mode d'existence antérieur" (J.-N. Aletti, *Saint Paul Epitre aux Colossiens* [Paris: Gabalda, 1993], p. 229).

25. See here B. Wannenwetsch, *Political Worship: Ethics for Christian Citizens* (Oxford: Oxford University Press, 2004), pp. 281-97.

thy; it does not belong to the economy of "empty deceit" (Col. 2:8); it is not "beguiling speech" (2:4) — marketplace rhetoric, the speech of "the mind of flesh" (2:18). To hear the gospel is to hear the truth, and this hearing is something that *has* taken place. The apostle tells his addressees that they *"have* heard," and speaks of "the day you heard and understood" (1:5, 6), and of "the gospel which you heard" (1:23) — the past tenses here indicate both the decisive interruption of a disordered economy of communication by the Word concerning Christ, and the fact that the church's present continues to be determined by that Word. The Word of Christ having been spoken, nothing remains unaltered.

(2) What has been heard in the economy of the divine Word can, therefore, be variously described. It is "the word of the truth" which is "the gospel" (Col. 1:5): the divine announcement of the hopeful truth that in Christ God is blessing creatures and directing them to their destiny in the kingdom of God. Or again, it is audible and intelligible grace, grace that "you heard and understood" (1:6). In the gospel and its proclamation grace occurs as a communicative act in which hearing and reason are drawn to attend to that which benefits creatures in a wholly unexpected and undeserved way. Grace *speaks* its blessing, and so establishes the saving rule of the Word.

(3) The domain of the Word is the place *to which* the Word has come (Col. 1:6). The Word is a gift from beyond human communicative practices, both original and eschatological. It is present not naturally but by virtue of a movement within the perfect life of God, which is the manifestation to the saints of the divine mystery (1:26-27). As mystery, the Word entirely exceeds the capacities of human speech, being beyond articulation or interpretative appropriation. If it is known, therefore, it has to be by a divine act of manifestation, an act which, moreover, elects and separates its recipients as "saints," taking them out of their customary course. In this way, the domain of the Word is a location of the divine *glory*, that is, the overwhelmingly rich majesty of God setting itself before creatures (1:27).

(4) Yet this manifestation of glory is audible, it takes contingent form as human address. That is, in the domain of the divine Word there are creaturely speech activities of which we may say: in them there is a "making known" of the Word in which both God and creatures act.

This co-action takes place, first, in apostolic speech. The gospel is God's audible grace learned from a fellow creature — in the case of the Colossian believers, from "Epaphras, our beloved fellow servant" (1:7).

Apostolic speech is *ministerial* (Col. 1:7; cf. 1:23, 25), serving the primary divine self-manifestation as an accompanying creaturely indication. Of itself, apostolic speech can say nothing; but it is not of itself, since it is the exercise of a "divine office" (1:25), a work of commissioned administration in which the apostle is given responsibility for seeing the Word through its full course. Such apostolic speech is therefore fitting when it is an enactment of "faithful ministry" (1:7), unswervingly steadfast in its allegiance to the Word by which it is preceded and which it is summoned to speak again.

Second, the divine Word is made known as it becomes a settled presence in the Christian assembly. "Let the Word of Christ dwell among you" (Col. 3:16). The Word, that is, engenders in the community of saints practices that form their moral agency: teaching, admonishment, singing, prayer. In this sense, the Word does not take place without that which the community does with the Word. But this "indwelling" does not mean that the Word is as it were folded into the formative practices to which it gives rise. Even as it is administered by the apostles and active in the community's public gatherings, the Word remains "the Word *of Christ*" — not simply the Word *about* Christ (though that sense is also there) but the Word whose speaker is Christ himself, inalienably his to utter, and only on that basis the Word of his ministers. His Word, spoken by him, *vivifies* the enterprise of moral community.

(5) The Word of Jesus Christ, active in the common life of the church, is *fruitful* (1:6). It is a productive Word, which has its term not simply in being uttered but in making moral history. Thus in its form as apostolic proclamation, the Word's end is human perfection: by it, creatures are moved to the fulfillment of their nature, namely, maturity in Christ. This movement embraces moral knowledge — "knowledge of [God's] will in all spiritual wisdom and understanding" (1:9) — and moral conduct — "leading a life worthy of the Lord, fully pleasing to him, bearing fruit in every good work" and just so "increasing in the knowledge of God" (1:10). The Word of Christ instructs, forms, and claims. It is a sanctifying Word. By this Word, Barth remarked, we are "caught at work."[26]

So far, then: Jesus Christ is the exalted one who constitutes all things, the communicative one who is present in his Word. How do

---

26. Barth, *Ethics,* p. 15.

these realities shape Christian conduct? By way of answer we look in more detail at the moral hinge of Colossians, 3:1-4.

III

> If then you have been raised with Christ, seek the things that are above, where Christ is, seated at the right hand of God. Set your minds on things that are above, not on things that are on earth. For you have died, and your life is hid with Christ in God. When Christ who is our life appears, then you also will appear with him in glory.

The opening four verses of Colossians 3 serve as a bridge from argumentation to explicit exhortation. This rhetorical function expresses the theological significance of the passage, which sums up the moral situation of believers before the letter turns more fully to instruction.[27] "Situation," we should note, not simply "perspective":[28] the Christological statements concern not just a way of looking at reality but a new reality itself. We may shy from saying that these verses communicate an ontology, perhaps on the grounds that this would suggest an over-realized eschatology in which moral exhortation had lost its point. But what Lightfoot calls a "new sphere of being"[29] is spoken of, and *only* on this basis does the subsequent paraenesis makes sense: "the

---

27. "More fully," because 3:5 does not mark a move to a new concern for ethics, but an intensification of what has been present in the preceding chapters. Hering notes that the conventional division of Colossians into 1:1-3:4 and then 3:5-4:6 "reflects the *relative* density of sheer theological or paraenetic material contained in each respective 'half' of the letter" but does not indicate a clear division of "dogmatic" and "ethical" passages (*The Colossian and Ephesian Haustafeln in Theological Context*, pp. 61-62). What unites the two "halves" of the letter is the theology of Christ's dominion. "Just as there is the unfolding of the universal scope of the dominion of Christ in the first two chapters of the letter, the third and fourth chapters give an exposition of the ways in which the lordship of Christ includes all areas of our life. Teaching and exhortation are thus closely bound to one another. As Christ is Lord over all (1:15-20), so his own people should do all in the name of the Lord Jesus (3:17)" (E. Lohse, *Colossians and Philemon* [Philadelphia: Fortress, 1971], pp. 3-4).

28. "Perspective" is J. Dunn's term in *The Epistles to the Colossians and Philemon* (Grand Rapids: Eerdmans, 1996), p. 202.

29. J. B. Lightfoot, *St. Paul's Epistles to the Colossians and to Philemon* (London: Macmillan, 1975), p. 275.

believer's being-raised-with-Christ defines the believer's horizon and modalities of action."[30]

In what history does the Christian exist and act? Answer: "You have been raised with Christ" (Col. 3:1). The Christian's moral history is shaped by reference to two past events: the resurrection of the Son of God, and the co-resurrection of the believer. Moral time now is therefore doubly defined: by Easter Day, and by the unleashing and actualizing of its transfiguring power in creaturely history at baptism. These two events are sheerly creative; in them, the redeemed moral life comes to be. This counter-indicative ontological force of the language of co-resurrection cannot be tempered into metaphor:[31] God has indeed made the believer alive (1:13; see Eph. 2:4-6). Moreover, location precedes action. Christ's significance for the moral history of the believer is condensed into the prefix "with" (συν-). Christ is not model or instructor or commander of some antecedent moral history that in some respect he modifies; rather, he *constitutes* creaturely reality by binding it into his own. "Christology has invaded all the dimensions of Christian existence. Above all it shows that for the author of Colossians the dimension of ethics is one in which the received fullness manifests itself, made to be shared"; "the believer's ethical activity comes from her situation, which is that of being alive with the same life as Christ."[32]

Yet there is no simple identity of believer and Lord; any such identity would, of course, render moral history superfluous. Believers are, as it were, in the moral interval between their resurrection-exaltation and their coming final glorification. This interval is shaped by both the aorist of having-being-raised, and the imperative: "Seek!" It is not that the aorist indicates something potential, a promise that "can only come to life in the process of 'seeking.'"[33] "Seeking" is required because

---

30. Aletti, *Saint Paul Epitre aux Colossiens,* pp. 215-16; Grässer's comment that the author "does not write a dogmatics but an *ethics*" seriously misconstrues not only the ethics of Colossians but the letter as a whole (E. Grässer, "Kolosser 3, 1-4 als Beispiel einer Interpretation secundum hominem recipientis," in *Text und Situation. Gesammelte Aufsätze zum Neuen Testament* [Gütersloh: Mohn, 1973], p. 130). By contrast, Pokorný rightly emphasizes that "the more the completion of salvation is emphasised, the more paraenesis is extended" (*Die Brief des Paulus an die Kolosser* [Berlin: Evangelische Verlagsanstalt, 1987], p. 136).

31. As it is by Dunn, *The Epistles to the Colossians and Philemon,* p. 203.

32. Aletti, *Saint Paul Epitre aux Colossiens,* pp. 216, 217.

33. E. Schweizer, *The Letter to the Colossians* (London: SPCK, 1982), p. 173.

resurrection with Christ has already taken place. The "seeking" is thus not a matter of struggling to obtain but of keeping a searching eye upon the things that are above. To envisage one's moral history as "seeking" is to enact roles and responsibilities (such as those set out in Col. 3:5–4:6) in such a way as to reduplicate the entire alteration that has taken place in Christ and into which the Christian has been drawn. It is to pursue his reality and our end in him. In this way, it is the moral movement corresponding to *nos extra nos:* we really are, and we really are outside ourselves.

What are the objects of this "seeking" that constitutes a basic act of moral existence in the domain of Christ and his Word? "The things that are above" (Col. 3:1, 2). To seek these realities is not to escape from creaturely relations. "Above" and "below" are not equivalent to "transcendent" and "temporal" — indeed, whatever else may be said of the so-called Colossian heresy, it appears to have fallen into precisely this all-too-worldly notion of the "above," which *inflamed* fascination with the flesh rather than checking it (2:23). To seek what is above, therefore, is to be directed in one's moral history by the reality which grounds that history and toward which that history moves, namely "Christ is." This seeking is not apart from the mundane realities of holy action — dealing with desire, governing speech, forbearing others, handling church, domestic, and economic relations. These realities are not of themselves "things that are on earth" (3:2) any more than rigorous devotion and bodily self-abasement are "things that are above" (2:23). Truly to seek what is above is not to flee embodied social existence but to see it as caught up in the entire reorientation of created life in the kingdom of Christ.

Because of this, once again, the instruction on common life in the church (Col. 3:5-17) or the *Haustafel* by which it is followed ought not to be read as relatively detachable conventional material awkwardly inserted after the Christological metaphysics. The paraenesis is rather the natural amplification of the Christology, a summons to practical compliance with the moral logic of ἐν κυρίῳ (the point is reinforced by the repeated references to Christ as κύριος in 3:12–4:1). As "Lord in heaven" (4:1), Christ is "before all" — *ante omnes . . . ante omnia . . . primogenitus;*[34] and his primacy is also a moral reality, that on the basis of which and toward which believers act. The distinctiveness of what

---

34. Tertullian, *Adv. Marc.* V.xix.

the gospel has to say is not simply at the level of motivation, but lies in its understanding of the nature of created reality and of moral action as falling within the *dominium Christi.*

"Seeking" is therefore an active, willed orientation to Christ and all things in him, which the apostle calls a "setting of the mind" (Col. 3:2) — a sustained effort of attention, a fixing upon a specific object in order to perpetuate truthful perception and proper use of temporalities. This fixing of the mind also entails a kind of asceticism: "not on things that are on earth." To act in such a false way would be to neglect the proper finality of created reality, and so fall into intemperance and crazy attachments that inhibit moral growth toward Christ in whom all things have their end.

But why should believers enact their moral histories in this way? Why should they reduplicate this order of being? Because this order of reality ("where Christ is," Col. 3:1) is not only external to them; it is also their own most proper reality: proper first to Christ, and so by derivation — that is, by Christ's self-communicative goodness — proper to them also. This is already stated in verse 1, in the astounding, unqualified claim: "You have been raised with Christ," and it is expanded in verse 3 by the no less astounding or unqualified claim: "You have died." The believer is no longer a participant in the unregenerate life-realm; that history is now closed. If it lives on — and the exhortation of the letter assumes that it does so — it can only be as a half-life, an absurdity, a lack of conformity to what has been made of us. And what has been made of us is that we "have" our lives in a way that is at once an unsettling of our desire to possess ourselves and also a restoration of creaturely nature and vocation. "Your life is hidden with Christ in God" (3:3). The prepositions here, σὺν and ἐν, indicate the ontological condition of the regenerate: their life is extrinsic to them, not *in se* but *ab extra.*

Here creatureliness is restored as the old nature has been killed and a new nature put in its place. But the restoration awaits its final end. The all-important backward reference in the paraenesis ought not to be mistaken for an over-realized eschatology. There is still moral time, stretching forward to the consummation of all things. "God's eschatological act has already taken place; he has called man from death to life," comments Lohse; but "this life is not conveyed to man as the divine fullness and power of immortality. Rather, it is the summons to obedient appropriation which results from having acquired salvation."[35] The new nature remains in some measure hidden; it does not share in the self-evidence of the things that are on earth. The believer's moral life is thereby burdened by a certain dishonor, for it is action within a non-evident situation, stretching out toward a blessing that goes largely unrecognized. Yet this pathos is a necessary corollary of the fact that with Christ, in God, the believer does indeed have life. "It is worth noticing," remarks Calvin, "that our life is said to be hid, so that we may not murmur or complain if our life, buried under the ignominy of the cross and various distresses, differs nothing from death, but may patiently wait for the day of revelation."[36] In distress we retain our location "with Christ" — and "what is more to be desired than that our life dwell with the very fountain of life?"[37]

Further, this limitation is not final: "When Christ who is our life appears, then you also will appear with him in glory" (Col. 3:4). The occlusion of life in Christ and its attendant ignominy is an episode in the wider history of the manifestation of the reality established in him and moving toward its climactic moment, the *appearing* of Christ, which will also be the appearing and glorification of those who share his life. "A beautiful consolation, that the coming of Christ will be the manifestation of our life."[38] Christian moral history is qualified not only by the world's negation of its true basis and direction, but also and above all by a promise. The substance of the promise is (most objectively) "Christ . . . is our life" and (as a determination of our own existence) "with him."

To sum up:

> The human existence of all of us is not really enacted at an undefined point in empty space, but in proximity, fellowship, even brotherhood with the human existence of Jesus Christ, and therefore with God's own human existence. In Jesus Christ we can see our human existence wide open to heaven, irradiated, purified, held and sustained from above, not rejected by God, but in a love that inter-penetrates all things affirmed by him in the way in which he affirms himself. And this view is not a mere theory, or vision, or moral ideal, but the unlimited and unconditional truth of our hu-

35. Lohse, *Colossians and Philemon*, p. 132.

36. Calvin, *The Epistles of Paul the Apostle to the Galatians, Ephesians, Philippians and Colossians* (Edinburgh: Oliver & Boyd, 1965), p. 346.

37. Calvin, *Galatians, Ephesians, Philippians and Colossians*, pp. 346f.

38. Calvin, *Galatians, Ephesians, Philippians and Colossians*, p. 347.

man existence, irrespective of what we deserve or achieve in our be-
haviour or attitude to this love.[39]

IV

By way of brief conclusion, what does the foregoing suggest about the
bearing of Christology upon creaturely moral history? Three things
might be noted. First, theology does well not to segregate what it has to
say about Jesus Christ from what it has to say about Christian conduct.
This, not in the hope that an ethically oriented Christology will somehow make Christ a cultural force to be reckoned with (that way lies
misery), but because of the reality which Jesus Christ is. He is the one
in whom redeemed creatures have come to be set on the way to fullness
of life. The moral lives of the redeemed do not take place in a sphere
apart from but in and with him. His being as Lord, his preeminence in
all things, is also to be seen in the moral mystery of "Christ in you."
Christology is a moral undertaking, but not in such a way that Jesus
Christ's identity is first realized or filled out in human moral activity,
as if he were amorphous until given moral definition by our conduct.
His identity is antecedently and infinitely full, and therefore limitlessly
potent. Moral Christology begins from apprehension of "the riches of
the glory of this mystery, namely Christ in you, the hope of glory" (Col.
1:27). His inherent glory glorifies, and part of the glorification of creatures is their sanctification.

Second, the gospel of Christ's resplendent glory relieves creatures
of the task of making their own moral histories. It does so by setting
before them the fact that in Christ's death and resurrection they are
made — that Jesus Christ is the actuality of the ἐνέργεια τοῦ θεοῦ (Col.
2:12). Faith in this divine energy, not self-realization, is fundamental to
the *esse* of the believer, and therefore to his or her *agere*. Christ's death
and resurrection certainly make believers to be makers — there is no
termination of moral history — yet not makers *ex nihilo* but *creatures*
who live with Christ in God. This is why the apostle can present the
shape of redeemed moral existence as a repeating of the given baptismal pattern of death and resurrection, rather than as the fashioning of
a wholly new reality. The moral history that stretches out before the re-

---

39. K. Barth, *Church Dogmatics*, II/2 (Edinburgh: T. & T. Clark, 1957), p. 558.

deemed is not indefinite; it has a distinct form. This form is one they must, indeed, disclose to themselves by apprehending and inhabiting it; but it is not one of which they are in a final way the creators. Creaturely moral history is a function of the gift of life, which in Christ flows to us from the inexhaustible fountain of God's own life.

Third, in Christian moral theology, the metaphysical task has material precedence over the paraenetic. The order of moral (not just dogmatic) theology is, first: "Him we proclaim," and then by (necessary) derivation "warning every man and teaching every man in all wisdom, that we may present every man mature in Christ" (Col. 1:28). Admonition and instruction derive from the continuing public annunciation of *him, this one*. It is certainly the case that proclamation, admonition, and instruction constitute a sequence that must be followed through to its end if the mystery of the divine Word is to be fully apprehended, for the creaturely term of that mystery includes a moral element: ἵνα παραστήσωμεν πάντα ἄνθρωπον τέλειον ἐν Χριστῷ. And, further, the derivative elements of admonition and instruction may often be first in the order of discovery, and on occasions may legitimately assume priority in the order of exposition. But they cannot be first theology; they must be undertaken in conjunction with Christian moral metaphysics. And Christian moral metaphysics is a joyful science, for it contemplates the loveliest reality, which is Jesus Christ who is all and in all.

3. Trinity, Christology, and Community

Kathryn Tanner

In contemporary theology, when issues of social ethics are raised, issues that concern the proper character of human community, the Trinity rather than Christology often takes center stage. What the Trinity is like is thought to establish how human societies should be organized; the Trinity is taken to be the best indicator of the proper relationship between individuals and their community; and so on. Jürgen Moltmann, John Zizioulas, Miroslav Volf, Leonardo Boff, and Catherine LaCugna are all important names in this regard.[1]

Although theological judgments here seem quite simple — for example, if the persons of the Trinity are equal to one another then human beings should be too — figuring out the lessons of the Trinity for social questions is a fraught task, full of complexities and perils. I systematically explore these complexities and perils here, in order to conclude that Christology is the better theological locus for clarifying the proper character of human relations in Christian terms.

---

1. See especially Jürgen Moltmann, *The Trinity and the Kingdom* (New York: HarperCollins, 1991); John Zizioulas, *Being as Communion* (Crestwood, NY: St. Vladimir's Seminary Press, 1993); Miroslav Volf, "'The Trinity Is Our Social Program': The Doctrine of the Trinity and the Shape of Social Engagement," *Modern Theology* 14, no. 3 (1998): 403-23; Leonardo Boff, *Trinity and Society* (Maryknoll, NY: Orbis, 1988); and Catherine LaCugna, *God for Us* (New York: HarperCollins, 1991).

Inflated Claims for the Trinity

My first caveat about the Trinity as the locus for questions of social ethics has to do with inflated claims made for the Trinity in contemporary theology. Many contemporary theologies overestimate, for instance, the progressive political potential of the Trinity. Monotheism, it is alleged, supports monolithic identities and authoritarian forms of government in which power is held exclusively by a single leader or group. An internally diverse triune God, in which persons share equally with one another, avoids these dangers. Or so the story goes.[2]

Overlooked in this common contrast between the sociopolitical implications of monotheism and trinitarianism are the complexities of such theological claims (Can monotheism and trinitarianism, for example, be this easily distinguished?), their fluidity of sense (Can't monotheism or trinitarianism mean many different things?), and the possible variety of purposes that each might serve. To limit myself to the last consideration for the moment: monotheism need not be all that bad in its political implications. Of course it can suggest rule by one: one God, one lord — meaning one human lord. But monotheism can also suggest (particularly when understood to deny that divinity is a general category of things) that no one shares in divinity and therefore that no one can stand in as God's representative: "no lord but God."

Trinitarianism, moreover, is not often — to say the least — historically associated with an egalitarian politics and respect for diversity within community. Trinitarian thinking arose in tandem with Christian support for an increasingly centralized Roman imperial rule, once Christianity became the state religion under the Emperor Constantine. Indeed, the major theological arguments in favor of imperial rule were not at all obviously monotheistic but presumed a diversity of divine principles or powers. Thus, Eusebius in probably the most famous of these, his "Oration in Praise of the Emperor Constantine," argues that the emperor has near absolute authority to govern the whole known human world as the agent and representative of the Word — a second divine principle among many — who rules the cosmos from on high at the supreme God's say-so.[3]

2. See Erik Peterson, *Der Monotheismus als Politisches Problem* (Leipzig: Jakob Hegner, 1935); Moltmann, *Trinity and the Kingdom,* pp. 192-202; Boff, *Trinity and Society,* pp. 20-24.

3. Eusebius of Caesarea, "Oration in Praise of the Emperor Constantine,"

Behind this poor historical showing lies the ambiguous socio-political potential of trinitarian theology itself. Many aspects of classical trinitarianism seem at least politically awkward on their face. Contrary to respect for difference, for example, divine persons are equal to one another because in some very strong sense they are the same. Short of tritheism, it is difficult to argue that divine persons are different from one another in the way human persons properly are — able to go their separate ways, distinguished by their own particular projects and interests, never in exactly the same place at the same time, distinct individuals sharing a common humanity in a general sense, but not the same one humanity in the way the divine persons are the same one and indivisible divine being or substance, and so on. Taken as an indication of proper human sociability, here it seems that humanity is subsumed by community with others. (Perhaps for this reason most advocates of a trinitarian social or political program err, to my mind, in the direction of a very strong communitarianism — that is much of the point of looking to the Trinity for social guidance.)

The common theological view that divine persons are constituted by their relations, along with the idea of their indivisibility in being and act, is simply hard to square with a politics that would like to foster the agency of persons traditionally effaced in relations with dominant members of society — women, racial or ethnic minorities, those overidentified with social roles in which their own needs and wants are given short shrift. Moreover, the order among divine persons, no matter how complex, tends to differentiate person by their unsubstitutable functions or places. The Holy Spirit, for example, has to go third in the liturgically favored, biblically derived formula, "Father, Son, and Holy Spirit." The order among divine persons is therefore ripe for justification of human hierarchy. It easily supports fixed social roles and the idea that people are equal despite the disparity of their assignment to such roles. And so on.

The turn to the economic Trinity — the Trinity's working for us in the world as the New Testament recounts it — is no help on this score, although lots of socially and politically progressive trinitarian theologians seem to think it is. New Testament accounts of Jesus' relations with the one he calls Father are much more subordinationalist in flavor than accounts of the so-called immanent Trinity usually are: Jesus prays to the

---

trans. E. Richardson, in *Nicene and Post-Nicene Fathers,* vol. 1, ed. Philip Schaff and Henry Wace (New York: Christian Literature Co., 1890).

Father, subordinates his will to the Father, defers to the Father, seems ignorant on occasion of what only the Father knows, etc. (See, for example, John 14:28; Mark 13:32; Mark 10:18; Luke 18:19; Matthew 19:17.) This sort of hierarchical relation between Son and Father, a relationship of inferior to superior, very obviously suggests the propriety of human hierarchy.

Finally, the inclusion of gendered imagery in classical characterizations of the relationships among the persons of the Trinity themselves and in their workings for the world has enormously problematic social and political ramifications. The pervasive Father-Son language of the New Testament in particular always holds the potential for rendering women second-class citizens of the church or effacing their contributions altogether. Granted, Father-Son language is always given a quite limited theological rationale in classical trinitarian theology. The point is very much not to import gender into God. That is quite explicitly denied: "the divine is neither male nor female (for how could such a thing be contemplated in divinity. . . ?"[4] The significance of the imagery is quite often limited simply to the idea that the one comes from the other and is of the very same substance with it — equal to it and not other than it. The intent is to distinguish the second person from a creature that also comes from God but is not equal to God. "Making" language therefore trumps "kinship" language when the Father's relations with the world are at issue: the Father does not act like a Father exactly in creating the world; the Father makes the world and doesn't beget it from his own substance.

The gendered imagery in classical trinitarianism is always played off, moreover, against other forms of biblical imagery of a quite impersonal sort — light and water imagery, for example. Paired with these other images, the meaning of Father-Son imagery is therefore often quite abstract, not specific to its gendered character. No one set of biblical images, furthermore, is privileged; they mutually modify one another in their theological import.[5] For example, light imagery is usually

---

4. Gregory of Nyssa, *Commentary on the Song of Songs*, cited by Verna Harrison, "Male and Female in Cappadocian Theology," *Journal of Theological Studies* 41 (1990): 441; see also Gregory Nazianzen, "Fifth Theological Oration" (31.7), cited and discussed by Harrison, "Male and Female," pp. 456-57.

5. For a clear expression of this principle, see Gregory of Nyssa, *Against Eunomius*, Book 8, sections 4-5, trans. W. Moore and H. A. Wilson, in *Nicene and Post-Nicene Fathers*, vol. 5, ed. Philip Schaff and Henry Wace (New York: Christian Literature Co., 1893), pp. 204-10.

considered far better than Father-Son imagery in conveying the inseparable, indivisible character of the two. But whatever the theological intent, the rhetorical punch of the language in practice is another thing altogether; and nothing erases the sorry history in which the importance of such language has been magnified all out of proportion, in defiance of these quite circumscribed understandings of its theological point.

Granted too that in classical trinitarian thinking this is a Father who acts like a mother: he births or begets the Son. The term used to sum up the activity of origination remains gendered male (probably because "father" is the dominant gendered term in the New Testament), but the activity itself seems much more in keeping with what only women can do — give birth. Notwithstanding the ancient biological theory in which the father is responsible for the substance of the child — the mother being a mere container for what the father contributes — what is of theological interest here is the way the Son issues immediately out of the Father like a child being birthed from its mother. It is the closeness of the relationship, in other words, that is at issue, the absence of any temporal or spatial distinction in the relationship of origin. Birth as the primary metaphor for developing whatever the Father is doing in relation to the Son is therefore quite strong in classical trinitarianism — for example, in Hilary.[6] One might even say, following Psalm 120:3, as Hilary does, that the Son is begotten of the Father's womb.[7] And Jesus' mother, Mary, an actual woman, consequently becomes a prime analogy, since her birthing, like the Father's birthing of the Son, happens in the absence of any contribution by a sexual partner: the Son — the second person of the Trinity — has only a Father in the way the Son incarnate had only a mother.[8]

This sort of gender-bending use of imagery associated with both sexes — a Father with a womb — might very well present the best hope for avoiding the theological reinforcement of male privilege. Gendered imagery is "exceeded" in a "baffling of gender literalism."[9] "Roles are

---

6. See Hilary of Poitiers, *On the Trinity,* Book 6, sections 9 and 35; Book 9, section 36, trans. E. W. Watson and L. Pullan, in *Nicene and Post-Nicene Fathers,* vol. 9, ed. Philip Schaff and Henry Wace (New York: Charles Scribner's Sons, 1899), pp. 100, 111, 167.

7. Hilary, *On the Trinity,* Book 12, section 8, pp. 219-20.

8. Hilary, *On the Trinity,* Book 12, section 50, p. 231.

9. Janet Martin Soskice, "Trinity and Feminism," in *The Cambridge Companion to Feminist Theology* (Cambridge: Cambridge University Press, 2002), p. 146.

reversed, fused, inverted: no one is simply who they seem to be. More accurately, everyone is *more than* they seem to be . . . the Father and the Spirit are more than one gender can convey."[10] Nothing stops, however, talk of a Father with a womb from simply erasing the contribution of real women by usurping their place: a man can do everything now! The genders are not being bent here in a strictly reciprocal way. The Father is not simply more than any one gender — male or female — can convey, but is already as Father everything that the other gender ordinarily suggests. The divine Father may act in the way a human mother does; and a human mother — Mary — may give birth in a close parallel to the way the divine Father gives rise to the Son. But the genders are still clearly distinguished by ranking them across the division of human and divine. Women generally and Mary in particular may be privileged over men as the closest analogue on the human plane to divine generation, but they are nevertheless bested on a divine level by what only a Father is said to do. Quite commonly, moreover, the use of both paternal and maternal language merely reinforces gender stereotyping. The Father is also a Mother because he is nurturing and compassionate and slow to anger, following, e.g., Isaiah 49:15; 66:13.[11]

One might try to avoid gendered imagery altogether. But even when absolutely equal trinitarian persons of unassigned gender are made the basis for social and political conclusions, the essential relatedness of those persons easily leads to heterosexism. The importance of differences between male and female for the identity of human persons can simply be presumed and substituted within a trinitarian account of the essential relatedness of persons to suggest that the identity of a woman depends on her relationship to a male counterpart.[12]

Clearly, then, trinitarianism can be every bit as socially and politi-

10. Susan Ashbrook Harvey, "Feminine Imagery for the Divine: The Holy Spirit, the Odes of Solomon, and Early Syriac Tradition," *St. Vladimir's Theological Quarterly* 37, no. 2-3 (1993): 114.

11. See, for example, Boff, *Trinity and Society*, p. 171.

12. Miroslav Volf, *Exclusion and Embrace* (Nashville: Abingdon, 1996), p. 187. Volf moves illegitimately here from a necessity of conceptual reference (from the fact that one term is defined with reference to another) to a necessary relation of fact (women must actually be related to men, e.g., married to them, in order to be themselves). The logical slippage involved becomes readily apparent when one considers other cases where terms are defined with reference to one another but where it would be absurd to infer a requirement of actual intertwined lives of intimacy: heterosexuality, for example, develops as a concept in relation to homosexuality, and so on.

cally dangerous as monotheism. Everything depends on how that trinitarianism (or monotheism) is understood and applied. The only trinitarianism that is clearly more socially and politically progressive than (some forms of) monotheism is trinitarianism within a very specific range of interpretations and modes of application. Those lauding the political merits of trinitarianism over strict monotheism eventually make clear that this holds only for trinitarianism when *properly* understood and employed — in other words, for the sort of trinitarianism they are actively trying to construct. What these theologians are trying to do, indeed, is systematically modify as many of the socially and politically problematic aspects of classical trinitarianism as they can.

Thus, Moltmann and Volf argue that the persons of the Trinity are not simply constituted by their relations without remainder.[13] Following Moltmann, politically progressive trinitarian theologians, such as Leonardo Boff, downplay irreversible orders among the trinitarian persons in favor of perfectly reciprocal perichoretic relations — relations of indwelling — among them: the Father is in the Son just as the Son is in the Father, etc. It is these perichoretic relations that do the heavy lifting. The reversibility of those relations, rather than identity of substance, is what accounts for the *equality* of the persons. And those perichoretic relations come to replace politically problematic alternatives, such as identity of substance, as the basis for the Trinity's *unity*.[14]

The theological merits of these politically progressive theologies hinge on how good the arguments are for such theological moves. One argument in their favor is simply the fact that these moves support a progressive social and political viewpoint — and I have no interest in denying the importance of that. But these social and political considerations hardly override the many theologically problematic features of the sort of trinitarianism typically advanced. Inexplicably to my mind, for example, no one has adequately addressed how the heavy load that perfectly reciprocal perichoresis carries in these theologies is compatible with their equally strong emphasis on the biblical economy, in which Jesus seems clearly to be acting in a non-mutual relation of subordination to the Father (e.g., the Son prays to the Father, but the Fa-

---

13. For example, Volf, "The Trinity Is Our Social Program," p. 410; Moltmann, *Trinity and the Kingdom*, pp. 172-74.

14. See, for example, Boff, *Trinity and Society*, p. 84; and Zizioulas, *Being as Communion*, p. 134.

ther does not pray to the Son; the Son does the will of the Father, but the Father does not do the will of the Son, etc.). In other words, not all the relations among the persons of the Trinity in the biblical narration of them seem even close to being reciprocal ones, in which the persons can change places with one another, and little explanation is offered for this; that fact is for the most part just ignored.[15]

The very heavy emphasis on perfectly reciprocal relations among the members of the Trinity and severe downplaying of any idea of their fixed positions in an order (for example, the persons are often now said to be all equally origins of one another, even if they are always properly named in the order Father, Son, and Holy Spirit[16]) seem, moreover, hard to reconcile with the usual ways of making clear that the persons are distinct from one another. The most common way in the history of theology is to talk about their being related to one another in some non-interchangeable way — the Father is related to the Son as the one begetting him but in doing so he is specifically the Father and not the Son — and to make a distinction on that basis between communicable or shareable properties (what all the persons exhibit qua divine) and incommunicable ones (when the Father gives the Son everything in begetting him that does not include the character of being Father).[17] Most socially and politically progressive theologies simply start from the assumption of distinct persons, taking this for granted as a feature of the biblical witness, and go on to talk about the unity of the Trinity on that basis — as a function of how closely related the persons are to one another. But if the relationships they have with one another allow for no distinctions among them, it is hard to see how such a starting assumption helps. Their relations work to undercut the distinctiveness of the persons that is simply assumed at the start, and there is no remaining way to shore it up.

Other moves made by socially and politically progressive trinitarian theologians suggest, to the contrary, that the persons of the Trinity are *too* distinct from one another. Moltmann, for example, maintains that the existence of the persons of the Trinity is distinct from their relations.[18] It is simply impossible, Moltmann maintains, for persons to

15. See Boff, *Trinity and Society*, pp. 138-39, where every biblically narrated relationship among the persons is said to involve their being in one another.

16. Boff, *Trinity and Society*, pp. 138-39.

17. See Boff, *Trinity and Society*, pp. 88-89, for an explicit rejection of the latter.

18. Moltmann, *Trinity and the Kingdom*, p. 172.

be their relations, in the way an Augustinian or Thomistic account of trinitarian persons as subsistent relations would have it. But this is simply to give the trinitarian term "person" (a rather ill-defined place-holder for whatever there might be three of in the Trinity) the modern sense of "human person" and then insist on taking it quite literally. It is impossible for human beings to enter into relationships unless they already exist; we have to exist before we can relate to other people. Or, to make the distinction between existence and manner of existence per-haps more properly (as Moltmann himself does in a later article), we can be said to exist because of certain relationships — in virtue, say, of being born of a particular mother and father — whatever the characters we come to have by way of subsequent relations with others.[19] But why assume any of this must hold for divine persons?

Quite a bit more argument than Moltmann offers would be nec-essary to justify the use of a modern sense of "person" here with impli-cations diverging so markedly from previous uses of personal language in trinitarian theology. Personal terms have long been employed to talk about the persons of the Trinity — Father and Son are the prime exam-ples. But (as Boff, pace Moltmann, properly points out in support of the use of the modern sense of person to discuss the three) that was to suggest the very constitution of such persons in and through their rela-tions with one another — there is no Father without this Son and no Son without this Father.[20] The point was to highlight their essential or constitutive relationality; personal language was certainly not used to distinguish the existence of a person of the Trinity from the *way* it ex-ists in relation to another.

Taken this literally, the argument clearly suggests tritheism. The persons of the Trinity become very much like human persons. And therefore the Trinity itself becomes a collection — tightly interwoven to be sure — of distinct persons on a very close — too close — analogy to a society of human persons.

19. Jürgen Moltmann, "Theological Proposals towards a Resolution of the *Filioque* Controversy," in *Spirit of God, Spirit of Christ*, ed. Luke Vischer (London: SPCK, 1981), pp. 164-73.

20. Boff, *Trinity and Society*, pp. 88-89, 115-16.

From God to Humans

No matter how close the similarities between human and divine persons, differences always remain — God is not us — and this sets up the major problem for theologies that want to base conclusions about human relationships on the Trinity. The chief complication is how to move from a discussion of God to human relationships, given those differences.[21] How exactly, in short, does a description of the Trinity apply to us? Three more specific problems arise here.

First of all, the differences between God and us suggest we do not understand very well what we mean when using ordinary language to speak of the Trinity. What the Trinity is saying about human relations becomes unclear, because the meaning of the terms used to talk about the Trinity is unclear. Divine persons are equal to one another but in what sense? The persons are "in" one another but what does "in" mean here? Divine persons are distinguished from one another by the character of their relations but who understands exactly what that character is? So, Hilary: "Begetting is the secret of the Father and the Son. If anyone is convinced of the weakness of his intelligence through failing to understand this mystery . . . he will undoubtedly be even more downcast to learn that I am in the same state of ignorance."[22] What indeed does even the language of "person" suggest, if with Augustine we have to say that "the formula three persons was coined, not in order to give a complete explanation by means of it, but in order that we might not be obliged to remain silent."[23] Because God is not very comprehensible to us, and certainly not fully so, discussion of the Trinity, all by itself, seems of little help in better understanding human relationships: what is difficult to understand — the proper character of human society — is explicated with reference to what is surely only more obscure — the character of divine community.

The second problem is that much of what is said about the Trinity simply does not seem directly applicable to humans. The differences

21. See Miroslav Volf, *After Our Likeness* (Grand Rapids: Eerdmans, 1998), pp. 191-200; and his "Trinity Is Our Social Program," pp. 403-7.

22. Hilary, *On the Trinity*, Book 2, section 9 (p. 55), following the more felicitous translation in Boff, *Trinity and Society*, p. 174.

23. Augustine, *On the Trinity*, Book 5, chapter 9, in *Nicene and Post-Nicene Fathers*, vol. 3, ed. Philip Schaff (Grand Rapids: Eerdmans, 1956), p. 92, following the more felicitous translation in Boff, *Trinity and Society*, p. 143.

between God and humans stand in the way. Many of these differences that prevent a direct application have to do with the essential finitude of human beings. Human society could therefore take on the very character of the Trinity in these respects in which they differ only if people were no longer human.

So, for example, it seems bound up with their essential finitude that human persons can only metaphorically speaking be in one another, if that means having overlapping subjectivities in the way the persons of the Trinity do.[24] Because all the other members of the Trinity are in that person, when one person of the Trinity acts the others are necessarily acting too. Clearly this does not hold for human persons: I may enter into or identify empathetically with the one I love, but that does not mean I act when my beloved does.

Divine persons, moreover, seem much more relational than human beings. Human persons can never be as closely tied to their relations with others as persons in the Trinity are commonly thought to be — and that is the case even were one to think (as I do not) that it is proper to make a real distinction between the existence and character of trinitarian persons.[25] Thus, it would be very unusual to suggest that trinitarian persons temporally precede the relations among themselves that make them what they are, in the way this happens in human relations. Human beings have no character to begin with, as that is decisively shaped by what happens to them later; I therefore exist prior to those relationships with duplicitous significant others, for example, that end up making me a bitter, distrustful old person.

Character, moreover, in human beings is not as bound up with actual relations with others. I can be defined by certain general relational capacities before, and whatever the way in which, these capacities are actualized in my relationships. For example, my character might be constituted by the tendency to be suspicious before, and whether or not, my relations with others give me good grounds to be that way. For much the same reasons, the character formed in me in virtue of my relations with others remains even when the relations that gave rise to it end: my character remains despite, for example, the deaths of the people and communities who have contributed most to it. The relational character-

---

24. Volf, *After Our Likeness,* pp. 209, 211.

25. See Thomas Weinandy, *Does God Suffer?* (Notre Dame: University of Notre Dame Press, 2000), pp. 115, 119, 128, 134-35, 140, 207-8.

istics of trinitarian persons, to the contrary, are much more tightly a function of actual relationships: the Father, for example, is not defined as someone with the general capacity to beget someone or other, but as the Father who is and remains such only in begetting this Son.[26]

The character of a human person, furthermore, takes different forms in the course of relations with different people. I always have the capacity to be more or other than I am right now: I have the capacity, for example, to be enormously engaging and incredibly funny (unlike now); and the capacity to be hateful when made the brunt of ridicule. And therefore to know a human person in her relations with you is to know her only incompletely. Theologians generally do not want to say anything quite like that of the Trinity: trinitarian persons are fully themselves in their relations with one another and with us; trinitarian persons are not in themselves, for example, other than the persons they show themselves to be to us.

Despite their intense relationality, trinitarian persons, moreover, remain irreducibly distinct from one another in ways that human beings cannot imitate. Father and Son remain absolutely different from one another in the Trinity, so to speak, because, unlike the case of human fathers and sons, here the Father has never been a Son — the Father is always Father — and the Son never becomes a Father in turn — the Son is always Son. The terms father and son in the Trinity do not, in short, indicate general capacities, which a variety of individuals might exhibit, but are person-defining properties. In the human case, I am different from my mother in that I am my mother's daughter but I can also become like my mother by becoming the mother of a daughter myself; and therefore in being different from my mother I am not absolutely different from her. The human relations that distinguish people never simply define them and therefore one can lose the way one has been identified in virtue of those relations (one's identity as a daughter, say, once one's mother has been dead for thirty years) and take on others (the identity of a mother to one's own daughter) while remaining oneself. But persons of the Trinity are too tied to their specific relationship, for example, of being Father and Son, to do this. They are too absolutely what they are — Son or Father — and too absolutely distinct from one another in such a relationship for that to be possible.

26. See Gilles Emery, "Essentialism or Personalism in the Treatise on God in Saint Thomas Aquinas?" *The Thomist* 64 (2000): 551-53.

Indeed, in the Trinity relations of tremendous intensity never threaten the individuality of the persons in the way relations like that threaten to blur the identities of human beings. Unlike the case of trinitarian persons, the finitude of humans seems to require the policing of boundaries between themselves and others that breaks off relationships. I will never be my own person unless I can break away from the incredibly intense relationship I have with my mother. In the Trinity, to the contrary, the persons are absolutely different from one another in the very intensity of the relationships they have with one another. It is because the relationship is so intense for them both, so to speak, that the Father can only be a Father and the Son only a Son.

Finally, human finitude also seems to entail that humans give of themselves so that others may gain in ways that often bring loss to themselves. In the case of trinitarian persons, to the contrary, their perfect equality is usually thought to involve giving without loss and receiving without increase. The first person of the Trinity does not give all of itself to the second at any cost to itself; and the second does not receive from the first what is not already its own.

One could argue, as I have done elsewhere, that loss in giving to others on the human plane is a function of a world in disarray and not a necessary consequence of simple finitude.[27] It is possible in principle for the world to be arranged in ways that make giving to others a benefit to oneself. But this simply brings us to the third problem: Direct translation of the Trinity into a social program is problematic because, unlike the peaceful and perfectly loving mutuality of the Trinity, human society is full of suffering, conflict, and sin. Turned into a recommendation for social relations, the Trinity seems unrealistic, hopelessly naïve, and, for that reason, perhaps even politically dangerous. To a world of violent, corrupt, and selfish people, the Trinity seems to offer only the feeble plaint, "Why can't we all just get along?"

So, how is the gap between the Trinity and sinful, finite human persons to be bridged in ways that allow us to see its implications for human community? One strategy for bridging the gap is to supplement the move down from the Trinity when envisioning human society, with a move up from below.[28] In other words, given what one

27. See my *Economy of Grace* (Minneapolis: Fortress Press, 2005).
28. Volf, *After Our Likeness*, p. 200; and his "Trinity Is Our Social Program," pp. 405-6.

knows about human beings, one can figure out the extent to which human relations might imitate trinitarian ones. The Trinity tells us what human relations should be like ideally. The understanding of humans as creatures and sinners tells us what sort of approximation of the ideal we are in fact capable of. The danger of such a strategy is that the Trinity fails to do any work. It does not add anything to what we already know about the real possibilities for human community, given the human limits and failings we live under.

The other major strategy for closing the gap looks to the economic Trinity for help.[29] One does not have to bring an account of the Trinity together with what one knows about the limits of human life to figure out how human relationships could come to approximate trinitarian ones. The economic Trinity — how the Trinity acts in saving us — instead makes that clear, because what one finds in the economic Trinity itself is the Trinity brought closer to what humans are capable of. For example, in the economy the Trinity appears as a dialogical fellowship of love and mutual service between Jesus and the one he calls Father — the kind of relationship that human beings could imitate in keeping with their finitude — in contrast, say, to perfectly mutual indwelling or perichoresis.

The same goes for sin. The economic Trinity is the Trinity entering a world of sin and death. Apart from any theological speculation, the economic Trinity itself therefore gives a clue to how trinitarian relations should be lived out in a world of sin. For example, those relations have the broken and sorrowful character of a Father losing his own Son by way of a death undergone for the sake of others.

The same sort of problem that beset the previous strategy resurfaces here, however. The closer trinitarian relations seem to human ones in the economy, the less the Trinity seems to offer advice about how to move beyond what we already expect of human life, given human limits and failings. The Trinity simply confirms what we already know and solidifies our chastened hopes under the circumstances. We all have some sense of what dialogical relations of loving fellowship are like. We all know about the way death severs relationships and about how obedience to a good cause often comes at the price of sacrifice in troubled times. And the Trinity offers us nothing more.

---

29. See Moltmann, *Trinity and the Kingdom;* and LaCugna, *God for Us.*

Do We Model Ourselves on the Trinity or Participate in It?

My own strategy for closing the gap also looks to what the Trinity is doing for us — what is happening in the life of Christ, in short — to answer the question of how the Trinity applies to human life. The Trinity itself enters our world to close the gap, but not (as the previous strategy suggested) by presenting us with a form of the Trinity we can imitate; the Trinity does not close the gap by making itself over in a human image of community that we can imitate — dialogical fellowship, say. Instead, in Christ the Trinity enters our world to work over human life in its image, through the incorporation of the human within the divine trinitarian life. By joining us to those relations, Christ gives us the very relations of Father, Son, and Spirit for our own. By becoming incarnate, the second person of the Trinity takes the humanity joined to it into its own relations with Father and Spirit, and therefore in Christ we are shown what the Trinity looks like when it includes the human and what humanity looks like when it is included in the Trinity's own movements — the character of a human life with others when it takes a trinitarian form, as that is displayed in Jesus' own human life.

The gap between divine and human is not closed here by making the two similar to one another, but by joining the two very different things — humanity and divinity, which remain very different things — into one via Christ, via incarnation. Trinitarian relations need not be like human relations in order for humans to be taken up in this way into them, and therefore the problematic tradeoff mentioned earlier is avoided: the more trinitarian relations seem close in character to human ones (and therefore relations that human beings could imitate) the less the Trinity tells you anything you did not already know about them. Gone, too, is the basis for hope in the idea that trinitarian relations are sufficiently close to human ones to be imitated by us. Now hope is fueled by how *different* the trinitarian relations, in which we are to be incorporated, are from anything with which they are familiar under the constraints of finitude and sin. The difference between the Trinity and us now holds out hope for a radical improvement of the human condition. The Trinity is not brought down to our level as a model for us to imitate; our hope is that we might one day be raised up to its level.

Finitude is no longer a problem either. Finitude does not make trinitarian relations inaccessible to us since human relations come to image trinitarian ones as they are swept up into them and not as they become like them in and of themselves. Human relations need not somehow become more than human themselves in order, thereby, to approximate the Trinity. Human relations, which remain fully human, only image the Trinity as they are joined up with its own life. Humans do not attain the heights of trinitarian relations by reproducing them in and of themselves, by mimicking them, in other words, but by being taken up into them as the very creatures they are. They come to share a divine form of existence, not their own by nature, by becoming attached to it.

The usual strategy of looking to the economy — the Trinity at work in the world — seems stuck on the idea that the Trinity appears to us in the economy as a model for our imitation because it fails to follow the economic workings of the Trinity all the way down to their impact on us. In other words, that strategy stops with relations among trinitarian persons in the economy — for example, the Son incarnate doing the will of the Father — and makes them a model for human ones rather than following through on what the economy of the Trinity itself is suggesting about human relations. Jesus' life, in short, exhibits not just the sort of relations that humans, in the image of the Son, are to have with Father and Spirit — relations of worshipful dedication to the Father's mission, empowered by the Spirit — but, in his relations with other people, Jesus also shows how those relations with Father and Spirit are to work themselves out in community with other people. If one wants to know how a trinitarian life impacts one's relations with other people, this second part of the story is very obviously the place to look: Jesus' relations with other people constitute the sort of human relations that the economy of the Trinity itself specifies; Jesus' way of life towards other people as we share in it *is* the trinitarian form of human social life.

It is not at all clear, however, that Jesus' relations with other people are trinitarian by following the trinitarian pattern of his relations with Father and Spirit. The human being Jesus relates to Father and Spirit in much the way the second person of the Trinity does. Because Jesus *is* the second person of the Trinity, he retains as a human being the same sort of relations with Father and Spirit that he has as the second person of the Trinity. This is a very direct translation of trinitarian relations into a human form. But none of that is true for Jesus' relations with other people; they are simply not the direct translation of trinitarian relations into a human form in the same way.

Indeed, if one takes into account the whole story of the economy — both parts of it — and avoids isolated attention to what is narrated about the relationships among the trinitarian persons, it is not at all apparent that the one side establishes the pattern for the other: Jesus' relations with Father and Spirit do not appear in any obvious way to be the model for his relations with other human beings in the story. Rather than establish the pattern for human relationships, Jesus' relations with Father and Spirit are — quite obviously — the sort of relations that it is appropriate for humans to have with Father and Spirit. One is to worship the Father following the precedent of Jesus' own prayers, carry out the will of the Father as human beings filled up with, empowered by, the Holy Spirit as Jesus was, which means working for the well-being of others in the way Jesus did, and so on. But why think one will relate to other humans in the process in anything like the way one is relating here to Father and Spirit?

Let me make the same rather obvious point in light of the way we are incorporated within the trinitarian life by being joined to Christ. When humans are incorporated into the Trinity through Christ, different people are not spread out across the Trinity to take on its pattern; instead, we all enter at the same point, we all become identified with the same trinitarian person, members of the one Son, sons by the grace of the Holy Spirit; and move as a whole, as one body, with the second person of the Trinity in its movements within the dynamic life of the Trinity. The Trinity does not therefore in any obvious way establish the internal structure of human community, the unity of the Trinity being what makes human society one, the diversity of the persons establishing its internal complexity. Instead, the one divine Son and the one divine Spirit are what make human society one; we are one, as the Pauline texts suggest, because we all have the same Spirit and because we are all members of the one Son. And the diversity of this human community is internal to the one Spirit and one Son, so to speak; the diversity is a diversity of gifts of the Spirit and of that one Son's bodily members. Rather than establishing the pattern of unity and diversity in human community, the Trinity establishes more what that one united but diverse body of spirit-filled sons by grace does, how it moves; the whole body of Christians moves together in the way any single human being, united to Christ's own life, follows a trinitarian dynamic.

There are of course New Testament passages that suggest the unity between Son and Father is what unity in human community is to be like: Jesus asks his Father "that they may be one as we are one" (John 17: 11, 22). Rather than read these passages as some brief for understanding the unity of human persons on an analogy with unity among persons of the Trinity, one can, however, take them to be indicating simply the centrality of Christ, and of his relations with the Father, for our relations with the Father. That is, Christ is one with the Father, perfectly doing the Father's will, and we should all be one by being one with the Father as Jesus is — united in doing the Father's will in the way Jesus does it.

The way Jesus images in a human form the relations among Father, Son, and Spirit has an effect, of course, on his relations with other people: Jesus relates to other people in highly unusual ways, which have everything to do with his relations to Father and Spirit. The way the persons of the Trinity relate to one another over the course of Jesus' life, relations among the divine persons in which we are to share by being united with Christ in the Spirit, bring with them changed relations among human beings. The Son is sent by the Father into the world, and empowered by the Spirit, to carry out a mission that brings him into relationship with us. A life empowered by the Spirit in service to the mission of the Father for the world means that Jesus is with and for us, and that we, in turn, are to be with and for one another, in the way that mission specifies.

The character of that mission, as Jesus' own way of life makes clear, is to inaugurate a life-brimming, spirit-filled community of human beings akin to Jesus in their relations with God: the mission means bringing in the kingdom or new community that accords with Jesus' own healing, reconciling, and life-giving relations with others. This way of being is what the trinitarian relations as they show themselves in the economy — Jesus' praying to the Father and serving the will of the Father in the power of the Spirit — amount to in human relational terms. Jesus' relations with Father and Spirit make his whole life one of worshipful, praise-filled, faithful service to the Father's mission of bringing in the kingdom; that is to be the character of our lives too, both in and out of church, as we come to share Jesus' life. We are to participate in the Father's mission for the world, mediating the life-giving Spirit of Christ, through union with him. Glorified, worked over into Christ's image so as to take on his shape in relations with other human beings, we are to form the citizens or members of a new kingdom or community with Christ as both the director and forerunner of the sort of new lives we are to lead together.

The question then becomes what the kingdom has to do with the Trinity that works to bring it about. To what extent is the kingdom, in other words, not just the consequence of a trinitarian life like Jesus' in relation to Father and Spirit, bound up, part and parcel of it for that reason, but also reflective of the Trinity's own character? A lot depends here on exactly what one thinks the kingdom is like. I would venture that the kingdom is like the Trinity in that both are supremely life-affirming of all their members, organized to bring about the utmost flourishing of all. Both are paradigmatic instances of what I have called elsewhere a community of mutual fulfillment in which the good of one becomes the good for all.[30] The Trinity is coming to us to give us the sort of life-giving relations of mutual flourishing that the Trinity itself enjoys.

There is an analogy then with the Trinity, but not a very specific one. What one gets out of the Trinity here for an understanding of the kingdom one might also find by treating any number of other theological topics — the incarnation, for example. The incarnation too — but in a significantly different manner from what one finds in the Trinity — sets up a kinship, in this case between humanity and divinity, a community of now mutual fulfillment in that the human is to benefit from what the divine already enjoys — divine life. In some ways, indeed, the incarnation is a better model for the sort of human community or kingdom to be set up: when every human being becomes one in Christ this overrides in a significant sense forms of already-established kinship that would otherwise keep people apart; this is an unnatural community, one might say, in much the way human and divinity in Christ are an unnatural community, made up of what is naturally disparate and dissimilar. More like the relationship between humanity and divinity in Christ than the Trinity, this is a community of previously diverse persons brought together only by something different from them that they all share — Christ.

---

30. Tanner, *Economy of Grace*.

4. The Whole Christ and the Whole Human Being: Dietrich Bonhoeffer's Inspiration for the "Christology and Ethics" Discourse

Bernd Wannenwetsch

The Primacy of "Critical Christology"

In this essay, I'd like to investigate three christological formulae *(Christus totus, Christus praesens, Christus pro me)* as to their critical significance for Christian life and moral discourse. I will stress the critical significance of these christological formulae not only over against christologically underdetermined types of Christian moral discourse, but also for their capacity to challenge the idealist or foundationalist tendencies that often characterize the debates on Christology and Ethics. It is my contention that a christologically saturated account of the Christian life will steer clear of the temptation to conceive the moral discourse that accompanies it as an exercise of *application:* whether this means applying traces of Christ's "personality" (the idealist or pedagogical temptation) to the moral life or a web of doctrinal propositions that map out a complete picture of reality (the foundationalist temptation).

My analysis will be developed in close conversation with Dietrich Bonhoeffer, since I can hardly think of a theologian or moral theologian better equipped to sensitize us to the critical requirements of the "Christology and ethics" discourse — as well as to its manifold and often unnoticed temptations. I will begin by scrutinizing Bonhoeffer's main moves in his 1933 Lectures on Christology,[1] which can be shown to have shaped his approach to moral theology in a variety of ways. Al-

---

1. Dietrich Bonhoeffer, *Christology,* introduced by E. H. Robertson, trans. J. Bowden (London: Collins, 1966).

though his massive *Ethics* fragment, written a decade later, contains substantive passages in which Bonhoeffer reflects on christological issues and their significance for the work of the moral theologian, familiarity with his earlier and more detailed lectures will be of critical importance to understand the christological framework within which Bonhoeffer situates Christian moral life and moral discourse.

The first structural observation that we are offered by looking at the table of contents bears some conceptual weight: it is very telling that Bonhoeffer spends the majority of his time and energy addressing what he calls "critical Christology," whereas the sections on "constructive Christology" are comparatively brief. Why this prerogative of critical Christology? Why prioritize the mode of doctrinal discourse that answers the question of who Christ is by addressing a multitude of wrong and unhelpful avenues in which this question has been approached? There must be more to this than the epistemological truism that constructive thought often unfolds best when forced to respond to provocations of heterodox claims, the argumentative repulsion of which eventually becomes the matrix for orthodoxy's refinement of its own stance.

The primacy of critical Christology in Bonhoeffer's account, I suggest, might be understood on the basis of Calvin's claim that the human heart is a factory of idols,[2] relentlessly projecting the complex of our desires and anxieties onto a screen-like sky, populating it with a pantheon of deities that resemble these desires more than they reign over them. This process of religious gestation is, as Bonhoeffer understood, not alien even to Christianity, insofar as Christianity, too, is involved in "doing religion."[3] Although "religion" is no more than the

---

2. "*. . . hominis ingenium perpetuam . . . esse idolorum fabricam.*" John Calvin, *Institutes of the Christian Religion* (1559), 1.11.8; cf. 1.5.12. Calvin's famous definition draws on Luther's characterization of the human being as *"animal rationale habens cor fingens."* The human being is, according to Luther's reflection on Genesis 8:21, a being furnished with reason that has a heart that imagines, pictures, and invents. *Luther's Works* (St. Louis: Concordia, 1955-86), vol. 2, p. 123.

3. Cf. the first stanza of Bonhoeffer's poem "Christians and Pagans": "Men go to God when they are sore bestead, pray to him for succour, for his peace, for bread, for mercy for them sick, sinning, or dead; all men do so, all: Christians and unbelieving." Dietrich Bonhoeffer, *Letters and Papers from Prison*, enlarged edition, ed. Eberhard Bethge (London: SCM Press, 1971), p. 348. On Bonhoeffer's account of religion and Christianity, see Bernd Wannenwetsch, "Christians and Pagans: Bonhoefferian Reflections Towards the Second Naiveté of a 'Converted' Religion or Christologically Mediated Creatureli-

"garment" of Christianity,[4] the actual entanglement of church and religion gives us reason to reckon with a vivid culture of christological or Jesu-logical "productivity" in terms of private and collective idiosyncrasies, projections and apologetic strategies that typically appear to be a few steps ahead of the church's doctrinal discourse in its attempt to test, adopt or correct such products. Hence we understand why the christological discourse got to be mainly "critical," if not polemical; and the assumption it could be otherwise — the academic theologian's sabbatical fantasy of a period of quiet and undisturbed working toward a constructive system of "positive Christology" — cannot but appear somewhat naïve.

Turning to the actual content of Bonhoeffer's Christology Lectures, I'd like to begin with a quotation from a letter to Eberhard Bethge from April 1944 that strikes me as a most useful summary of Bonhoeffer's agenda, even for the 1933 Lectures. "What is bothering me incessantly is the question what Christianity really is, or indeed who Christ really is, for us today."[5] This is indeed *the* question to ask, according to Bonhoeffer, both in Christology and for the Christology and ethics discourse. *Who* is Christ — not *what* he is, or *how* he is the god-man; who *is* Christ — not who *Jesus was*. What matters is the *Christus praesens*, not a figure of the past that could serve as an inspirational moral exemplar. The emphasis is decisive in a further respect, too: Who is Christ *for us* — not Christ *per se*, but precisely *pro me*. The *numerus* matters, too, in Bonhoeffer's expression: the Christ *pro me* is not "for me" in terms of an individualized egotism of salvation, but very decidedly for *us* — in the ecclesiastical plural. Finally: Who is Christ for us *today?* Bonhoeffer's famous concern for the "concreteness" of Christian ethics beyond formalism and casuistry is rooted in his quest to get in touch with reality as it really is.[6] An ethics that does not abstract from

---

ness," in *"Who Am I?" Dietrich Bonhoeffer's Theology Through the Lense of His Poetry*, ed. Bernd Wannenwetsch (London: T. & T. Clark, 2009, in press).

4. *Letters and Papers from Prison*, p. 280.

5. *Letters and Papers from Prison*, letter of 30 April 1944, p. 279.

6. "Christ did not, like an ethicist, love a theory about the good; he loved real people. . . . Thereby we are turned away from an abstract ethic and toward a concrete ethic. We can and should speak not about what the good is, can be, or should be for each and every time, but about *how Christ may take from among us today and here*." Dietrich Bonhoeffer, *Ethics*, ed. Clifford Green, Dietrich Bonhoeffer Works 6 (Minneapolis: Fortress Press, 2005), pp. 98f.

reality must be rooted in an account of reality that does not abstract from the one who has insurmountably determined it as mediator and redeemer of all things.

The 1933 Lectures on Christology

We shall now investigate, from the Christology Lectures that the young *Privatdozent* delivered at the University of Berlin in 1933, how Bonhoeffer understood the three formulae and their inner connectedness. All three: *Christus praesens, totus Christus,* and *Christus pro nobis,* are seen as answering the one question: Who is Jesus Christ? — each one for itself, and all together.

Not *what* is or *was* Jesus Christ, but *"Who is Jesus Christ for us today?"* Since the *logos* is not an idea, but the incarnate, it would for Bonhoeffer be "a godless question" to ask: "How can it be possible you exist?" Only the question: "Who are you?" acknowledges the strangeness and otherness of the person we encounter. Yet this question, which is dramatically intensified when the crucified one appears as the resurrected,[7] can be put in two mutually exclusive ways. It can be the question of one who knows that he has been encountered and that the question he asks the other person is pointing back to himself: "You being who you are — who, *then,* am I?" But the question "Who are you?" can also be asked in a way that really means to ask *how* to deal or cope with the other, or eventually even how to get finished with him.[8]

The primacy of the "who" question over the "what" and "how" questions is based on the fact that, as Bonhoeffer puts it, "there is no access to man unless he reveals himself of his own accord."[9] Any other approach would be — at best — failing to arrive at the person or — at worst — mean violent intrusion. If granting that self-revelation — or in classical philosophical terms, "appearance" — is the only basis on which we can get to know a person, we must, however, not conflate the order in which the recognition of person and work occurs: "I have access to the work of Christ," Bonhoeffer states, "only if I know this person who does this work. It is essential to know the person if the work is

7. *Christology,* p. 34.
8. *Christology,* p. 36.
9. *Christology,* p. 38.

also to be known. If Jesus was the idealistic founder of a religion, I can be elevated by his work and stimulated to follow his example. But my sins are not forgiven. . . . Jesus' work leads to despair in myself, because I cannot imitate his pattern. But if Jesus is the Christ, the Word of God, then I am not primarily called to emulate him; I am encountered in his work as one who could not possibly do this work myself."[10]

Here Bonhoeffer points to a crucial implication for the Christian moral discourse, implicitly drawing on Luther's distinction between imitation of Christ *(imitatio Christi)* and conformation with Christ *(conformatio cum Christo)*. Later we shall see what this suggests for the possibility for Christians to do virtue ethics, based on emulation and habituation. Before we get to this, however, we must alert ourselves to the wider context in which Bonhoeffer situates this insight. The main lesson to learn from the traditional christological controversies, as Bonhoeffer analyzes them, is that two avenues must be avoided, both of which represent the "how" question: either to think of Christ in terms of an abstract being, a Christ "per se" (the Scholastic temptation); or to think of Christ in terms of his efficient power, as a sheer *pro me* (the Protestant temptation).

In the church's Greco-Roman period, the "what" and "how" questions tended to be couched in the framework of "substance/accidence" (Christ's divinity as substance, Jesus' humanity as accidence),[11] and it was the narrowness of this framework that provoked the rise of a series of heretical movements the church had to ward off — although the churches did not always manage to transcend the framework. Bonhoeffer narrates the history of christological controversies up to the Chalcedonian decisions with great determination and confidence of judgment. Over against the stereotypical liberal-Protestant reservation with the Chalcedonian formulae (seen as subjecting Christian thought to Greek philosophical frameworks) Bonhoeffer stresses that they must actually be understood as a liberation from the straightjacket of Greek philosophical conceptuality.[12]

In rejecting the Monophysite and Nestorian heresies, the Chalcedonian definitions took recourse to negative language in detailing how the two natures can be thought to coincide in the one person of Christ. The wisdom of the *particula exclusiva* approach, for Bonhoeffer, is pre-

10. *Christology,* pp. 38-39.
11. *Christology,* p. 81.
12. *Christology,* pp. 104-5.

cisely that it determines the limits of the "what" and "why" discourse once and for all times, freeing up again the sense of the "divine mystery" of the god-man that can only be approached by the categorically different question of "Who is Jesus Christ for us today?"

"After the decision of Chalcedon, it is no longer permissible to objectify the divinity and the manhood in Christ and to distinguish them from each other as entities. We cannot form a concept of God and then draw boundaries within it."[13] The problem with the formulae of the patristic church was not, as liberal Protestantism suggested, that the use of an ontology of substance physicalized what should have been understood as a moral relation *(sittlich)*; rather, the mistake was based, as Bonhoeffer puts it, on "the way in which the nature of God and the nature of man were spoken of in a theoretical, objectifying way, so that these natures were regarded as two entities, distinguishable from each other, which afterward come together in Jesus Christ." But, as Bonhoeffer explains further, "the relationship between God and man cannot be imagined as a relationship of entities; it can only be thought of as a personal relationship. Moreover, nothing can be known of either God or man before God has become man in Christ."[14]

If we are prepared to follow Bonhoeffer thus far in acknowledging that the christological discourse can only be pursued appropriately if the existential connection of the inquirer with the one who is inquired of is part of the inquiry process itself, as opposed to observational and objectifying modes of inquiry, the question still remains: "How could the person of Christ be recognized and known other than by his work?" At this point, Bonhoeffer voices a sharp verdict: "This objection contains a most profound error."[15] And this for two reasons: the first is that the work of Christ is not unequivocal. It can be interpreted and has been interpreted as the work of a moral or religious hero, or even as a work of blasphemy, to name just two extremes. The historical deeds of Jesus of Nazareth — irrespective of the historiographical problem of accounting for them — do not speak unambiguously. History as such is not revelatory of, but rather a hiding place for the truth of Christ and his work. "No, he did his work in the incognito of history, in the flesh."[16]

---

13. *Christology,* p. 91.
14. *Christology,* p. 105.
15. *Christology,* p. 39.
16. *Christology,* p. 39.

Therefore, Bonhoeffer insists there can be only one way of accessing the person of Christ, and that is at the very locus of his revealing presence in the here and now: the church. Only here, at the divinely assigned locus of his presence, can Christ be approached and experienced without ambiguity. Any other approach is bound to remain partial (such as the search for the historical Jesus) and will never get to the whole Christ. Only *Christus praesens* is *totus Christus,* and vice versa: the whole Christ is always the present Christ. Personal presence, in turn, is articulated in temporal, spatial and relational terms, which again reinforces the claim of the sole accessibility of Christ in and as his body, the church.[17]

Hence we arrive at a triadic conclusion that, I believe, characterizes Bonhoeffer's account accurately: the present Christ is the whole Christ is the Christ *pro me*. In regards to the Reformation motto of *pro me,* Bonhoeffer guards himself against a twofold misunderstanding of the presence of Christ, both sides of which are of massive importance for our understanding of the Christian life and its concomitant moral discourse. The first misconception is to construe presence as effective power, resembling the dynamist heterodoxy; the other is to construe presence as representation, the problematic exemplified by the so-called *Extra Calvinisticum.*

To think of Christ's presence in terms of *dynamis,* effective power, tends toward thinking of him in an impersonal way. Interestingly, Bonhoeffer finds this same mistake in those (nineteenth-century) theologies that tended to emphasize the "personality" of Jesus. This rhetoric, he states, actually aims at "the opposite of what is meant by person. 'Personality' is the fullness and harmony of the values that are combined in the phenomenon of Jesus Christ. 'Personality' is fundamentally an a-personal concept. It ends up in the neuters 'power' and 'value.' But in that case, the christological question is obliterated."[18] This last qualification owes much to the way in which Bonhoeffer sees the "personality talk" relating to the framework of questions that he previously discussed: "The questions which are put about personality are 'How?' and 'What?'; about the person, the question is 'Who?'"[19]

Bonhoeffer also stresses how this modern christological underdetermination, represented in the theologies of Schleiermacher and

17. *Christology,* p. 43.
18. *Christology,* p. 44.
19. *Christology,* p. 44.

Ritschl, mirrors a particular approach to the order of person and work: if the phenomenon of Christ is being accessed by way of inquiring about his "personality," it must be done by looking at the work first, and from there only to the person. The implication of this approach, though, is that the resurrection can no longer be described as constitutive in any strong sense. The dead Jesus can just as well "be thought of" and remembered "like Socrates or Goethe."[20]

Luther, on the other hand, followed a very different rationale when he began to think of Christ's presence under the impression of his resurrection and ascension. Bonhoeffer quotes the Reformer: "When he was on earth, he was far from us. Now he is far from us, he is near to us."[21] The core problem of the aforementioned liberal accounts Bonhoeffer finds not in their overemphasizing of the *pro me*, but in their understanding of this formula according to a dynamist rationale (thinking from work to person). The actual significance of the *pro me*, though, is that it points out the inevitable existential relatedness in which the person of Christ appears and is to be thought.

> Christ is Christ not as Christ in himself, but in his relation to me. His being Christ is his being *pro me*. This being *pro me* is in turn not meant to be understood as an effect which emanates from him or as an accident; it is meant to be understood as the essence, as the being of the person himself. . . . That is, Christ can never be thought of in his being in himself, but only in his relationship to me. That, in turn, means that Christ can only be conceived of existentially, viz. in the community. Christ is not a Christ in himself and additionally still in the community. He who alone is the Christ is the one who is present in the community *pro me*.[22]

Bonhoeffer finds this core distinction between a (primarily) ontological perspective and a (primarily) existential perspective neatly summarized in another quote by Luther: "So it is one thing if God is there, and another if he is there for you."[23]

Both major ways in which Christian theology has been less than faithful to the personhood of Christ — the Scholastic reduction of it to

20. *Christology*, pp. 44-45.
21. *Christology*, p. 45, no reference given.
22. *Christology*, pp. 47f.
23. *Christology*, p. 48; Luther: WA (Weimar Edition) 23, p. 152.

a "being per se" and the Protestant reduction of it to efficient power whether in its pietistic (individualist salvation) or liberal (inspirational personality) variant, suffered, as Bonhoeffer sees it, from the same problem: both types miss the full personhood of Christ by configuring the truth of the logos as a timeless category — an idea. The Word, in the biblical sense, is not an idea but always an address: "not timeless truth," as Bonhoeffer states, but "truth spoken in the concrete moment, the address which puts a man in the truth before God."[24]

It is precisely this concreteness that the Word assumes as address which is insurmountably present in the sacramental life of the church. And it is here that we see Bonhoeffer's next critical move emerging: his critique of presence conceived as representation. "The Word in the sacrament is an embodied Word. It is not a representation of the Word. Only something which is not present can be represented."[25] The traditional debates surrounding the so-called *Extra Calvinisticum* illustrate this problem. If, as theologians of the Reformed wing of the Reformation assumed, Christ as logos-person needed to be thought as present externally to the actual Eucharistic consumption, according to a surplus of the logos' being over its own embodiment, we are faced, according to Bonhoeffer, with yet another variant of the christological "how" question.[26] In fairness to the Reformed tradition, Bonhoeffer notes that the Lutheran counter-position did not fully escape from the problematic framework of the how question. Although, in Bonhoeffer's view, the Lutheran understanding was more faithful to the incarnation, the idea of Christ's ubiquitous presence according to the *genus repletive* made it, again, too difficult to think of him as person.[27]

Thus, Bonhoeffer summarizes his main intention: "The question *how* that can be must be changed into the question *who* this person is. The answer is: the historical one *(geschichtliche) and* the crucified, the resurrected *and* ascended one, the God-human, revealed as brother *and* Lord, as creature *and* as creator."[28]

---

24. *Christology*, p. 51.

25. *Christology*, p. 54.

26. "This *extra-Calvinisticum* is the result of the question 'How?'" *Christology*, p. 56.

27. *Christology*, p. 57.

28. *Christology*, p. 59. Translation altered, as Bowden's version fails to render the emphasis on the conjunction "and" that I italicized.

Christus praesens — *totus Christus* — *Christus pro me*

We are now going to look at the three christological formulae — *Christus praesens, totus Christus, Christus pro me* — in turn, with a more pronounced view on their significance for the Christian moral discourse. I suggest doing so in close connection with another triad, offered by Bonhoeffer himself, which invites itself as a structuring principle. We can relate any one of the christological formulae to one of the three ways in which, according to Bonhoeffer, Christ is embodied in the church: as word, as sacrament, and as congregation.[29] In a series of very condensed summaries, these relations amount to the following critical patterns:

For the *present Christ,* to live as his body, the concrete Christian congregation *de loco et tempore,* affords a twofold vigilance: a vigilance against "representational accounts of the moral life" as they are found in social-activist agendas (of mostly Reformed types) which are typically characterized by the language of "making present," "realizing," "applying," or "campaigning"; the second critical vigilance afforded by the *Christus praesens* is over against uncritical theological adaptations of classical virtue approaches, in particular when these are based on a variant of the *imitatio Christi* tradition.

For the *totus Christus,* we focus on his presence in the sacrament. In it, Christ gives himself unreservedly and completely, to be consumed, in a correspondingly holistic fashion, by the whole human being of mind, soul, and body. Hence the formula *totus Christus* is prone to challenge any compartmentalizing either in Christology or in human life — a temptation that ethical theories are prone to give in to otherwise. Fragmentation enables instrumentalizing. Bonhoeffer's sacramentally grounded resistance to compartmentalizing accounts crystallizes in his moral concept of "the responsible life" that he thinks best characterizes the interaction of the "whole Christ" with the "whole human being."

Finally, I suggest interpreting the moral significance of Bonhoeffer's account of the *Christus pro me* from the perspective of the third way in which Christ is present in the church: as Word. The existential relatedness that the formula *pro me* expresses, understood as not only benefiting from but first of all being addressed by Christ, affords a critical stance over against foundationalist accounts of the moral life, in that

29. *Christology,* p. 47.

Christ's Word *pro me* is to be understood in a primary way as *critical interlocution* to, not a constructive basis of human moral discourse. It is the external Word of judgment that calls human beings out of their habitual patterns of self-assurance.

Whereas in soteriology, the *pro me* is precisely reassuring the believer so as to deliver her from insecurity and doubt, in moral matters the same liberating character of the Word frees her from the temptation of organizing an ethical topography in such a neat and comprehensive fashion as to allow for a moral life beyond doubt. While we cannot anachronistically expect Bonhoeffer to employ non-foundationalist language, his concept of "mediation" points in that direction. Christ the mediator is the critic of all attempts at immediacy: in human relationships as much as in moral theorizing.

We can now attempt to visualize the connection that the three christological formulae have with the three modes of the presence of Christ in the church in a diagram. In so doing, we can also include the respective exemplary moral concepts that Bonhoeffer sees developing from within these respective contexts. The diagram also highlights certain aspects of Bonhoeffer's participation in the German resistance movement as they can be understood to biographically reflect and "fit" the moral concepts respectively.

Formula:	*Christus praesens*	*totus Christus*	*Christus pro me*
Location:	congregation	sacrament	word
Moral concept:	conformation	responsibility	mediation
Biography:	taking on guilt	vs. escapism	open to judgment

Christ Present as Congregation

Overcoming Moral Idealism The concrete Christian community is, as Bonhoeffer puts it in his lectures, "his only *gestalt* between the ascension and the second coming."[30] Hence he locates the ethical center of Christology in ecclesiology, since the church as the body of Christ is the concrete and sensory way in which the *gestalt* of Christ is experienced within space and time. "The starting point of Christian ethics is the body of Christ, the form of Christ in the form of the church, the

---

30. *Christology*, p. 59, translation altered.

formation of the church according to the form of Christ."[31] In listening to the word and celebrating at the Lord's Table, the congregation is made so fully one with Christ as his body, that Christ's presence need not (and cannot) be "represented" in a significatory way. "The community is therefore not only the receiver of the Word of revelation; it is itself revelation and Word of God. Only insofar as it is itself the Word of God can it understand the Word of God."[32]

In other words: the church in its existence as body is a "letter of Christ" to the world (2 Cor. 3:3). The church exists as Christ's presence in the world by virtue of its sacramentality. Therefore, we may conclude, there is nothing to "represent" here: either in terms of the liturgy as human action that merely "mirrors" on earth the union of hearts and logos that really happens up in the heavens *(sursum cordae)*, or in terms of an ethics that "lends credibility" to the claim of Christ's rule and presence through human action.[33] The church in its very living as Christ's body — *Christ's* body and Christ's *body* — renders false any idealist construal of the Christian life that aspires to a farfetched ideal out there, aiming at the best possible proxy values of "realizing" these ideals. As Bonhoeffer himself puts it: "God hates this wishful dreaming," as found in projects of church "development"[34] or in "Christian programs" of "Practical Christianity."[35] For Bonhoeffer, idealism, in all its variants — including moral idealism — is a blunt conceptual denying of the presence of Christ as congregation.

Challenging an Ethics of Emulation The same sacramental realism comes to bear on Bonhoeffer's account of the church as the locus of Christian formation: "Formation" *(Gestaltung)*, he states, "occurs only by being drawn into the form of Jesus Christ, by *being conformed to the*

31. *Ethics*, p. 97.

32. *Christology*, p. 60.

33. Presence in a sign is at the same time presence and absence of the signified. And in regards to the moral life, it will typically be more the absence than the presence of Christ that becomes a motivation for ethics to actively "fill the gap" that the "not yet" of the presence in the sign leaves open. See further on this problem: Bernd Wannenwetsch, "Ecclesiology and Ethics," in *The Oxford Handbook of Theological Ethics*, ed. Gilbert Meilaender and William Werpehowski (Oxford: Oxford University Press, 2005), pp. 57-73.

34. Dietrich Bonhoeffer, *Life Together/Prayerbook of the Bible*, ed. Geffrey B. Kelly, Dietrich Bonhoeffer Works 5 (Minneapolis: Fortress Press, 1996), p. 36.

35. *Ethics*, p. 92.

unique form of the one who became human, was crucified and is risen."[36] Already, in the opening paragraphs in his *Ethics* fragment, Bonhoeffer stresses that the question Christian ethics is supposed to ask is not: "How can I be good?" or "How can I do something good?"[37] Rather: "*The subject matter of a Christian ethic is God's reality revealed in Christ becoming real among God's creatures,* just as the subject matter of doctrinal theology is the truth of God's reality revealed in Christ."[38]

In that Bonhoeffer emphasizes the idea of passively *being* conformed to Christ over against attempts to (actively) make something of oneself by emulating Christ's deeds, he seems to be pointing to a problem that is similar to that which moral philosophy has long known as the so-called "Meno problem." For the classical Greek philosophers a commitment to the principle that same can only be recognized by same made *some* level of virtue necessary for the individual in search of a virtuous person worth emulating. So, simply put, how is one to *become* virtuous without *being* already virtuous? The hint that Aristotle gave to answer this problem was social moral convention. Before you begin to watch and emulate their virtuous actions, you can recognize the virtuous persons due to the fact that they are held in high esteem within the polis. This structure is paralleled in the conventionalism of liberal Protestant accounts of moral formation that typically conceived of moral formation as an educational process in which the religious *a priori* that exists *in nuce* in every person is developed and brought to flourishing through the inspirational impact of a religious genius.

However, the problem with the idea of Jesus as moral exemplar whose works are to be emulated is that it assumes these works can be taken on their own, in abstraction from the person of Christ. Yet since the work is determined by the person, emulation of individual deeds would at best produce semblances of Christ's deeds; it would be as it was with Simon the sorcerer in Acts 8, who, in offering money to the apostles for the gift of the Holy Spirit so that he could do the same works that he had watched them do with ogling fascination, revealed that he was actually interested in the *phenotype* of their powerful deeds only. Yet, to be healed by Christ is not "a healing experience" that could, at least in theory, be reproduced by any other highly skilled prac-

36. *Ethics,* p. 93.
37. *Ethics,* p. 93.
38. *Ethics,* p. 49.

titioner, but a Christ-experience that gives the healing a unique quality in the first place.

Discipleship, understood properly, is unlike virtue habituation through emulation. In fact, when Jesus sends his disciples to preach in the villages, to heal or to cast out demons, they do this as those who travel under the auspices of Jesus' own *exousia* — his powerful authority that he sends along with them; the disciples are, strictly speaking, doing "his deeds" rather than their own. Accordingly their "moral" aim must be to simply stay within the sphere of their calling and do what comes to hand, instead of aiming at perfecting their vocational skills through exercise so as to eventually rival or transcend the master's own virtuosity in them.

The same would be true of the attempt to emulate Christ's attitudes. They too cannot be isolated from their bearer and hypostasized as "values" that could be reproduced. Yet, we might hear an objection being raised at this point: Does not Paul, in Philippians 2, precisely summon the congregation to mimic Christ's kenotic disposition when he says: "Your attitude should be the same as that of Christ Jesus"? Two observations are required here. First, Paul is summoning the congregation to simply be what they are, which is "at one" with Christ: of one mind and body with him. Second, as the actual content of the Christ hymn that follows this summons reveals, the imperative toward mimesis is ironically broken. That hymn, which elaborates upon Christ's "attitude," does not point to Jesus' good works on earth, but rather to Christ's exclusive soteriological "work," that is, his mission of incarnation, cross, and resurrection. Ironically, Paul seems to be asking the believers to precisely emulate that which cannot be emulated — apart from *being* made one with Christ himself, which cannot be achieved by emulation at all.

This is the bedrock insight of Luther's famous distinction between Christ as *exemplum* and Christ as *sacramentum*, which the reformer emphasized in a clear and irreversible order: only if Christ is recognized *first* as God's mysterious, efficacious gift[39] that renews the

---

39. This same distinction in Luther is also rendered as between *bonum* and *exemplum*. "Christ as a gift nourishes your faith and makes you a Christian. But Christ as example gives your works a workout. They do not make you a Christian, but they proceed from you, you who have already been made to be a Christian." *Luther's Works*, vol. 31, p. 357. Cf. Oswald Bayer, *Martin Luther's Theology: A Contemporary Interpretation*, trans. Thomas H. Trapp (Grand Rapids: Eerdmans, 2008), pp. 63-64.

human heart *(sacramentum)*, can it *then* happen for those thus united with him that they find Christ-like attitudes, patterns of thought, and emotions growing in and among themselves. What Luther sought to defend by this christological formula — "sacrament first, exemplar second" — was not an abstract priority of salvation over sanctification or of human receptivity over activity; what he sought to defend was rather Christ's *ongoing activity as a living* sacrament, as opposed to his being reduced to a *historical* role of exemplifying moral values. In keeping with this distinction, Luther was reluctant to embrace the medieval tradition of imitation of Christ *(imitatio Christi)* and suggested instead to speak of the Christian life as the process of being con-formed with Christ *(conformatio cum Christo)* — an idea that came to feature centrally in Bonhoeffer's account of the Christian ethics.

Toward the end of the analysis of any one of the christological formulae and their moral significance, I suggested looking at how each one of these was reflected in Bonhoeffer's own biography, and in particular in his work for the German resistance movement. One of the most striking — and controversial — concepts that Bonhoeffer introduced, and that came to illuminate biographical decisions he made, is the idea of "taking on guilt" on behalf of others. This is particularly interesting in our context, as it looks, on the surface, like a straightforward imitation of Christ's own "vicarious representation of mankind." To make things even more puzzling, Bonhoeffer explicitly states that such action is only possible because Christ has entered human guilt and hence has become the one in whom all vicarious representative action is grounded. Jesus showed real love for human beings that could not "abandon human beings to their guilt"; and accordingly, responsible action "springs from the selfless love for the real human brother or sister — it cannot seek to withdraw from the community of human guilt."[40]

We shall further analyze the notion of "willingness to become guilty" for the sake of others later on when we take a look at the two other christological formulae. At this point however, it suffices to say that Bonhoeffer understood this concept as including the willingness to suffer. But in keeping with his emphases on the *Christus praesens* and the becoming conformed to him, the point of suffering guilt for the sake of others was not to suffer *as* Christ suffered, but rather to suffer *with*

---

40. *Ethics*, p. 275.

Christ, to "watch with him in Gethsemane"[41] or — in Apostolic language — "to fill up in our flesh what is still lacking in regard to Christ's afflictions, for the sake of his body, which is the church" (Col. 1:24).

Totus Christus *and the Whole Human Life*

Challenging a Moral Anthropology of Separation "For the christological question, of its very nature, must be addressed to the whole Christ, the one Christ."[42] The focus on the sacrament that I propose to adopt in this section points to the two sides of the holism at stake: according to the Lutheran emphasis on *manducatio oralis,* the actual sensual consumption of the Eucharistic elements that enter the mouth of the communicants, the *whole* Christ gives himself into consumption by the *whole* human being of soul, mind, and body. As Bonhoeffer puts it in his correspondence from Tegel prison: "The Bible does not recognize our distinction between the outward and the inward. . . . It is always concerned with *anthropos teleios,* the *whole* man. . . . The 'heart' in the biblical sense is not the inner life, but the whole man in relation to God."[43]

Over against the separation of the religious from the secular sphere which effectively turns the concern of Christ into a "provincial affair"[44] and belies the "unity of the reality of God and the reality of the world established in Christ,"[45] Bonhoeffer reminds his readers: "The will of God, as it was revealed and fulfilled in Jesus Christ, embraces the whole of reality. . . . Faith in this Jesus Christ is the single source of all good."[46]

In his own time and country, Bonhoeffer found missing precisely

41. The quotation echoes the line in Bonhoeffer's poem "Christians and Pagans" where he highlights what genuinely distinguishes the former from the latter: "Christians stand by God in his hour of grieving." *Letters and Papers from Prison,* p. 349. In his letter to Bethge from 18 July 1944, Bonhoeffer explains: "Jesus asked in Gethsemane, 'Could you not watch with me one hour?' That is the reversal of what the religious man expects from God. Man is summoned to share in God's sufferings at the hands of a godless world. . . . This being caught up into the messianic sufferings of God in Jesus Christ takes a variety of forms." *Letters and Papers from Prison,* pp. 361-62.

42. *Christology,* p. 40.

43. *Letters and Papers from Prison,* p. 346.

44. *Ethics,* p. 57.

45. *Ethics,* p. 59.

46. *Ethics,* p. 75.

that holy simplicity whose gaze would be firmly fixed on this single source of good. The various moral attitudes that existed among the German people — "sense of duty," "private virtue," "conscientious-ness," and so forth — proved to be insufficient — "rusty weapons" — to the task of resisting the Nazi temptation.[47] Each of these attitudes, in some way, allowed for a typically "divided gaze." One eye may well have been set on the neighbor and her plight while another eye was fixated on one's own integrity and self-protection, or the overriding concern for one's own moral self.[48] The "man of private virtue" is a particularly illuminating type, as he embodied this divided gaze that allowed him to dwell in two different spheres at the same time — his private life and his public existence — when the beatific vision of one allowed him to turn a blind eye to the atrocities of the other.[49]

Over against the existence of such a *"di-psychos,"* a being of a divided soul, and its tumbling into moral disaster, Bonhoeffer commends a combination of simplicity and wisdom[50] — the only moral attitude, in his view, that could again bring "ground under our feet."[51] As an abstract ideal, though, even this unity of simplicity and wisdom would be bound to fail as well, but Bonhoeffer thought it possible when grounded in Christ. "Only because there is one place where God and the reality of the world are reconciled with each other . . . is it possible there and there alone to fix one's eyes on God and the world together at the same time. This place . . . lies in Jesus Christ, the reconciler of the world."[52] Only a Christology that resists any reductionism and represents the *totus Christus* (Christ as the No *and* Yes to human life, in judgment and reconciliation) can be met with a moral response able to resist the flight into any of those moral self-images ("man of duty,"

---

47. *Ethics*, p. 81.

48. On the problem of the "moral self," see Bernd Wannenwetsch, "Responsible Living or Responsible Self? Bonhoefferian Reflections on a Vexed Moral Topic," *Studies in Christian Ethics* 18 (2005): 125-40.

49. The "banality of evil" as represented by Adolf Eichmann and characterized by Hannah Arendt was a case in point, as the "architect of the Holocaust" and cold-blooded chief mechanist of mass destruction was, when put to trial in Jerusalem in 1961, found to be anything but a monster, but irritatingly normal, a reportedly good husband, father, and neighbor in his "other (private) life." See Hannah Arendt, *Eichmann in Jerusalem: A Report on the Banality of Evil* (Harmondsworth: Penguin Classics, 1994).

50. *Ethics*, p. 81.

51. *Letters and Papers from Prison*, p. 3.

52. *Ethics*, p. 82.

"man of private virtue," etc.) that effectively divert human allegiance to a number of conflicting authorities instead of to God alone.

Overcoming Moral "Christologies of Separation"   It is most interesting to see that Bonhoeffer understood this same connection as operating the other way round, too: only the uncompromised wholeness of a moral existence lived in "simple" (undivided) obedience to Christ will safeguard the christological discourse from eventually becoming "partial," i.e., reducing Christ to a Christ of "cheap grace" (a mere "yes"), a mere giver of moral advice, or a prototype of Aryan superiority, and so on. Since Ethics and Christology share the same subject matter — "the form of Christ taking form in the world"[53] — in their interdependence both discourses provide ever-new material for critical scrutiny by the respective other.

Bonhoeffer's formula of *totus Christus/totus homo,* the whole Christ, responded to by the whole human person, serves as a criterion of testing on each side of the correspondence for overt or subtle forms of reductionism. This calls for a particular alertness to discern how the one-sided emphasis on a particular christological aspect or moment engenders a correspondingly narrowed account of the moral life — be it an incarnationalist theology resulting in a random celebration of everything "material" or "bodily," or a theology of the cross, promoting an ideology of altruistic self-sacrifice, or a theology of the resurrection, eventually endorsing variants of moral or cultural triumphalism.[54]

A Christology that seeks to keep up with the doctrinal standard of "the whole Christ" will consequently be instrumental in the unmasking of such reductionisms. This standard is, however, not functioning in such a way as to seek or engender a "balanced" approach in which all moments are neatly arranged and equally weighted; rather it functions polemically, when, for example, a triumphalist emphasis on the resurrection needs to be countered with a solid theology of the cross, lest we end up with an ethics not of the resurrected one, but an ethics "of resurrection," itself hardened to a principle. As we are never in a position where we could start from scratch, but always have to respond to a concrete situation that is mostly likely characterized by a certain over- or underemphasis of any of such moments, the *totus*

---

53. *Ethics,* p. 102.
54. "The glory of the new life is hidden with Christ in God" (Col. 3:3), quoted in *Ethics,* p. 95.

Christus formula will in most cases actually appear as a critical calling into question rather than as a constructive principle itself.

Responsible Action Following up from our attempt to match Bonhoeffer's conceptual world with his biographical decisions, we hit on another of Bonhoeffer's core moral concepts in the context of his emphasis on the *totus Christus*: responsibility. "This life, lived in answer to the life of Jesus Christ (as the Yes and No to our life), we call *'responsibility.'* This concept of responsibility denotes the complete wholeness and unity of the answer to reality that is given to us in Jesus Christ, as opposed to the partial answers that we might be able to give, for example, from considerations of usefulness, or with reference to certain principles."[55]

Whereas the insistence on one's own moral integrity prevents one, as Bonhoeffer sees it, from actually making the neighbor's concerns the driving principle of one's action, responsible action is genuinely free for the neighbor, precisely as it is free from self-concern. Responsible action can be expected to arise from those who do not "seek to avoid becoming guilty" and therefore do not "place their personal innocence above their responsibility of other human beings."[56] Acting responsibly in allowing selfless love of neighbor to override any concern for the self, including the quest for an uncontaminated moral self, included for Bonhoeffer the willingness to "take on guilt"[57] for the sake of others. This moral commitment became all too real for Bonhoeffer when, for example, his involvement in smuggling Jewish individuals across the Swiss border in the famous "Operation Seven" required him to be prepared to fake documents, deceive and lie to the border guard, and more of same.

Yet it was precisely this willingness that led, in turn, to the discovery of what Bonhoeffer called true worldliness. "I'm still discovering right up to this moment, that it is only by living completely in this world that one learns to have faith. . . . By this-worldliness I mean living unreservedly in life's duties, problems, successes and failures, experiences and perplexities. In so doing we throw ourselves completely into the arms of God, taking seriously, not our own sufferings, but those of God in the world — watching with Christ in Gethsemane."[58]

---

55. *Ethics*, p. 254.
56. *Ethics*, p. 276.
57. *Ethics*, p. 282.
58. *Letters and Papers from Prison*, pp. 369-70.

Christus pro me *and the Divine Word*

Overcoming Immediacy and Self-Justification We now turn to the last formula: *Christus pro me.* Earlier we saw how Bonhoeffer understood this as Christ's existence as living Word that addresses his creatures and calls them to a life "for others." Responsible action, then, is the appropriate moral response to the address that is Christ: to his life, work, and person. "At the risk of my life, I give an account . . . for what has happened through Jesus Christ. Primarily, therefore, I do not take responsibility for myself, for my actions: I do not justify myself (2 Cor. 12:19). Rather, I take responsibility and answer for Jesus Christ."[59]

In this formulation we encounter what is perhaps the most exciting turn in Bonhoeffer's moral Christology: when he characterizes the active answer to Christ — the moral life — as accounting for Christ in the world, *instead* of accounting for oneself before the world. To act vicariously for others, and be willing to take on guilt on behalf of others, is revealed as perhaps the only path that steers us away from living a life of (more or less subtle forms of) self-justification.

Bonhoeffer's determination is to throw himself upon the merciful judgment of God. In so doing, he does not anticipate that very judgment by mounting a solid philosophical or theological defense of an intended course of action *ex ante,* by recourse, for example, to a justifying moral principle. Instead of a matter of self-assured absolution, Bonhoeffer conceived of his involvement in the conspiracy as "an act of repentance"[60] on behalf of his people and his own sharing in their trial and guilt.

For Bonhoeffer, to forgo any attempt at justifying oneself through moral reflection that aims at a totally unambiguous "go ahead, you will be justified in what you do," means to live open to God's judgment instead of anticipating it. It means, in other words, to accept Christ as the mediator of all things — the Christ that "gets in between": between our moral knowledge and our moral action, between the other human being and myself, and even between myself and myself. Christ the mediator shuns any claim at immediacy that human beings are so prone to make. Christological mediation is the most wholesome of all detours, as it is the only way to arrive at the

---

59. *Ethics,* p. 255.
60. *Ethics,* p. 13, editors' introduction.

other, at myself, at moral action that side of exploiting and distorting violence.[61]

The Christ that "gets in between" is precisely Christ, the Word — the Word that actively addresses us and withstands our attempts at domestication through interpretation. Put in the language of the Reformation, we may say that Christ the mediator and critic of immediacy is the word that we encounter as *verbum externum et alienum,* the external and strange word. While it is true that in Christ we encounter the God who has made himself known, and not an anonymous *deus absconditus,* Christ remains strange to us, as much as he is familiar; he remains not-ours, as much as he is totally ours.

This emphasis on the distance in which Christ remains to us — in, with, and under his proximity — can, I believe, open up a way in which Lutherans can appreciate the moment of truth in the *Extra Calvinisticum* and its interest in the sovereignty of Christ. If not understood in terms of a quasi-substantial surplus of Christ's person over what has become human of it, but as the perennial resistance of Christ against any form of domestication, the meaning of the *Extra Calvinisticum* could even be seen as complementary with the meaning of the Lutheran counter-position. The latter can, I suggest, be understood as dealing with the same problem of domestication. Although the Lutheran emphasis on the *manducatio oralis* was historically generated as a polemical reaction to the Calvinist stressing of a christological reserve in regard to Eucharistic consumption — Christ as giving himself as *totus Christus,* but not *in toto:* not completely and exhaustibly — the sensuality of the Lutheran motto appears to point to a convergence in purpose, at least. If Christ is conceived as giving himself totally and unreservedly into the consumption by the believing community, the very

---

61. Bonhoeffer's emphasis on christological mediation as a critique of immediacy appears in several contexts of his thought, including his account of community in his reflections on "Life Together." "Perhaps the contrast between spiritual and emotional, self-centred reality can be made most clear in the following observation. Within the spiritual community there is never, in any way whatsoever, an 'immediate' relationship of one to one another." *Letters and Papers from Prison,* pp. 40-41. "Spiritual love . . . knows that it has no direct access to other persons. Christ stands between me and others. I do not know in advance what love of others means on the basis of the general idea of love that grows out of my emotional desires. All this may instead be hatred and the worst kind of selfishness in the eyes of Christ. . . . Contrary to all my opinions and convictions, Jesus Christ will tell me what love for my brothers and sisters really looks like." *Letters and Papers from Prison,* p. 43.

materiality of this consumption (chewing, tasting, swallowing, digesting) mounts, in its own way, an obstacle to domestication, insofar as bodily consumption eschews the distance between consuming subject and consumed object that domestication requires.

The Word as Interlocutor vs. Foundationalist Concepts of "Christology and Ethics" These insights are also of utmost importance for the moral "use" we make of Christology: Christ is not the *foundation of* our moral knowledge, but the *interlocutor to* our moral discourse[62]; he is not the one to assure us, but the one to challenge us, not the one who *is* near, but the one who *comes* near:[63] Christ, the mediator.

The gospel narratives confirm this point when they tell of the notorious strangeness of Jesus — for his family, for his hometown, and even his "true family," his disciples. Over and over again, these narratives tell of Jesus' failing to meet the expectations: of the people, the religious elite, or again of his own disciples. He appears scandalous at one time and opaque at another time, never to be pinned down, fixated, or domesticated. Yet, the radical foreignness and challenge that Christ will continue to be for us is met by an equally radical coming near: while Jesus cannot be grasped whenever we want him and for whatever use we might have for him, Christ gives himself totally in the assigned time and space of his Eucharistic presence where the Word is as near as to be incorporated. The Word is stubbornly and wholesomely external for the principal reason that it is destined to be internalized eventually; yet to be internalized not in such a way as to be domesticated by human interpretation or "putting it into action," but — just as John of Patmos had to eat the scroll (Rev. 10:9) — to domesticate us into the household of those who live by consuming the living Word that transforms them from within.

---

62. The resistance that the incarnate Word represents, in particular for the moral life and discourse, has been emphasized with particular fervor by Hans Ulrich in his book *Wie Geschöpfe leben. Konturen evangelischer Ethik* (Münster: LIT Verlag, 2005). Cf. also the multi-authored volume, *The Theological Ethics of Hans G. Ulrich: Critical Reflections on Wie Geschöpfe leben,* ed. Susan Frank Parsons, Studies in Christian Ethics 20 (London: Sage, 2007).

63. "The word is near you, on your lips and in your heart (that is the word of faith)" (Rom. 10:8).

Conclusion: Eucharistic Ethics and the Idealist Temptation

We conclude then, with the grain of Dietrich Bonhoeffer's theology: that christologically saturated ethic *is* a Eucharistic ethic. Dietrich Bonhoeffer understood that a Christian ethic whose subject matter is "how Christ may take form among us today and here" must begin with "Christ as he exists in the world," that is, as his body in space and time: the church.

In saying that christological ethic is a Eucharistic ethic, I am not claiming that the practice of taking the Eucharist is an action that must then be realized in our moral life. In fact, the Eucharist is neither a *thing* nor a bit of knowledge that can be utilized in moral deliberation. Rather, questions about the moral life will be assessed according to the standard by which a proposed course of action can be said to "fit" the Eucharistic life — whether or not our human actions can harmoniously coexist with the Eucharist which is Christ's presence at the same time it is the presence of his judgment, the Yes and No, No and Yes to our lives. Christologically saturated ethic does not ask "What would Jesus say?" (if he was present) or even worse: "What would Jesus have said?" (if he was still alive), but rather: Does this or that instance of human conduct "belong" here — in the presence of Christ, *Christus praesens, totus Christus, Christus pro nobis?*

If we were to characterize the main target of this analysis then, it would not be inappropriate to see it primarily addressing what I would call the "idealist temptation": both in the Christian life and in the discourse on Christology and ethics. A first — and more obvious — critical gain could be had in regard to the problematic of accounts that present Jesus as moral ideal or exemplar and eventually replace Christology with pedagogy. To address this, we have seen Bonhoeffer draw out the significance of Luther's shifting of emphasis from *imitatio Christi* to *con-formatio cum Christ* as well as his understanding that Christ needs to be taken first as *sacramentum* before he can be taken as *exemplum*. We have seen how Bonhoeffer elaborates on these distinctions, by watching him interpret three classical christological formulae in such a way as to close the door for reductionist accounts, both in Christology and ethics, whether romanticist, historicist, or compartmentalist in kind: the "whole of Christ" who is calling forth the response of the "whole human being" is at the same time the *Christus praesens* and the *Christus pro nobis.*

A second, perhaps less obvious critical gain of our analysis can be marked in regard to a more subtle temptation that is inherent in the

Christology and ethics discourse itself: precisely as it succeeds in warding off the "pedagogical" temptation of reducing Christ to a moral exemplar, it seems easily susceptible to another form of idealism — the construal of the interrelatedness of both discourses that assumes that "if only we get our Christology right, the proper ethics will be easily derived from it and follow suit."

Since both discourses share the same subject matter: "Christ taking shape in the world" (as mediator of creation, reconciliation, redemption as well as of sanctification), the interdependence of Ethics and Christology must be understood as a lively process of mutual instruction and challenge. This insight should make us cautious of the idea that the positive relation between Christology and ethics can be sufficiently represented in a balanced doctrinal account that details what christological "moment" or *datum* engenders what moral claim. The representation of the *totus Christus* that drives the process of Christ-formation cannot be domesticated in any discourse, since it is not an idea, a principle, a system that "re-presents" Christ in the word, but Christ's own self-giving in and through the Spirit. This is the reason why the stressing of the crucial role of worship in which the whole Christ gives himself to his people by addressing mankind as a whole in all their faculties (emotional, rational, will) as the one who is praised and prayed to, listened to (proclamation), and eventually incorporated (Eucharist), must amount to a serious methodological caveat.

Only this encounter with the whole Christ in the complexity and mediation of worship allows us to not misrepresent the constitutive role of Christology for Christian moral thought and life and vice versa. In abstraction from this *locus theologicus,* the well-meaning discourse on Christology and ethics to which this essay happily contributes is prone to eventually end up *substituting* for the process of conformation with Christ rather than endorsing it.

Since, as Bonhoeffer reminded us, sanctification belongs to the subject matter of Christology from the outset, the discourses on Christology and on Ethics need to be aware and ward off the idealist temptation to initially secure individual grounds of expertise that will only in a secondary step be brought into relation with the respective other. Such a Christology and ethics debate would not be worth having, because it would methodologically reestablish a Christology of separation and ethically promote a "thinking in two realms," no matter how doctrinally sound their individual formulation might be.

5. Forgiveness as New Creation: Christ and the Moral Life Revisited

Lois Malcolm

Introduction

As Hannah Arendt has observed, forgiveness is Christianity's unique contribution to the Western world.[1] The Greeks did not have a concept of forgiveness, and although it may have had a role in Roman law, it was for the most part not a major category of human action in the ancient world. Jesus of Nazareth brought forgiveness to the forefront. Not only did he create controversy by forgiving other people's sins — taking on the power that God alone had to forgive sins[2] — but he also enjoined his followers to forgive one another, and even made God's forgiveness of them contingent on their forgiving others.[3] The Lord's Prayer enjoins God to forgive us as we forgive our debtors.[4] At the Last Supper, Jesus invites his followers to eat bread, "my body," and drink wine, "my blood of the covenant, which is poured out for many for the forgiveness of sins."[5] After his resurrection, Jesus grants his disciples the Holy Spirit who will enable them to forgive and retain sins.[6] After his ascen-

1. Hannah Arendt, *The Human Condition* (Chicago: University of Chicago Press, 1998), pp. 236-43.

2. See Luke 5:21-24; cf. Matthew 9:4-6 and Mark 2:7-10. See also Arendt, *The Human Condition,* p. 239.

3. See Matthew 6:14-15; see also 18:35 and Mark 11:25. See also Arendt, *The Human Condition,* p. 239.

4. See Matthew 6:9b-13; cf. Mark 11:25; Luke 11:2-4.

5. Matthew 26:26-28.

6. John 20:22-23; see also Luke 24:44-49.

sion, Jesus sends the Holy Spirit who propels the disciples with a message — from Judea to Samaria to the ends of the earth — that calls people to repent and be baptized so their sins may be forgiven and they too may receive the Holy Spirit.[7]

While forgiveness has been at the heart of Christian faith and practice over the centuries, it is interesting to note that it has also become a central theme in contemporary scholarly and popular literature. Given the reality of conflict throughout the world, forgiveness and reconciliation are increasingly becoming topics of interest in philosophy[8] and politics.[9] Moreover, forgiveness is also becoming a major theme in psychological literature and its self-help variants, literature that attends to its import not only for interpersonal relationships at home or at work but also for one's individual growth and sanity.[10]

In this paper, I examine the relationship between Christ and ethics by arguing, from a reading of Paul's Christology, that Christian forgiveness cannot be divorced from the new age the crucified and raised Christ has ushered in, a "new creation" that Christians believe we have a foretaste of even on this side of the eschaton.[11] In my interpretation of

---

7. See Acts 1:8 and 2:38, where the response to Christian proclamation includes repentance, baptism, forgiveness of sins, and reception of the Holy Spirit (see also 8:16; 10:44-48; 19:1-6).

8. See, e.g., Jacques Derrida, *On Cosmopolitanism and Forgiveness,* trans. Mark Dooley and Michael Hughes (New York: Routledge, 2001), and Charles L. Griswold, *Forgiveness: A Philosophical Exploration* (Cambridge: Cambridge University Press, 2007).

9. See, e.g., Peter Digeser, *Political Forgiveness* (Ithaca, NY: Cornell University Press, 2001), and Martha Minow, *Between Vengeance and Forgiveness: Facing History after Genocide and Mass Violence* (Boston: Beacon Press, 1999).

10. For psychological work on forgiveness, see Robert D. Enright and Richard P. Fitzgibbons, *Helping Clients Forgive: An Empirical Guide for Resolving Anger and Restoring Hope* (Washington, DC: American Psychological Association, 2000); Robert D. Enright, *Forgiveness Is a Choice: A Step-by-Step Process for Resolving Anger and Restoring Hope* (Washington, DC: American Psychological Association, 2001); Michael E. McCullough, Kenneth I. Pargament, and Carl E. Thoresen, eds., *Forgiveness: Theory, Research, and Practice* (New York: Guilford Press, 2001); and Everett L. Worthington, *Dimensions of Forgiveness: Psychological Research and Theological Perspectives,* Laws of Life Symposia Series, vol. 1 (West Conshohocken, PA: Templeton Foundation Press, 2000), *Forgiveness and Reconciliation: Theory and Application* (New York: Brunner-Routledge, 2006), and *Handbook of Forgiveness* (New York: Brunner-Routledge, 2005).

11. See Galatians 5:6; 6:15. Paul's use of "new creation" echoes Isaiah 65:17-25. Paul understands salvation as God's re-creation of the world (see Rom. 8:19-23; 2 Cor. 5:17-19; see also Rev. 21:5). For an earlier treatment of this relationship, see Jürgen Moltmann,

this Christology, I also draw on two secular appropriations of Christian notions of forgiveness that have creativity at the heart of their understanding of forgiveness.[12] I develop this argument in four sections. First, I locate my argument in relation to contemporary debates in Christian ethics and in political thought. Second, I examine two major secular appropriations of Christian understandings of forgiveness — as a form of psychological creativity (in Julia Kristeva)[13] and as a form of political creativity (in Hannah Arendt).[14] Third, I examine Paul Ricoeur's complex and detailed account of the "Adamic myth" in Paul's theology, an account that explicitly demonstrates by way of close readings of biblical traditions how the forgiveness and justification identified with Jesus' death and resurrection cannot be divorced from an eschatological context.[15] Finally, I discuss the ethical implications of the profound link within Christian faith between forgiveness of sins and new creation.

A Context for My Argument

I situate my argument by way of a contrast with two conceptions of Christian ethics. Several decades ago, in a book called *Christ and the Moral Life*, James Gustafson analyzed different ways theologians have related Christology to ethics. In that book, he developed a typology

---

"Justification and New Creation," *The Future of Creation: Collected Essays* (Philadelphia: Fortress Press, 1979), pp. 149-71.

12. For an account compatible with my argument, see F. LeRon Shults and Steven J. Sandage, *The Faces of Forgiveness: Searching for Wholeness and Salvation* (Grand Rapids: Baker Academic, 2003). For an influential theological critique of the psychological use of forgiveness, see L. Gregory Jones, *Embodying Forgiveness: A Theological Analysis* (Grand Rapids: Eerdmans, 1995).

13. See Julia Kristeva's essays on "Can Forgiveness Heal?" and "The Scandal of the Timeless," in *Intimate Revolt: The Powers and Limits of Psychoanalysis,* trans. Jeanine Herman (New York: Columbia University Press, 2002), pp. 14-24, 25-42. See also "Dostoyevsky, the Writing of Suffering, and Forgiveness," in *Black Sun: Depression and Melancholia,* trans. Leon S. Roudiez (New York: Columbia University Press, 1989), pp. 173-218. For other relevant works by Kristeva, see *Hannah Arendt,* trans. Ross Guberman (New York: Columbia University Press, 2001); *New Maladies of the Soul,* trans. Ross Guberman (New York: Columbia University Press, 1995); and *Powers of Horror: An Essay on Abjection,* trans. Leon S. Roudiez (New York: Columbia University Press, 1982).

14. See Arendt, *The Human Condition,* pp. 236-47.

15. See Paul Ricoeur, *The Symbolism of Evil,* trans. Emerson Buchanan (Boston: Beacon Press, 1967).

based on three central ethical concerns: the sources of the moral good, the self's agency, and criteria for moral judgment and action.[16] Christologies that depict Christ as "creator and redeemer" focus on how Christ is the source of the good in Christian ethics. Those that focus on Christ as "justifier" and "sanctifier" focus on how Christ is the source of the self's moral agency. Those that focus on Christ as "pattern" and "teacher" focus on how Christ is the criterion of judgment and action in the Christian life.

In this essay, I take one of these themes, "Christ as justifier," as the answer to the three main questions, but in doing so I argue for a somewhat different construal of "Christ as justifier" than the one Gustafson outlined. Drawing primarily on Martin Luther and Reinhold Niebuhr, Gustafson defines justification as freedom. Defined negatively, this freedom is a freedom from legalism. Defined positively, this freedom enables one to love the neighbor, to be open to the present and the future, and to be realistic and pragmatic.[17] I agree that justification entails these things; nonetheless, I stress something Gustafson does not. Following the apostle Paul, I argue that justification cannot be divorced from the new eschatological age he identifies with Christ's cross and resurrection. This new age, or new creation, has an embodied and corporate character that includes not only Christ's work as justifier and sanctifier, but also enacts Christ's creative and redemptive power and provides, albeit in a fashion that continually seeks to discern what is most fitting in each situation, a concrete criterion for judgment and action — Christ's cross and resurrection.

I make this case in response to a recent trend in Christian ethics in North America, a trend exemplified in the work of Stanley Hauerwas, which stresses the distinctive character of the biblical narrative and the centrality of the Christian community especially in shaping the virtues required of the Christian life.[18] Although I have no disagreement with any of these emphases — they clearly are central components of any thoroughgoing conception of Christian ethics and

---

16. James Gustafson, *Christ and the Moral Life* (New York: Harper & Row, 1963).

17. Gustafson, *Christ and the Moral Life*, chap. 3.

18. See, e.g., the following by Stanley Hauerwas: *The Peaceable Kingdom* (London: SCM Press, 2003); *A Community of Character: Toward a Constructive Christian Social Ethic* (Notre Dame: University of Notre Dame Press, 1981); and *After Christendom* (Nashville: Abingdon Press, 1991). See also Stanley Hauerwas and William H. Willimon, *Resident Aliens: Life in the Christian Colony* (Nashville: Abingdon Press, 1989).

offer an important corrective to the more abstract and formal conception of "justification" presented in Gustafson's book — I nonetheless argue that they are incomplete. Paul's eschatology, with its focus on God's creative righteousness, is not simply about the distinctive narratives and virtues of particular Christian communities, although it encompasses them. It is about the universal activity of the "one" that later Christian theology would affirm is a triune God.[19] Although deeply embodied within human communities, this activity justifies and sanctifies by creating a "righteousness" (Rom. 3:21-26) that is radically distinct from any law or communitarian grammar that sustains particular groups of people — whether they be, in Paul's words, "Jew or Greek," "slave or free," or "male and female" (Gal. 3:28).[20]

The second context in which I would like to situate my argument is a broader discussion about the role of religion in public life. For this, I turn to Mark Lilla's historical analysis in *The Stillborn God* of the political and theological ideas that have shaped our understanding of the role of religion in public life within Western thought.[21] With the Thirty Years' War after the Reformation (1618-1648), a particular political argument emerged, in particular with Thomas Hobbes but also with David Hume and John Locke, that called for a "Great Separation" between religion and politics. Another strand of thought, exemplified by Immanuel Kant and G. W. F. Hegel, argued for a liberal conception of theology that could serve as the ethical substance for public life. In Lilla's view, this liberal faith — with its "stillborn God" — was so desiccated of religious passion that it created a vacuum after the First World War. Messianic theologies in Judaism and Christianity emerged to fill this vacuum — theologies that, at their best, were suspicious of modern democracies and, at their worst, were tolerant of some of the worst excesses of either Nazi socialism or communism.

In response to Lilla's concerns about messianic theology, I hope to make the case that Paul's conception of it, like that of the Gospels, is not of a political theology for governing the state. The crucified Messiah Christians worship was a failed political leader. The power of the

---

19. "God is one" (Gal. 3:20; Rom. 3:30), an allusion to Deuteronomy 6:4.

20. See also Alain Badiou, *Saint Paul: The Foundation of Universalism*, trans. Ray Brassier (Palo Alto: Stanford University Press, 2003), and Gunther Bornkamm, *Paul* (Minneapolis: Fortress Press, 1995).

21. Mark Lilla, *The Stillborn God: Religion, Politics, and the Modern West* (New York: Vintage, 2008).

new age he ushers in is the power of the Suffering Servant, whose weakness and death are the source of power and life for others. Any Christian uses of messianic theology that fail to meet the criterion of the cross are false. Although I will need to develop the case more fully elsewhere, I do hope, at least in a small way, to intimate some sense of how Christian ideas of forgiveness and justification might be relevant to public life even though — or precisely because — they do not involve the coercive use of political force.

Two Secular Accounts of Forgiveness and Creativity

Kristeva on Forgiveness and Agency

In order to understand better the relationship between forgiveness and creativity, I turn first to Julia Kristeva's work. A linguist and a psychoanalyst, Kristeva has throughout her work sought to understand how speaking subjects are always creating new meanings within old psychic and linguistic patterns, meanings that enact the "semiotic" (unconscious drives within us) by the "symbolic" (the structures and patterns of language, culture, and art we use to express ourselves). Her work on forgiveness, which explicitly draws on Christian themes, exemplifies this process.

Drawing on Ricoeur's *Symbolism of Evil,* Kristeva gleans three central themes in Christian conceptions of forgiveness for her work as a psychoanalyst, themes I will explore in more depth in my discussion of Ricoeur's work.[22] First, Christianity has a complex understanding of fault that encompasses not only a movement from communal *sin* to individual *guilt* but also retains more archaic conceptions of *defilement* by an external contagion from which one must be purified. Second, Christianity presupposes that Christ, as the innocent "Suffering Servant," undergoes an "absurd" and "scandalous" suffering. Not a punishment (as effect) for his sin (as cause), this suffering is, rather, a voluntary suffering (a gift) that becomes, by way of the transfer of others' sin onto him, a means by which these others receive pardon and healing.

Third, Christianity affirms that the "justification" or forgiveness

---

22. See Kristeva, *Intimate Revolt,* especially the essays "Can Forgiveness Heal?" pp. 14-25 and "The Scandal of the Timeless," pp. 25-42. Page numbers given parenthetically in this section will refer to this text.

this pardon and healing enact actually has efficacious power to bring about not only remission of sins but also rebirth or new life. Christ's forgiveness enacts a new subjective and intersubjective configuration whereby "guilt is extracted from judgment and time in order to be reversed in rebirth" (p. 16). In other words, Christ enters human misery not merely to receive its punishment or share in its pain, but rather also to "reverse" it by way of an "efficacy" that creates "meaning" where there is "lack." By faith, the Christian biblical and theological tradition interprets the apparently "scandalous" death of the innocent Jesus of Nazareth in terms of the bond of love between Father, Son, and Spirit. Within this bond of love, not only are human guilt and its time of judgment and punishment suspended, but something new is created and effected.

Interpretation is the concept Kristeva uses to relate a Christian understanding of forgiveness to what happens in psychoanalysis. Psychoanalysis also works with guilt and love. It seeks to reinterpret guilt — which, within a psychoanalytic framework, is defined as the ill-being linked with anxiety, trauma, depression, and more generally, a sense of lack — in relation to the bond of love enacted in the "transference" between the psychoanalyst and the analysand. By reinterpreting the guilt of ill-being, psychoanalysis seeks to undo the psychological apparatus that generated it. This interpretation enacts a secular forgiveness that accepts the semiotic drives that emerge out of the unconscious even as it seeks to sublimate those drives into new, healthier "symbolic" expressions. Forgiveness occurs within the transfer of love — the transference and counter-transference that occur between the psychoanalyst and analysand — a love that enables preverbal instincts and affects to be brought out into the open so that they can be given meaning. Such interpretation does not absolve the savage desires of the unconscious — for example, its desire to either reject or "abject" the self or murder others.[23] Rather, it seeks a "third way between dejection and murder." In psychoanalysis, we experience the forgiveness that enables us to confess our desire to kill instead of killing. Within the context of the relationship with the analyst, the analysand experiences an unconditional acceptance that enables her to "make sense" of "troubling senselessness."[24]

23. See Kristeva's treatment of "abjection" in *Powers of Horror: An Essay on Abjection*.
24. See also Kelly Oliver's discussion of Kristeva in *The Colonization of Psychic Space: A Psychoanalytic Theory of Oppression* (Minneapolis: University of Minnesota Press, 2004), pp. 185-94.

The communication between the analyst and the analysand is not merely verbal or intellectual. It takes place in a transfer of affects and instincts that are given meaning in the process of communication. The way analytic interpretation gives meaning through this transfer of affects is a form of *pardon* (*par* meaning "through"; *don* meaning "gift") that "has nothing to do with 'explication' and 'communication' between two consciousnesses. On the contrary, this par-don draws its efficacy from reuniting with affect through metaphorical and metonymical rifts in discourse" (p. 26). Forgiveness supports the transfer of affects and drives — the unconscious — into signification. It happens between two communicating bodies, what psychoanalysts call the "third." Agency in the forgiving process lies in this "third"; it lies neither solely in the analyst nor solely in the analysand. It is an effect of meaning experienced between two people. In this transfer, the meaninglessness of life, especially the meaninglessness of trauma, is "forgiven" by being given signification or meaning. It is, in Kristeva's words, the "coming of the unconscious to consciousness in transference" (p. 19). The suspension of judgment required for forgiveness — the suspension of the harsh, judging superego — facilitates the "sublimation" of the semiotic drive of the unconscious into language.

The pardon that enables this sublimation occurs within what Kristeva calls a "luminous phase" of "conscious atemporality," a "strange atemporal space" that reconfigures the cause-and-effect relationship of crime and punishment (pp. 25-42). Not the "strange space" of the savage, desiring unconscious, this "strange space" is a space that welcomes and accepts the savage unconscious so that it can give it meaning and thereby transform and heal it. In a fashion similar to the way in which the unconscious stops time in our lives by continually repeating patterns that enact desire and death — patterns deeply engrained in our bodies — so pardon stops time, but now in a way that seeks to reconstruct through love a new way of being with one's self and others (pp. 29-31).

Because this pardon is essentially about interpretation, it creates new forms. It has the effect of an action — a deed or a *poiesis* (new creation) — that expresses what "humiliated and offended individuals" have experienced in their "bruised emotions and bodies" (p. 20). This new form integrates sense and nonsense in a fashion, like Hegel's *Aufhebung*, that arises as "a positive jolt integrating a possible nothingness" (p. 20). By bearing the erosion of meaning, what Kristeva calls "abjection," pardon displaces the erosion of meaning even as it affirms and inscribes new meaning. When the analyst affirms "there is meaning," which for Kristeva is the "eminently transferential gesture," she helps create a "third" that exists for and through another (p. 20). In sum, forgiveness, and the "remission" it offers, results in "new birth" (pp. 19-20).

Arendt on Forgiveness and Action

Unlike Kristeva, Hannah Arendt has never put much stock in psychoanalysis. Nonetheless, her work on forgiveness has informed Kristeva's work and serves as an interesting point of comparison.[25] Arendt appropriates Christian forgiveness within the context of her understanding of what is distinctly *human* about "human action," what is distinctly creative and free about human action and not merely a response to predetermined patterns of cause and effect. In this regard, both Kristeva and Arendt link forgiveness with the creation of new "meaning." Kristeva links this creativity with psychological health and interiority; Arendt links it to public action and speech. For both, love sustains the possibility of a forgiveness that gives expression to new forms of life.

Arendt identifies two activities that explicitly enact such "human action": *forgiving* and *promising*.[26] Both activities directly break and move beyond cause-and-effect patterns. Forgiving enables us to deal with *irreversibility*, that is, the inevitable consequences of past actions. Promising enables us to deal with *unpredictability*, that is, the fact that we cannot foresee what will occur in the future. Further, both forgiving and promising take place within a context that is very different from a Platonic grounding for ethics, what justifies and limits our exercise of power in relation to others. Platonic ethics, Arendt observes, revolves around one's own individual capacity for self-control; it relates political action, and our relation to others in general, to the soul's right ordering of itself. By contrast, an ethics that involves forgiving and promising presupposes the presence of others and the synergy that takes

---

25. See Julia Kristeva, *Hannah Arendt*, trans. Ross Guberman (New York: Columbia University Press, 2003).

26. See Hannah Arendt, *The Human Condition*. Page numbers given parenthetically in this section will refer to this text.

place between oneself and others. It is intrinsically social, locating individual action within the context of pre-existing relationships.

If Kristeva draws on a Pauline conception of Christian justification, then Arendt explicitly draws on the teachings of Jesus. What she finds most helpful in Jesus' conception of forgiveness is that he links forgiveness to the creation of something new and not simply to penance, guilt, and the like. She makes this point drawing on three words in Luke 17:3-4,[27] words found throughout the New Testament. "Forgive" *(aphienai)* has to do with dismissing and releasing; "repent" *(metanoein)* has to do with changing one's mind, rendering the Hebrew *shuv* as return, tracing back one's steps; and finally, "sin" *(hamartanein)* has to do with trespass, missing the mark, failing, going away. Arendt also points out that Jesus arrogates the power of forgiveness to himself — the power to create anew, to bring about a new state of affairs. This threatens the "scribes and Pharisees" because Jesus arrogates to himself what only God has the power to do — forgive sins.[28]

Moreover, she notes, Jesus tells his disciples to forgive others in the same way because "if you forgive others their trespasses, your heavenly Father will also forgive you; but if you do not forgive others, neither will your Father forgive your trespasses" (Matt. 6:14-15). Further still, she observes that Jesus tells his disciples to forgive others unconditionally, regardless of the extremity of the crime. One is to forgive "seventy times seven" (Matt. 18:22; cf. Luke 17:4), even though Jesus also acknowledges the inevitability and seriousness of what Kant called "radical evil," unforgivable "offenses" or "occasions for stumbling" *(skandalon)*: "woe to anyone by whom they come! It would be better for you if a millstone was hung around your neck and you were thrown into the sea" (Luke 17:1-4).

Why, in Arendt's view, is such forgiveness so important to human action? Because trespassing is an everyday occurrence and we continually need forgiveness — the persistent "mutual release" from what we have done — to enable us to continue. As fresh release, forgiveness is the exact opposite of *vengeance,* our natural and automatic response to transgression. Vengeance involves both the agent and the sufferer of a

---

27. "Be on your guard! If another disciple *sins,* you must rebuke the offender, and if there is *repentance,* you must *forgive.* And if the same person *sins* against you seven times a day, and *turns back* to you seven times and says, '*I repent,*' you must *forgive*" (Luke 17:3-4, emphasis added).

28. See Luke 5:21-24; cf. Matthew 9:4-6 and Mark 2:7-10; and Luke 7:49.

misdeed in a "relentless automatism," an irreversibility that perpetuates a chain reaction that, far from putting to an end the consequences of the first misdeed, keeps everyone bound to a process of chain reactions that are both calculated and expected. By contrast, forgiving is an action that does not "merely re-act" but "acts anew and unexpectedly, unconditioned by the act which provokes it and therefore freeing from its consequences both the one who forgives and the one who is forgiven" (p. 241).

In addition, forgiveness and punishment both differ from vengeance in that they "put an end to something that without interference could go on endlessly" (p. 241). Still, they stand in a structural relation to each other since we are "unable" to "forgive" what we cannot "punish" and we are "unable to punish what has turned out to be unforgivable" (p. 241). In this context, Arendt comments on how "radical evil" is something we as human beings can neither forgive nor punish precisely because it dispossesses us of all power. Those who commit such crimes deserve to be cast into the sea, as Jesus said, with a "millstone" around their necks (p. 241). Only the Last Judgment can take care of such crimes, which, as Arendt notes, the New Testament defines not only in terms of forgiveness but also in terms of just retribution.[29]

Forgiveness is always an "eminently personal" affair. The sin, *what* was done, is forgiven for the sake of the sinner, the person *who* did it. Only love can forgive because only love fully accepts who one is. In the story of the sinful woman whom Jesus forgives, Jesus states, "her sins, which were many, have been forgiven; hence she has shown great love. But the one to whom little is forgiven, loves little" (Luke 7:47). Love possesses a clarity of vision that discloses *who* a person is and could be, and overlooks *what* she has been or done in the past (his or her qualities, shortcomings, achievements, failings, and transgressions). Nonetheless, such love appears to be "unworldly" and in fact "impossible" — indeed "not only apolitical but anti-political" (p. 242). Thus, drawing on Aristotle's conception of political friendship, Arendt suggests that "respect," a friendship without intimacy and closeness, plays a role in the political sphere similar to the role "love" plays in the interpersonal sphere. Operating from a standpoint not of intimacy but of distance,

---

29. See Matthew 16:27: "For the Son of Man is to come with his angels in the glory of his Father, and then he will repay everyone for what he has done." See also 5:17-20; 7:15-20. See also Romans 2:6; 1 Corinthians 4:5; 2 Corinthians 5:10.

respect enables us to have esteem for others simply because they are human beings and not because of their achievements or qualities (p. 243).

Finally, Arendt connects forgiving and promising with "natality,"
new life. Both activities, which arise directly out of our acting and
speaking with one another, function like "control mechanisms" that
enable us "to start new and unending processes" (p. 246). Without the
capacity "to undo what we have done and to control at least partially
the processes we have let loose," we would be the victims of "automatic
necessity," of "inexorable" natural laws. The "law of mortality" may be
the most certain and the only reliable law of lives spent between birth
and death. Nonetheless, there is another law that interferes with this
law — our "faculty of action," with its ever-present reminder that even
though human beings must die, they are not born "in order to die but
in order to *begin*" (p. 246, my emphasis).

From the standpoint of automatic processes, of natural cause-
and-effect relations, this capacity to create something new appears to
be a "miracle," albeit an "infinite improbability which occurs regularly"
(p. 246). In this regard, Arendt compares the originality of Jesus' teaching on forgiveness to Socrates' insights into the possibilities of
thought. When Jesus related the power to forgive to the power of per-
forming miracles, he put both forgiveness and miracles on the same
level and within the reach of human beings (p. 247). The same faith enables us both to forgive and to move mountains. The one is no less a
miracle than the other. Thus, the disciples can only say in response to
Jesus' command to forgive seventy times seven: "Lord, increase our
faith" (p. 247). For Arendt, the miracle that can save the world of human affairs from its normal, "natural" ruin is the "fact of natality."
New human beings, and with them new actions and new beginnings,
are continually born. This faculty of birth — of action that continually
creates anew — is what bestows "faith" and "hope," two virtues absent
in Greek antiquity, on human affairs. The most succinct expression of
this faith and hope is the gospel's announcement of "glad tidings": "A
child has been born unto us" (p. 247).

Justification and New Creation in the "Adamic Myth"

Arendt and Kristeva appropriate Christian concepts of forgiveness in secular terms. Kristeva's forgiven speaking subject is innocent and responsi-

ble, but not a sinner; the love that forgives in the "third" of transference and counter-transference is strictly a human love; and the forgiveness it confers enables a creativity that is primarily aesthetic, not moral. In turn, Arendt conceives of forgiving and promising as strictly human and not divine activities. Although forgiving and promise enable us to grapple in creative ways with the irreversible consequences of wrongdoing and the unpredictability of life, we, as human beings, nonetheless remain powerless in the face of "radical evil." We are incapable of either punishing or forgiving it. These points of difference between these secular appropriations of Christian forgiveness and a classically Christian understanding of forgiveness will become salient in the following discussion of Ricoeur's detailed analysis of the biblical traditions that inform Paul's Christology, which Ricoeur depicts as the "Adamic myth."[30]

Defilement, Sin, and Guilt

Kristeva has already introduced us to Ricoeur's complex threefold conception of human evil as a movement from *defilement* to *sin* and *guilt*.[31] *Defilement* links evil not with moral fault but with misfortune, disease, death, and failure. Like a stain, defilement infects us with something outside of us that makes us "unclean" (as in Isa. 6:5). Purification of some sort, which "washes," "cleanses," and "purges" us, rids us of what defiles us (as in Ps. 51:2, 7).

By contrast, *sin* links evil with violating a covenant "before God." Sin, therefore, violates a personal bond. The diverse range of biblical genres (from narratives to hymns, oracles, sayings, and laments) depict sin in the same way. They all make clear that sin violates an imperative, an imperative always set within the context of a word that summons, calls, or elects a people to a unique relationship with their God.

Objectively, this imperative within a summons takes the form of an infinite demand that is also a finite or limited imperative. The conjoining of infinite demand with a finite imperative has its most precise form in the Decalogue of Exodus 20:1-17. The utterances of the proph-

---

30. The classical locus for the "Adamic myth" in the New Testament is Romans 5:12-21 (see also 1 Cor. 15:21-26, 45-49).

31. See Paul Ricoeur, *The Symbolism of Evil*. Page numbers given parenthetically in this section will refer to this text.

ets also take this form — from Amos, Hosea, and Isaiah to Jeremiah and Ezekiel to the later reforms of Josiah and the codes of Deuteronomy, which are what Jesus quotes when he summarizes the law as two great commandments (Deut. 6:4-6). Beyond any expression in history or finite observance, God's infinite demand is a form of political nihilism: it brings all history and politics under judgment; it allows no room for self-justification, personal or corporate.

Subjectively, this imperative within a summons takes the form of divine wrath. Human beings cannot see God. Those who do encounter God in palpable ways experience great terror — for example, Moses at Horeb (Exod. 3), Isaiah at the temple (Isa. 6), and Ezekiel face to face with God's glory (Ezek. 1-3). Divine wrath does not vindicate ancient taboos; it is not the resurgence of primary chaos. Rather, the "wrath of God," the "day of Yahweh," is the countenance of God's holiness for sinful human beings, a holiness that is as just and righteous as it is powerful. This countenance — God's seeing us — causes us to perceive our lives and our actions from the standpoint of God's holiness. Nonetheless, because God's summons or election of a people always encompasses God's infinite demand, an announcement of promise always accompanies the announcement of imminent threat. The prophets present human choice with judgment and promise, destruction and salvation: "Seek the Lord and live" (Amos 5:6); and, "I have set before you life and death, blessings and curses. Choose life so that you and your descendants may live" (Deut. 30:19). Divine wrath reminds the people of the "truth" necessary for any reconciliation with God and others (Ps. 51:6).

Sin is the violation of the covenant, a quasi-personal bond. Thus, in a fashion analogous to the way purification rites cleanse us of what "defiles" us, so the pardon that restores this bond takes the form of a "return" *(shuv)* to the covenant. The Hebrew root words for sin have to do with "missing the mark" *(chatta't)*, "deviation from the straight road" *('awon)*, and "rebellion," "revolt," or "stiff-neckedness" *(pesha')* (p. 72). These images have to do with relations of orientation in space, not with infection from a harmful substance. Pardon follows a return to a right orientation. "Repentance" *(teshubah)* leads to restoration, the renewing of the primitive bond: "in returning and rest you shall be saved" (Isa. 30:15; see also Jeremiah and Hosea). Such "return" is a human choice, but the prophets also implore God to make the people return and, in many instances, emphasize God's side alone, depicting the "return" as the "effect of a love, of a *hesed* beyond all reasons (Deut 7:5ff.)" (p. 80). In

Jeremiah and Ezekiel, for example, "pardon" and "return" coincide with receiving a "heart of flesh" instead of a "heart of stone," and Second Isaiah articulates a "most acute sense" of the "gratuitousness of grace" in contrast to the "nothingness of creatures" (e.g., in Isa. 40:1ff.).

The prophets describe sinners' going away from God as a kind of "nothingness" — not a nothingness worked out in relation to a concept of being, but a nothingness linked with failure, deviation, rebellion, or going astray. The vanity of idols is like the "breath of air" that passes. It is light, empty, insubstantial, and futile — like dust or an exhalation (see, e.g., Isa. 41:24). Nonetheless, biblical traditions also depict sin as having a *positive* quality. Drawing on archaic images of defilement to describe the hold sin has on people, they depict sin not only as the violation of a personal and communal covenant, but also as a sickness and as something brought on by demons or evil spirits. In these instances, sin is a power that binds sinners, holding them in social and intersubjective captivity to a fascinating, frenetic, and evil force that not only hardens their intent to sin but also defiles them, making them impotent to change their situation.

In the face of this aspect of sin, we are not free to make a radical choice between good and evil. Rather, we need to be liberated from the captivity that holds us. Instead, then, of linking pardon only with return, biblical traditions also link pardon to the way slaves are liberated or "bought back" from slavery by way of a "ransom" given in "exchange" for their lives (p. 91). Three Hebrew root words each develop an aspect of this "exchange." *Ga'al* furnishes a chain of images, from avenging and protecting to covering or hiding, buying back, and delivering (p. 91). *Padah* alludes to the custom of "buying back the offering of the first born or slaves by ransom" (p. 91). And *kapar*, drawing on images of covering and effacing, connotes a ransom that releases one from a severe penalty or that saves one's life, images that also furnish the basic image of "expiation" (p. 92). Exodus, the liberation of the Israelites from slavery in Egypt, furnishes the primary event in Israel's history of "buying back" (Exod. 14; Deut. 26:5-10). Later traditions relate this image of liberation from slavery to images of God's theogonic victory over the waters of chaos (Ps. 106:9; 114:3).[32] Second Isaiah makes

---

32. In Psalm 106:9, God, in mighty power, "rebuked the Red Sea," an allusion that links the liberation from slavery in Egypt with depictions of the victory of God over the primeval waters of chaos.

the most explicit connection between God's creative power and the "exchange" God makes to "ransom" God's people in a new exodus out of Babylonian captivity (Isa. 43, 44), an "exchange" that is tied as well to the "return" of "the ransomed of the Lord" (Isa. 51:9-10).

Not only does God liberate us from the power of sin, but God also cleanses us from its defiling effects — the "punishment" we "bear" for it (Ezek. 14:10), its "subjective weight" and "objective maleficence" we experience in our bodies (p. 95). The priestly cycle of texts tends to link sin with "dread" and the "threat of death" — a "blow" or a "wound" (e.g., Lev. 10:6; Num. 1:53; 17:12; 18:3). Various rites of sacrifice in Leviticus deal with these "realistic" and "dangerous" aspects of sin (p. 95). As an "expiation" *(kipper)* for sin, sacrifice enacts the pardon that "buys back" and "ransoms" one from sin (Lev. 4:20, 26, 31, 35; 5:10, 13). Not a magical rite, biblical sacrificial expiation focuses on how, "as life, it is the *blood* that makes atonement" (Lev. 17:11, my emphasis) or "ransoms" (cf. Exod. 30:12, 15, 16).

Blood is what relates the "rite of expiation" to "faith in the pardon" that confession of sins and repentance presuppose (p. 97). As a *gift* "given" by God, blood is what restores the one confessing and repenting to a right relationship with God, a theme echoed in psalms that invoke God as the subject of expiation (78:38; 65:3; 79:9). Indeed, the very ritual of the "day of expiation" (Lev. 16) relates the "confession of sins" not only to "expiation," with its "multiple sprinklings," but also to the "rite of the goat driven into the desert to carry away the sins of Israel" (p. 98). In sum, the "ceremonial expiation" of priestly texts cannot be divorced from the prophetic linkage of pardon with themes of return and ransom.

Finally, as an awareness of sin and its defilement, *guilt* expresses the paradox in a Christian understanding of human fault: we are responsible for and yet captive to the sin that binds us. In spite of being created in God's image and therefore free, we find, as Luther would observe, that our will remains servile and bound. In Paul's words, "I do not do the good I want, but the evil I do not want is what I do" (Rom. 7:19). Long before the trajectory of philosophers who would reflect on existential alienation (from Hegel to Marx, Nietzsche, Sartre, and Freud), Paul understood how the law, when severed from the dialogical relation of the covenant, sets before us an accusation that, when atomized into an indefinite number of demands (what Hegel would call the "evil infinite"), alienates from ourselves. The "curse of the law," according to

Paul, comes upon "everyone who does not observe and obey all the things written in the book of the law" (Gal. 3:10-14). The law even leads us to sin, not because it is evil — the law in itself is good — but because we are impotent in the face of its demands. "Justification" is Paul's response to this dilemma, and it comes only from the "righteousness of God" disclosed "apart from the law" (Rom. 3:21) (pp. 139-50).

The Adamic Myth

"Justification" and the "righteousness of God" that enacts it must be set within the eschatological context of Paul's theology. The forensic declaration that one stands justified and righteous before God has to do with a future that has relevance for the present — an outward reality that has import for one's internal struggle with sin. Thus, Ricoeur relates justification to the broader context of what he calls the "Adamic myth" (Rom. 5:12-21; cf. 1 Cor. 15:21-26). Adam's "trespass," his grasping for what was God's alone (Gen. 3:3), brought death which "spread" and became an unavoidable condition for all (Rom. 5:12-13). By contrast, Jesus Christ, the "Second Adam," who "emptied" himself in spite of sharing equality with God (Phil. 2:7), enacts a "free gift" that leads to "justification and life for all" (Rom. 5:15-17).

Of course, Adam is not a central figure in the Old Testament. The narratives in Genesis place more emphasis on Noah and Abraham, and the prophets completely ignore him. Even Jesus does not refer to Adam — the Synoptic Gospels link evil to an evil heart or the work of an Adversary. Nonetheless, the twofold Jewish confession of sin — that God is good and human beings are responsible and not innocent — prepares the way for the Christian Adamic myth. Near Eastern theogonic myths depict the creation of the world as the liberating act of gods who struggle with chaos; evil as chaos is part of the origin of things and salvation or liberation from chaos occurs with the same act that creates the world. By contrast, in the Adamic myth, which draws on the Genesis stories of creation, God is good and creation is good; evil is not part of the origin of things. Wickedness emerges in human history — with human sin — and not in a theogonic struggle with chaos. Salvation, then, in its view presupposes a future eschatology that is distinct from the end of creation; it preserves a tension between a creation that exists now and a salvation that is yet to come (pp. 161-74).

The second Adam, Christ, enacts this future eschatology. He is the "perfect human being," the figure who will redeem "sinful human beings" who are responsible for their sin yet held captive by it. How does he emerge as an eschatological figure? For Paul, Abraham's call is an initial answer to the first Adam. He believes in God, who "reckoned" this belief "as righteousness" (Rom. 4:3; cf. Gen. 15:6). Even before the emergence of eschatology in biblical history, Abraham is involved in a covenant that integrates the disparate stories of his descendants — from Isaac, Jacob, and Joseph on to the trajectory of Israel's history — into a larger story of promise and fulfillment. Noah's covenant with God is yet another answer to the first Adam, although it brings to the fore what is universal in the covenant with Abraham — that all people are under the promise given to Noah. Later Christian baptismal imagery, with its enactment of burial and resurrection, will draw on the imagery of Noah's flood to signify not only God's wrath but also God's power to bring about a new creation (pp. 238ff.).

Postponed in the epochs of Israel's history — from Exodus, Sinai, and the wandering in the desert to the conquest and establishment of Zion with its Davidic monarchy — the promise to Abraham takes on a new form when Israel ceases to exist as an independent nation. The figure of a king, in an idealization of the Davidic monarchy, becomes "eschatologized" into a messianic figure (pp. 264ff.). The kingdom "founded in those times" transforms into "the kingdom to come" (p. 264). The earthly and political hopes identified with the Davidic monarchy become the expectation of a new age identified with the Son of David. Biblical traditions sanction the royalty of this future messiah with God's creative power to bring about a new creation, appropriating strands of Near Eastern creation combat myths, which sanctioned the royalty of ancient kings by linking the king's power with the creative and liberating act of the gods that banished chaos at the origins of time.[33]

In addition to this eschatologized messianic figure, two other biblical figures become prominent in later New Testament exegesis (pp. 265ff.). The first is the "Servant of Yahweh" of the "Suffering Servant

---

33. In their depictions of God's unique creative and redemptive power, biblical traditions echo ancient Near Eastern theogonic myths that sanctioned kingly power with their depictions of the defeat of the powers of chaos represented by floods and waters (see, e.g., Ps. 74:12-17; 93:3-4; 104:7-9; Job 38:8-11; Isa. 27:1; 51:9-10).

Songs,"[34] who will restore Israel's survivors. Although enigmatic (the "Suffering Servant" could refer to an individual or a nation), this figure exchanges his suffering for the sins of others: he "was wounded for our transgressions, crushed for our iniquities; upon him was the punishment that made us whole, and by his bruises we are healed" (Isa. 53:5). Neither merely the transfer of defilement onto a scapegoat nor simply the destiny of a misunderstood prophet, what occurs through the suffering of this figure is a voluntary gift, an expiation that enacts their pardon. The second historical figure is the "Son of Man" identified with the apocalyptic figure of Daniel 7. Also enigmatic (this figure could refer to an individual or a personified collective), the Son of Man is not the "first man" but the "Man of the end." Although a "replica of the first Man," created in God's image, he is nonetheless "new in relation to him" (p. 268). As judge and king, he will come at the Last Judgment "with the clouds of heaven" to establish "an everlasting dominion" over "all peoples, nations, and languages" (Dan. 7:13-14).

The Gospels bring these figures together in two affirmations. Not only does Jesus refer to himself as the Son of Man (Mark 13:26-27), but he also unites the idea of the "Son of Man" with the idea of "suffering and death," which had been a central theme for the Servant of Yahweh (pp. 269ff.). By bringing these two figures together, Jesus redefines a "theology of glory" by way of a "theology of the cross," linking the roles of "king" and "judge" to that of "pardoner" and "healer" (pp. 269ff.). Paul's Christology also appears to relate the themes identified with these two figures. Even the hymn in Philippians 2:5-11 appears to identify characteristics of the Son of Man ("he was in the form of God") with characteristics of the Servant of Yahweh (he "emptied himself . . . to the point of death").

Moreover, although Paul's Christology draws a parallel between the first and the second Adam (the fault of one brings judgment on all; the justice of one brings justice for all), he also makes clear that this parallel is not parallel at all. The "free gift" is very different from the "trespass" (Rom. 5:15). It enacts a "much more" that not only restores what existed before the first trespass but also "much more surely" brings about an "abundance of grace" (v. 17).

In sum, Paul's understanding of justification cannot be divorced

---

34. Scholars have identified the following texts as "servant songs": Isaiah 49:1-9; 50:4-11; 52:13–53:12.

from eschatological imagery. Justification by faith, with its "experience of pardon," is "so to speak, the psychological trace" of what happens in reality — the incorporation of believers into the "new Adam" as they are "transformed [μεταμορφοῦσθαι — metamorphosed] into the same image [εἰκών]" (2 Cor. 3:18) and "conformed [σύμμορφος] to the image [εἰκών]" of the Son (Rom. 8:29). Having "borne the image of the man of dust," we will also "bear the image of the man of heaven" (1 Cor. 15:49) (p. 275). Justification deals not only with juridical imputation, which echoes aspects of the contractual character of the covenant, but also with a messianic expiation that links the remission of sins with images of unbinding and purifying. Further, the image of cosmic judgment over all only amplifies these themes: the "one" is for "all" (Gal. 3:20). Although deeply personal, this eschatological judgment is also communal. It incorporates the prophets' call to "return" into a picture of eschatological judgment and acquittal. Baptized into Christ's death and resurrection, believers now belong to Christ's "body" (1 Cor. 12); they now share the "mind" of Christ (1 Cor. 2:16; Phil. 2:5). Finally, justification involves the redemption of bodies and the entire cosmos — the resurrection of the "body" (1 Cor. 15:35-58) and a "new creation" (Gal. 6:15).

However, as Ricoeur points out, the Adamic myth needs to be complemented by two recessive myths in biblical theology — the theogonic and the tragic — if it is to do justice to life's complexity. We have already alluded to the way the eschatologizing of the Davidic reign into hopes for a future messiah incorporates theogonic themes from Near Eastern creation myths. Nonetheless, the tragic also exists as a recessive theme in biblical theology. In Greek tragedies, tragic heroes suffer innocently and therefore question whether a simple theory of retribution — that supposes that if you do evil, you will die — can account for innocent suffering. Job, the Bible's epitome of a tragic figure, receives no answer for why he, a just man, has suffered so much. All he receives in response to his queries are the sea monsters, Behemoth and Leviathan, who as figures associated with a primordial chaos are tamed, and the experience of "seeing" the God whom he had only previously "heard of . . . by the hearing of the ear" (Job 42:5). Job's innocent suffering questions any facile theory of retribution. As Ricoeur points out, Job and Adam stand in sharp contrast. Adam's sin leads to just banishment. Job's innocence leads to unjust suffering. As a third figure, the Servant of Yahweh causes us to rethink both the theory of retribution identified with Adam and the conception of tragedy identified with Job. The

Suffering Servant's voluntary suffering — a senseless, scandalous suffering — is the expiation whereby both sin and suffering are replaced with pardon and healing.

In addition, as Job's own encounter with the sea monsters suggests, the tragic also hints at theogonic themes, which persist even today long after the naïve theogonies of the biblical Near East have died. Philosophers and worldviews continue to identify evil and tragedy with existence itself or, in philosophical terms, with a negativity that coincides with the very logic of being. By including in God's life the figure of the Servant of Yahweh, Christology incorporates suffering as a moment in divinity. This moment of abasement and annihilation in God's life completes and suppresses tragedy because God takes on the evil of the world. Christ becomes the "curse for us" (Gal. 3:13); the Son of Man is the one delivered up and subjected to futility. Yet, in this moment, the fate of tragedy is suppressed by being inverted. In theogonic myths, the child often murders the parents in order to overcome chaos. In the Adamic myth, Christ offers himself to God for others; as victim, he is thereby glorified. Fate is inverted by voluntary gift.

Christ and the Moral Life Revisited

How do we relate this Christology to ethics? Further, how might its similarities and differences with Kristeva's and Arendt's secular appropriations of Christian forgiveness shed light on who we are and how we should live?[35]

Creation, Sin, and Redemption

This Christology presupposes a particular understanding of God and the world. On the one hand, it presupposes not only that God is good, but that creation is good as well. Evil is not part of the origin of things. Moreover, it presupposes that, as those created in God's image, we can perceive and respond to the world God has created with discernment

---

35. See also Shults and Sandage, *Faces of Forgiveness,* which also seeks to integrate psychological and theological accounts around the virtues of "faith," "hope," and "love."

and judgment. Not only can we use language to generate insight into this created world — we can imagine and create new possibilities (artistic, technical, theoretical, and practical) — but we can also deliberate and decide how best to respond to it. We can encounter this world "responsibly," that is, not through "compulsion" but with "deliberation" and "decision."[36]

On the other hand, when we interpret and respond to what happens around us, we do so out of the concrete totality of all that constitutes who we are. This includes who we are as those shaped by nature, history, and even by ourselves (our past perceptions and responses to life). It includes the structure of our bodies, our psychic strivings, our spiritual character, the communities to which we belong, our past remembered and forgotten — in general the environment and world that have shaped and had an impact on us.[37] Hence, our freedom always has a given character. It always responds to what exists already.

This makes it difficult for us to ascertain precisely where personal responsibility for our lives actually begins. Kristeva's psychoanalytic insights into the "ill-being" we carry in our bodies speak profoundly of how the complex of defilement, sin, and guilt affects us. Defiled not only by what we have done but also by what others have done to us, we find ourselves enmeshed in a residue of personal and corporate guilt that contaminates us in deep, often unconscious ways. As her work as a psychoanalyst attests, our bodily and psychic instincts often drive our motives and actions at a level much deeper than our conscious awareness. This is why ancient notions of defilement are still relevant to our contemporary notions of sin and guilt. Moreover, as Paul and the Old Testament prophets asserted, our interests, whether they are social, cultural, political, or economic, affect what we think and do often at a level much deeper than our stated intentions. Even the natural world that surrounds us is infected to some extent by human defilement, a theme that echoes the "curse" found on the earth (of Gen. 3:17-19) or the "bondage to futility" about which Paul speaks (in Rom. 8:20). As the biblical imagery we have surveyed suggests, sin involves not only straying and wandering from our relationship to God and others but

---

36. See Paul Tillich, *Morality and Beyond* (Louisville: Westminster/John Knox Press, 1963). See also his *Systematic Theology*, vol. 1 (Chicago: University of Chicago Press, 1963), pp. 182ff.

37. Tillich, *Systematic Theology*, vol. 1, pp. 185ff.

being held in captivity as well. In line with prophetic and apocalyptic judgments, structures of evil govern this estranged world; demonic powers rule not only individuals, but also nations and nature.[38]

Christians believe that Jesus, as the crucified Messiah, liberates not only all people, but also all of nature, from these powers. Christ's crucified and raised body is the place in God's life where God's forgiveness is given — is transferred — to us. This body takes on the "curse" of sin that separates us from the one Jesus called Father. In a fashion similar to the way forgiveness is enacted in the transference that takes place between the analyst and the analysand, our forgiveness is enacted in the transference — the "exchange" — whereby Christ takes on our sin and gives us his life in its stead.[39] All of this, in trinitarian theology, takes place through the power of the Spirit who unites the will of the Son with the Father even when Jesus cries out "My God, my God, why have you forsaken me?" (Mark 15:34). The Spirit creates the "space" not only for this greatest difference and yet unity within trinitarian life, but also for our participation in Christ's crucified and raised body through baptism (Rom. 6:1-14). In this participation, we die to our sinful self and are raised by the same Spirit who raised Jesus from the dead. We now are a "new creation" in Christ. We find ourselves in the "space" of God's reign of justice and mercy, a "space" created and permeated by the Spirit, which makes our forgiveness of one another — as both victims and perpetrators — possible.

Ethical Implications

What, then, does this mean for ethics? We return to Gustafson's three questions about Christ and the moral life. What does this mean for our understanding of the *nature and locus of moral goodness*? In this Christology, the nature and locus of moral goodness lies in Christ's crucified and raised body. By way of our participation in this "third," Christ's body and the new creation or reign of God it enacts among us, we are not only reconciled to God but also reconciled to one another, as both

38. Tillich, *Systematic Theology,* vol. 2, p. 27.

39. On this "exchange," see Galatians 3:13 and 2 Corinthians 5:17. See also Hans Urs von Balthasar, *Theo-Drama: Theological Dramatic Theory,* vol. 4: *Action,* trans. Graham Harrison (San Francisco: Ignatius Press, 1994).

victims and perpetrators. In the space of this "third," the tangible locus in which we participate bodily through baptism, the Lord's Supper, and our daily dying and rising in Christ within the complexity of our everyday lives, we are freed from what holds us back from relating to one another as truly responsible and free subjects. Christ's body sustains the ongoing "natality" of which Arendt speaks. It sustains our "mutual release," our capacity to forgive and be forgiven in an unpredictable world with the promise of God's unconditional love (Rom. 8:38-39). Within it, what appears irreversible — the seemingly endless patterns of vengeance and punishment that capture us in cycles of cause and effect — is reversed.

Christ's crucified and raised body, which, in the Spirit's power, is the basis for our being able to have true community with one another, provides an even more substantial transfer of love than one finds in a psychoanalyst's office. It is the location, which we can see and tangibly ingest in bread and wine, where, in Kristeva's words, our "ill-being," the defilement and guilt of our sin, both personal and corporate, is released and re-created into new life. We now can respond creatively to the circumstances in which we find ourselves. Christ's body sustains our capacity to make conscious the fears and desires we dare not face — the fears and desires that propel us into sin — so that we can truly think, speak, and act as free ethical agents who are capable of valuing others as much as we value ourselves (Rom. 13:8-10).

Even though it justifies both victims and perpetrators, it also, as the Gospels make evident, clearly distinguishes between them, often by unveiling our distortions regarding who is truly righteous and who is truly sinful, who is inside the law and who is outside of it. Christ's death and resurrection clearly demarcate the distinction between the "old age" and the "new age," the first Adam and the second Adam, the "flesh" and the "Spirit." This contrast is not based on the law. Here "circumcision" and "uncircumcision" no longer count, only "faith working out in love" (Gal. 5:6). Even though this God's creative righteousness is enacted "apart from the law" (Rom. 3:21), it nonetheless enables us to fulfill the just requirement of the law (Rom. 8:4). Freed from the law, sin, and death, we now can use that freedom in service of others rather than simply for our own interests. Incorporated into Christ's body, we are given a very different "mind" for perceiving and responding to the world. Incorporated into a very different kind of power and wisdom, God's infinite power and infinite wisdom, we now are able to perceive and respond to one another from the standpoint of its infinite excess and not from the standpoint of our finite fears and desires.

We no longer need to see one another — or the leaders, slogans, and groups with which we align ourselves — as competitors for finite goods (1 Cor. 1-3). "All is yours," Paul avers, "past, present, and future, life and death" (3:23). The implications of this are great. Our participation in Christ's justification is a participation in God's creative righteousness. This divine righteousness endows us with a "moral creativity"[40] that also gives us the power to forgive — to release and heal (at least to some extent on this side of the eschaton) — the evil residue in our own bodies as individuals, as families, as communities, and even as participants in the natural world.

Second, what does this mean for the *character of the moral self,* our capacity for ethical agency? In this Christology, participation in Christ's crucified and raised body is what constitutes the moral self. Kristeva's depiction of how the love transferred between the psychoanalyst and analyst "forgives" the ill-being that hinders speaking subjects and releases their creative capacities provides a helpful analogue for what happens when sinners are justified by Christ's death and resurrection and thereby set onto new and more creative ways of being in the Spirit. Participation in Christ's body frees us to become responsible agents capable of deliberating how best to exercise our individual capacities in the service of the "common good" (1 Cor. 12:7). William Schweiker describes Christian responsibility as a "radical interpretation" of our circumstances in order to discern how best to use the power we have at our disposal in the service of the good; such radical interpretation discerns how best to integrate the finite goods we have at our disposal in the service of "respecting and enhancing finite life."[41] Participation in Christ's crucified and raised body carries us into an even deeper discernment of where God's creative righteousness is unleashing moral creativity within and among us, enabling us to forgive and heal the evil residue in our psyche and patterns of interaction.

Thus, Paul's ethical creativity differs from Kristeva's aesthetic creativity. For Kristeva, we are responsible and innocent. For Paul we are

---

40. See John Wall, *Moral Creativity: Paul Ricoeur and the Poetics of Possibility* (New York: Oxford University Press, 2005).

41. William Schweiker, *Responsibility and Christian Ethics* (Cambridge: Cambridge University Press, 1999).

responsible and guilty; what is forgiven is not merely psychological ill-being but radical evil — the fact that "in my flesh, I can will what is right, but I cannot do it" (Rom. 7:18). For Paul, we are not merely victims of the powers that keep us from doing what we know is right, but perpetrators whose very acquiescence to these powers hardens not only our captivity but others' captivity as well. For Paul, faith is never merely about individual salvation. It is about being incorporated into a body that consists of others as well. Justification may be "transmoral" in that it surpasses the law, but it does not do away with the law, in particular, its twofold summary in the commands to love God and one's neighbor as one's self; rather, it gives us the power to fulfill the law. Justification enacts a righteous self-identity that is always also an identity with others. It enables one not only to individuate as fully as one can and ought as a finite creature capable of free thought and action, but also to participate as fully as one can and ought in the lives of other finite agents, who are also capable of fully individuating and participating in relation with others. God's love is always universal in its scope, working "all things for good" not only for individuals but also for all people and even the cosmos (Rom. 8:28).

Third, what does this mean for the *criteria, norms, and values* that we turn to for guiding our judgments and actions? The criterion that guides our judgments and actions is, again, Christ's crucified and raised body, a body that opens up a new space — a new construal of the "in-between" among us — that allows for the continual creative undoing of dysfunctional patterns and unleashing of new life. This body sustains the most radical interpretation we can make of our lives: it enables us to discern how Christ's Spirit is resurrecting new life out of the defilement and guilt of our sin. As we appropriate and integrate the goods we have at our disposal, we are impelled to go even deeper in discerning how we can participate in the concrete ways God's forgiving and healing power actually transforms ill-being in our midst. As we daily die and rise in Christ, as we daily put to death the "sin" in our "bodies" so that "we too might walk in newness of life" (Rom. 6:1-12), our bodies become the location where, as Paul states, "death is at work in us" in order to bring about "life in you" (2 Cor. 4:12).

Relevant here is Arendt's understanding of how forgiving and promising give us the "miracle" of natality. Still, Christ's crucified and raised body undergirds the forgiving and promising Arendt speaks of with an eschatological hope in God's ultimate power to redeem all of life. Its creativity has the power to redeem what often appears to be our tragic vulnerability not only in the face of life's sheer capriciousness, but also in the face of radical evil itself. The New Testament interpreted Christ's suffering in terms of the suffering of the Servant of Yahweh and not in terms of the suffering of Job. Christ's suffering and death entails the "natality" of new creation. The wisdom and power of the cross is not merely "foolish" but also paradoxically "wise," not merely "weak" but also paradoxically "strong" (I Cor. 1:18-25).

Thus, Paul commends us to value hardships as much as we do the honors and pleasures of life: "We are afflicted in every way, but not crushed; perplexed, but not driven to despair; persecuted, but not forsaken; struck down, but not destroyed" (2 Cor. 4:8-9). Indeed, we are those who are "always carrying in the body the death of Jesus, so that the life of Jesus may also be made visible in our bodies" (v. 10). Thus, we must put to death any messianic pretensions to impose our will on others, and in so doing negate their freedom to act and think as those who are also created in God's image. Justification and the creative righteousness it enacts also judge — put to death — any creative use of power that fails to recognize its own potential for radical evil. Christ's messianic reign brings together both the Son of Man's judgment and power and the Servant of Yahweh's suffering and pardon.

Later work will need to spell out in much more detail the ethical implications of this Christology for ecclesial and political life. In this reading of Paul's theology of justification alongside two contemporary accounts of forgiveness, my intent has simply been to argue that (in Paul's theology at least) the pivot relating Christ and ethics centers on our participation in Christ's death and resurrection, a pivot that always links our justification to the new creation Christ's Spirit is enacting in our midst. Early Christians like Paul interpreted not only the scandal of Christ's death, the scandal of a crucified Messiah who died a political and religious failure, but also their own sin and sufferings in terms that fused messianic images of a future Davidic reign with images of the Son of Man and the Servant of Yahweh. By faith they confessed that, far from being tragic, Christ's suffering and death ushered in a new age in which the sufferings we now experience are the birth pangs of a new reign of God being enacted in our midst. By faith we too can radically interpret, that is, perceive and respond to, the seeming "futility" of our circumstances in this created world the way a mother experiences the pangs of giving birth to a child (Rom. 8:12-24).

As our source of the good, capacity for agency, and criterion for judgment, Christ's crucified and raised body not only forgives and cleanses us of all defilement, sin, and guilt, but also incorporates us into a new crucified and raised body. This gives us hope. Not a hope in utopian illusions, this hope is realistic — something we actually experience in our bodies — enabling us to affirm confidently that we can enact new ways of being, in spite of and in the midst of the ill-being we find within and around us. We can not only promise to respect and care for others and ourselves, but we can also forgive and be forgiven by one another when we fail, confident that whether or not we achieve success in human terms, "all things" do indeed "work for good" according to God's "purpose" for them (Rom. 8:28).

6. The Surprise of Judgment and Justice

Jan-Olav Henriksen

Introduction: My Points of Departure

Theology starts in the present: in the present tasks and challenges we face, and in the experiences we struggle to make sense of. It is always from the present situation that we confront the resources of the past and see whether they can help us. I have a double point of departure in addressing elements relating Christology and Ethics to each other, and accordingly, the combination of the two following perspectives has determined the way I will develop the argument that explores this relation in the present context.

The first element in my point of departure is the conviction that I suppose most people share, namely *that what we do matters*. It matters to those who are in need — those who are calling us to justice and who have no means by which their cry for justice can be heard. This is not an abstract claim: as I write (spring 2008) the people of Darfur are still in desperate need of help (and have been for a long time now), while billions of dollars are spent and thousands of soldiers engaged elsewhere in wars for which the financial means, if allocated differently, would have been sufficient to wipe out most of the world's health- and poverty-related issues, not to say provide the Darfur refugees with much-needed security. This situation mirrors how the prioritizing by those in power takes on absurd features, and it testifies to the fact that the cry for justice is not heard, and that what we do or don't do matters in significant ways.

Despite the feeling of helplessness this might impose on us, we nevertheless continue to believe that what we do matters. Is there a theological warrant for this conviction? The strong moral thrust of this situation, and the insights into what matters, are in many parts of Western culture strongly shaped by the Christian message. Not uniquely so, but the practices and teachings of Jesus probably have a lot to do with how people relate to and assess issues regarding justice and righteousness. One of the parables in Matthew underscoring the belief that what we do matters has to do with the "Judgment of the Nations." Set in a context in which Jesus calls for his disciples to be ready for the advent of the king and the kingdom, the parable also suggests that what we do matters in terms of our own final destiny. It is, as we shall see, a deeply disturbing parable in more than one sense.[1] Besides interrupting and challenging popular images, it also goes beyond the basic message that "It matters what you do."

Perhaps paradoxically, the second element in my point of departure is also shaped in response to a strong moral thrust, but one that is apparently critical of the Christian message. In a talk-show on television some years ago, a recently elected bishop in Norway was asked how he could defend a doctrine implying that many people will face damnation and rejection, while others will be welcomed into community with God. The question was presented with vehement indignation, as if this way of dealing with humans was utterly unjust and intolerable. Probably without knowing it, the host of the show was voicing a typical post-Enlightenment critique of New Testament conceptions of the last judgment. The bishop elect seemed totally unprepared for this type of question (a sign that this is perhaps not what bishops usually are prepared to defend in front of the general public), and was unable to give a clear and direct answer. Since then, I have been asking myself how we can make sense of the parables about the judgment in a way that would allow us to express the potentially fruitful insights such parables contain, and at the same time avoid the problems they seem to raise from a moral point of view. As will become clear, I will develop my argument in a way that attempts to safeguard the following concerns:

---

1. There are different reasons for the disturbing effect that the parable has, but it is nevertheless striking that this effect has even kept some of the most prominent New Testament scholars from dealing with it. Cf., for example, the lack of any extensive interpretation of it in N. T. Wright, *Jesus and the Victory of God*, Christian Origins and the Question of God, vol. 2 (London: SPCK, 1996).

- Justification and salvation are based on faith, not on works.
- What we do matters.
- Conceptions of judgment need to be developed in a way that makes the judgment appear as just, in accordance with our basic moral intuitions.
- The above is possible if we relate elements in Christology and ethics to each other, e.g., as I attempt to do in the following.

Some Presuppositions Concerning the Reading of the Parable

Let me suggest two important possible readings, both of them rather tempting if we approach the parable about the last judgment as found in Matthew 25. The first is to read the parable as suggesting a one-to-one relationship between works of merit on the one hand, and the righteousness that brings eternal life on the other hand. The other possible reading is a version of the former, serving to establish a kind of self-justifying attitude over against those who appear in the parable as not justified. As we shall see, neither of these interpretations seems to hit the mark.

The narrative of the "Judgment of the Nations" (as it is called in NSRV), calls for several important insights in terms of how to relate Christology and ethics. The thesis behind these explorations (and I underscore that the present piece is to be understood more as an exploration into *possible* readings than as an authoritative and final interpretation) is the following: The usual problems that emerge out of reading this parable become easier to solve if we read it within a framework that links Christology and ethics together. The justification by works that the parable seems to indicate, and that so many interpreters (especially within the Reformation strand of theology) have struggled with, appears somewhat different, or emerges within a different context, when seen in a wider framework that still needs to be developed.

The necessity for such a wider framework of theological (and not only textual) interpretation immediately gives rise to the question: What elements of Christology can contribute to such an understanding? I will suggest here that an understanding of *Christ as the true image of God* might especially help us here. The text itself offers some clues for that perspective.

Jesus as the True Image of God

The narrative starts with the proclamation of the eschatological advent of the Son of Man, a title that the synoptic authors usually use when Jesus speaks of himself in relation to God and/or of his own eschatological functions. This description of the Messiah goes back to the apocalyptic literature, and should here be seen as an expression of the close relationship between Jesus and God.[2] However, one immediate puzzle here is that their relation is expressed in the form of the Son of *Man.* Why is that? Would it not be a more likely description to use a title suggesting that Jesus was a descendant of God? My suggestion is that it is exactly when Jesus identifies himself as the Son of Man that it is possible to identify and understand his close relation to God, as well as his participation in humanity. This is due to the fact that only humans are described in the Bible as images of God. By directly relating himself to humanity in this way, Jesus confirms his relation to that which constitutes his own calling as well as that of all of humanity: the calling to be the image of God.

The evidence for calling humans images of God is scarce in the biblical literature. Nevertheless, the places where this notion is used are sometimes very central. The most obvious example is Genesis 1:27: "So God created humankind in his image, in the image of God he created them; male and female he created them." Widely used and referred to in contemporary theology, this designation of humanity nevertheless is not quite clear as to what it means, unless we understand it from its wider historical and cultural context. The approach that recommends itself, especially in the present context, is to provide a reconstruction of its main content, in the light of historical knowledge we now have access to. Such reconstruction would then imply the following factors:

The "image of God" might historically point back to stone markers that signified who was ruling in a certain area or country. Kings erected such markers, thus making themselves visible — and present — even when they were not physically present. Applied to the understand-

---

2. For a more extensive and clarifying treatment of how the different Messianic titles and functions relate to each other in a way that is also of importance to the systematic theological treatment of the present topic, cf. Lois Malcolm's essay in the present volume.

ing of humanity as the image of God, this would mean that humanity is visibly called to represent God and mark God's presence on the Earth, even when God is not physically present. Against this background it also becomes clear why humans are called to fill the earth in the following verse in Genesis 1: not to overpopulate the Earth, but to make clear that all of the Earth is God's creation and domain. In the context of the present parable, the Son of Man is also called the king (v. 34), thereby indicating that a representation of kingship is implied here.[3]

Furthermore, this designation of humankind must necessarily be understood in the light of God's calling of humanity. The designation "image of God" is relational, not something that humans have in themselves. Rather, the designation is *given* due to the relationship that God has established with humanity. The one called to be the image of God is called to be God's representative. As humans are *created* to be the image of God, this designation is given with their very existence. It is not something optional, but the very basis on which humankind must be understood theologically. The relational character of the *imago Dei* is not added to the act of creation, but is fully integrated with the act of creation. It thus serves as a designation of what it means to be human, and in our context it indicates that all the involved parties have one thing in common. As we shall see, the main issue then seems to be whether or not all parties are able to recognize each other as called to be and/or to become images of God.

This implies that humanity is given an unconditioned recognition by God, a recognition that cannot be eliminated but can be ignored. Accordingly, humanity can fulfill the calling to be the image of God or fail to live up to it. That is what Genesis 3 indicates in the story of the fall, which suggests that humans try to break out of their relationship with God. But no matter how much humanity fails this calling, it nevertheless remains valid — as a calling. This double option makes it necessary for biblical writers, and especially those of the New Testament, to differentiate between the images of God that we are called to realize, and the *true* image of God which is already realized in Christ.

Sin thus implies a double lack of recognition, and also has conse-

---

3. Cf. Gunnlaugur A. Jónsson, *The Image of God: Genesis 1:26-28 in a Century of Old Testament Research* (Stockholm: Almqvist & Wiksell, 1988).

quences for relations to other humans. By failing to recognize God as God, humans also reject their own calling to be images of God, and this leads to the failure to acknowledge the neighbor's needs as well. By now, it should be clear that this is a possible background for reading the text in question.

At this point, however, it is important to make sure that the understanding of humanity's lack of fulfillment of its calling *does not have a merely moral content.* It is not only a question about what we do or don't do, but about how we recognize God, ourselves, and the neighbor. Hence, we already have a clue here for reading the parable as something more than an instance of moral agency or lack of it. The narrative has more to say. Accordingly, it is not only what humans do or don't do that makes them fail their calling. Rather, in light of the *imago Dei*'s relational character we should understand the failure from a human point of view. This lack of recognition, however, should not be seen as a total dissolution of the relationship; God's calling is still valid, and God is still relating to humans as *imago Dei*. The failure is thus one in which the lack of full unity between God and humans is manifested. How can we, against this background, understand the conditions for this unity?

As indicated negatively already, the *unity* between God and humanity is constituted on the one side by God's recognition of humanity as called to become his image, and on the other side by humanity's recognition of this calling, and implicitly, by humanity's recognition of God. The fundamental structure in this process of recognition manifests itself in the awareness of the difference between humans and God (echoed in the words of Jesus in Mark 10:18). Humans cannot partake in their vocation without being aware of the fact that they are not themselves God. This goes even for Jesus as part of humanity.

Putting oneself in a position where one takes over the functions of God might, if this difference is forgotten, be an ultimate expression of *sin.* Such functions might then be expressed in terms of, e.g., *determining who is righteous,* or attempting to secure the means for upholding one's position socially, religiously, or otherwise. Or it might simply have to do with ignoring God's call to show concern for the neighbor, a call that might suggest you are not the center of the world. As we can see, these ways of living and acting are addressed by the parable of the Judgment. To put it in Lutheran terms: it is when humans start trusting in themselves and their own work and merits that they make themselves into God. They thereby reveal that they do not trust in God's recognition, designation, and calling of them, and prefer to understand themselves outside of this relation.

The *recognition of difference from God* is thus an indicator of humanity's identity as the image of God.[4] Simultaneously, this recognition of difference is the condition for its unity with God. It is by allowing God to be God that human beings can become fully human, and it is by becoming fully human that humans can bear full witness to the glory, love, and grace of God. The goodness of human life is, then, not only to be found in obedience to the law, but is present when humans allow for God's grace, mercy, and love to become manifest in the world — including in their own lives. That is something not secured by human agency only. These qualities can even become present to, and in, humans who are beyond what we can call the capacity for agency. Hence, goodness and glory transcend the law, and are revealed as elements of excess and surplus that go far beyond what can be established on "reasonable" grounds for agency, or by what can be conditioned by mutual agreements between agents. The grace, mercy, and love of God, to whom humans are called to testify, is the presupposition for faithful agency, and not the result of it, or a mere result of the acts according to the law. A *testifying* agency (fulfilling the calling to serve as the image of God) requires a faithful recognition of the world as the place where God reveals these qualities.

Contrary to Nietzsche's dictum "If there were Gods, how could I then cope with not being a God?"[5] the human being who lives according to her vocation to become *imago Dei* understands and recognizes herself from the necessary difference between God and humans, and embraces this way of living. The calling to become God's image thus presupposes the *boundary* between God and humans, and recognition of the fact that humans can never be God. The attempt to become like God destroys humanity's calling (cf. Gen. 3:3-5). Humanity exists *according* to its calling only when we are aware that we are not, and cannot be, like God. To be living as the image of God is to live in such a way that the glory and grace of God are revealed. It is not to try to establish such

4. This is a point strongly emphasized in W. Pannenberg. Cf. Wolfhart Pannenberg, *Systematic Theology*, vol. 2 (Edinburgh: T. & T. Clark, 1991).

5. Cf. Friedrich Wilhelm Nietzsche and Alfred Baeumler, "Auf den Glückseligen Inseln," in *Also Sprach Zarathustra: Ein Buch für Alle und Keinen* (Stuttgart: Alfred Kröner, 1953).

glory on our own merit.[6] This is why the New Testament can call Jesus the true image of God (Col. 1:15), and even the firstborn of all creation. Christ was the first to fulfill this calling toward which all of humanity is directed.

Goodness in human life manifests itself in what happens when humans live and receive life according to this calling, and thereby let God be God. The gifting of this goodness suggests that it is not constituted by human agency, nor is it exhausted in human action, although it emerges through others: goodness is in the receiving of a gift as much as in being creative, thriving, comforting, and in sustaining relationships of love and recognition. The *inexhaustible* character of goodness and desire for goodness also points to how humanity's existence as *imago Dei* is rooted in a reality beyond what can be grasped, fully articulated, or calculated.

The point is elaborated in J. Kosky's analysis of Immanuel Levinas. Kosky discusses the relation between goodness and desire in Levinas, and says the following:

> The infinite is good, above all, in that it does not accept what desire offers but directs this desire to an other, *Autrui*. The Good thus compelled disorients desire, turning it away from the infinite which aroused it and which it wants, in order that the infinite might escape a present shared with desire. The infinite is "Good in this very precise, eminent sense: He does not fill me with goods but compels me to goodness, which is better than to receive goods."[7]

The goodness that transcends desire (and whose source is God) can thus itself be a source for the goodness we are called to show our neighbor. The combination of presence and transcendence of goodness in human life is one of the main reasons why Christianity could find an ally in Platonic thought. This character of goodness might also shed some light on our attempts to develop a framework for a more positive approach to the notion of desire in Christian theology: as desire is always directed toward the *assumed* good, the question becomes to what extent we can see desire as something to be fulfilled, or as something

---

6. This is a main point in Christof Gestrich, *The Return of Splendor in the World: The Christian Doctrine of Sin and Forgiveness* (Grand Rapids: Eerdmans, 1997).

7. Cf. Jeffrey L. Kosky, *Levinas and the Philosophy of Religion,* Indiana Series in the Philosophy of Religion (Bloomington: Indiana University Press, 2001), p. 181.

that lets us exist in a position of enjoyment without full consummation. The enjoyment implied in not being able to fully reach the desired
"object" might thus stem from the recognition of the character of *difference* in the object: by recognizing that this object (goodness, or even:
God) is different from what is present and nevertheless also expresses
itself in the present, desire is given a different character that no longer
relates to the desired as an extension of itself, but as the announcement
of otherness.

In spite of its transcending character, this makes goodness something *internal* to human life, as goodness announces itself in our desire
for it. This desire can then also be said to be an expression of the calling
humans are given by their very existence. Jesus responded to this calling toward goodness in the way he acted with others. It is by seeing him
as the true fulfiller of the vocation to be *imago Dei* that we are consequently able to interpret what he did as expressing the goodness of
God. Thereby — and by still marking the difference between himself
and God, as witnessed in Mark 10:18: "Why do you call me good? No
one is good but God alone" — Jesus fulfils his calling by bearing witness to the goodness of God: when goodness expresses itself in his life,
it witnesses to the goodness of God.[8]

In order to understand the designation *imago Dei* as a calling, we
must see that *it is a gift that has to be realized and recognized as gift.* When
the character of gift is not given priority, the *imago Dei* easily ends up
being understood as the capacity of humankind to *do* this or that. Only
as *an unconditional and determining gift* prior to all that humans can be
and do can this designation be a marker of human dignity, God's unconditional recognition and gift to every human being.

As a gift given with our existence, the unconditional character of
the *imago Dei* might be expressed from our point of view in the pure,
trusting reception of it. Humans live as images of God by receiving in
trust and openness. The way the gift is received is, however, not a condition for it to be a gift. But, as Kathryn Tanner points out, some gifts
call for an appropriate response. She also underscores the element of
joy, gratitude, and freedom inherent to the gift itself, not as a kind of
obligatory return:

8. This is developed further in my recent book: Jan-Olav Henriksen, *Desire, Gift,
and Recognition: Christology and Postmodern Philosophy* (Grand Rapids: Eerdmans, 2009).

It would be odd to say, for example, that the gift of a delicious meal for twelve obligates your eating it and sharing it with eleven friends; that is just an appropriate response to what it is. There is no external constraint being placed on the recipient; this response emerges from the recipient's own reaction to the gift, from what the gift means to the recipient. If a return to the giver seems the right thing to do, that is not because of a condition placed on the transaction, because this was the deal going into an exchange that began with the gift's being handed over to you, but because of what the gift is, how good it is. The gift's goodness is what inclines one to affirm that fact, to thank the one who brought it, to praise and honor the giver for her kindness and generosity. One doesn't make a return like that to the giver because one has to, but out of a free and joyful testimony to what one has received from another's hands. The more unconditional that giving was — the giver had no prior relationship with you, the giver could have avoided having anything to do with you, you hadn't done anything for them, and so on — the more wondrous the sense of gratitude and joy.[9]

Receiving a gift usually implies recognizing the giver as well. To receive in faith the gift of being the image of God is, accordingly, to recognize God as the source of our own designation, calling, and destiny, which allows for the joyful response. It is possible to say that due to his recognition of this giver, Jesus appears then to be the true human being; something is realized in him that had never previously been realized in the same manner. His unity with God is related to how he recognizes God and God's calling of him.

The preconception of *imago Dei* developed here thus serves as a hermeneutical tool for understanding Jesus as a true human. We thus combine the scriptural resources on the *imago Dei* with our systematic reconstruction and with the concrete actualization of this calling in the life of Jesus. What it means to be truly human is not seen, then, as something realized solely out of Jesus' example. Rather, Jesus can be understood as a true human because he makes visible what it means for all humans to be truly human and to live as images of God.

We are now in a position to see more clearly what it might mean to say that Jesus is a true human, an understanding that emerges from

9. Kathryn Tanner, *Economy of Grace* (Minneapolis: Fortress Press, 2005), p. 69.

seeing him as the true image of God. By fulfilling his calling, and by bearing witness to God's giving and recognition, Jesus does what any representative of God is called to do. But every human except him fails to fulfill this calling. The true humanity of Christ is thereby something that differentiates him from God, who sends him; but this differentiation does not jeopardize his *unity with God* — rather it expresses, confirms, and realizes it. The unity that Christ manifests with God is from this point of view not exceptional in that it discloses a total discontinuity with the rest of humanity; rather it is in continuity with the designation and calling for all of humanity.

The approach we have developed might suggest that the unity of Jesus with God — along these lines — can be taken as something related to the life-conditions of every human being. It allows for recognizing humanity in Christ, as well as Christ in humanity. It is Jesus' concrete fulfillment of his calling to be the image of God that leads to his crucifixion, and it is against this background that we can understand his vindication by God in the resurrection. In this perspective, the resurrection might be seen as confirming the unity already apparent in Jesus' ministry. The suggested approach thus also indicates a warranted claim for Jesus' unity with God apart from how we understand the historicity of his resurrection.[10]

If there is any "will to power" expressed in the ministry of Jesus as he realizes his designation of *imago Dei*, it is the will for a *different* power: one that is not aimed at control and subjection, but at empowering others to become more fully images of God — by letting them receive community, relationship, and grace. A systematically developed understanding of *imago Dei* such as the one above suggests that it involves a true recognition of the other. The power of God lies in being the source of goodness and grace, not in an ability to subvert human freedom and community. I make this point in order to provide a further background for justice in the parable's account of judgment.

The understanding of God implicitly witnessed in the ministry of Jesus thus turns out to have an ambiguous character: on the one hand God is the gifting one who reigns by shaping community and offering

---

10. This last remark should not be taken as an indication of my rejection of the historical basis of the claims for Jesus' resurrection. It is rather meant as suggesting that there is something about the reality of God to be experienced and understood in Jesus regardless of how one understands the issue of resurrection.

people chances to live a life unbounded by exclusion and marginalizing, by sin and suffering. On the other hand, allowing for the consequences of our reconstruction here, God is also vulnerable: to be able to realize God's kingdom in the world, God is in need of representatives who are witnessing to God's gifts. If that does not happen, God is not voiced and remains silenced; God's presence is not expressed or manifested. God's presence and the manifestations of God's power are thus not something given and secured; they are always partly, at least, dependent upon someone responding to God's calling. God is not manifested as a necessary power, but as a possibility for something different. This understanding of God is linked closely to how humans fulfill their destiny: *God's destiny in the world is dependent on how humans respond to God's designation of them as images of God. The specific and unique character of Jesus' life was that he was able to manifest this possibility in an unforeseen manner, in a way that changed the world.* This change was not due to coercive power, but to the power of love evidenced in the ministry of Jesus.

The previous analysis then provides us with an angle from which we can understand Jesus as the self-revelation of God: it is because Jesus voices and manifests the power of God as he does that we can say he is God's self-revelation. Jesus does not reveal *himself,* he never points to himself, but always to the one who has sent him. He does this in accordance with God's calling, and hence, it is ordained by God that Jesus reveals God in the way he does. We shall now look further into what the above reflections mean for our understanding of the Judgment.

The Parable of the Last Judgment Reread: Christ as Judge and Witness to Justice

> [Jesus said to his disciples:] "When the Son of Man comes in his glory, and all the angels with him, then he will sit on the throne of his glory. All the nations will be gathered before him, and he will separate people one from another as a shepherd separates the sheep from the goats, and he will put the sheep at his right hand and the goats at the left. Then the king will say to those at his right hand, 'Come, you that are blessed by my Father, inherit the kingdom prepared for you from the foundation of the world; for I was hungry and you gave me food, I was thirsty and you gave me some-

thing to drink, I was a stranger and you welcomed me, I was naked and you gave me clothing, I was sick and you took care of me, I was in prison and you visited me.' Then the righteous will answer him, 'Lord, when was it that we saw you hungry and gave you food, or thirsty and gave you something to drink? And when was it that we saw you a stranger and welcomed you, or naked and gave you clothing? And when was it that we saw you sick or in prison and visited you?' And the king will answer them, 'Truly I tell you, just as you did it to one of the least of these who are members of my family, you did it to me.' Then he will say to those at his left hand, 'You that are accursed, depart from me into the eternal fire prepared for the devil and his angels; for I was hungry and you gave me no food, I was thirsty and you gave me nothing to drink, I was a stranger and you did not welcome me, naked and you did not give me clothing, sick and in prison and you did not visit me.' Then they also will answer, 'Lord, when was it that we saw you hungry or thirsty or a stranger or naked or sick or in prison, and did not take care of you?' Then he will answer them, 'Truly I tell you, just as you did not do it to one of the least of these, you did not do it to me.' And these will go away into eternal punishment, but the righteous into eternal life." (Matt. 25:31-46)

The question "Who is righteous?" is answered in several of Matthew's parables; the one about the judgment of the nations is usually considered the most important. The parable presents us with a crux, especially from a Protestant angle: Is Jesus here claiming that humans will be judged according to what they *do,* after all, and do we then have to conclude that everything said about the grace of God is rendered invalid?

In the following, I will present an interpretation highlighting two interrelated issues: one is related to *recognition* (which we have already prepared for), and the other to *differentiation.* As for differentiation, Matthew strongly indicates that what humans do or don't do has implications for the outcome of their lives. To suggest otherwise would be to say that in the end there is no justice for those who suffer. Hence, differentiation between good and bad deeds (or lack thereof) is a main concern here — not in itself, but for the sake of justice for those who suffer.

Consequently, one has to ask if the existential meaning of the parable is not primarily to underscore that God takes seriously the suffering of those who are not shown mercy and compassion by their neighbors. Given that we identify the judge (named by Matthew as "the Son of Man" — an eschatological dimension he attributes to Jesus) as Christ, God's representative, the point of the judgment is that Christ recognizes those who are suffering and gives them their right. Without such judgment, there is no real recognition of those who suffer, or of suffering and injustice in general. The judgment makes us see, and helps us verbalize both the injustice and justice.

That this might be a main point of the parable is suggested by the detailed description of the different forms of injustice addressed by "the Son of Man" and repeated more or less four times in the parable. Against this background of securing concrete justice we then may look at how the judgment is carried out. It appears, as we shall see, that those who are judged are judged according to how they identified and recognized the neighbors' needs and the injustice they suffered.

At this point the relevance of our previous discussion of gift seems relevant: those who are positively recognized by the judge are recognized because of actions that they did not themselves perceive as done for a specific economic purpose. They lack an understanding of what they have done in terms of *what their actions are giving in return.* They have not acted in order to achieve goods for themselves, but solely for the sake of the other, for the sake of sharing goods, as they have recognized others as belonging to the same community as themselves; they have recognized the humanity of others as equal to their own. A religious conception of merit, retribution, or reciprocity seems to be totally outside the scope of their actions, which is why their surprise is so large when they learn their actions have the implications pointed to by the judge.

The lack of *personal motive* for doing good to others need not preclude an internal relationship between the one doing good and the recipient of that deed. Moreover, it is possible to see how the good deed is marked by, or even constituted by, a perceived relationship on the side of the agent. This relationship in turn also reveals itself as a relationship with the judge (Christ): the judge says that "what you did to the least of these that are members of my family, you did to me." This suggests that God's justice has a triadic structure: it is based in God's gifts, which humanity is called to share with the neighbor. Anyone who keeps these gifts for him- or herself or uses them for private (religious) purposes contradicts this triadic structure, and thereby violates the open and positive community that all these gifts are meant to serve.[11]

There *is* a return here, but it is not linked to an "economic" circle by the one who invests his or her actions or deeds.[12] Rather, the return is freely given, a point not only marked by the words of the giver, but also by the recipients' wonder and surprise when confronted with the gift of the kingdom: this is something unexpected and hence, something outside their perception of the context for action. This non-necessary connection between reward and action suggests not only that the inheritance of the kingdom must be understood as a gift of grace, but also that the actions rewarded have some kind of quality or content not realized by those who performed it. The lack of calculation makes the beneficence a real gift as well. The surprise expressed at the positive judgment turns into a question of recognition: "When was it that we saw you?" This question of recognition is not only about being able to recognize Christ, but also a question about who belongs to the community of Christ. The response of the judge makes this clear: when the suffering one is visited, fed, given clothes, etc., Christ himself is visited, fed, and given clothes. This suggests that there is an internal link between three parties, and that Christ is the non-present third party in the relationship between the one who gives and the one who receives. He is nevertheless not openly recognized. How can we come to terms with this puzzle? I suggest that the answer to the puzzle consists of three parts:

The first part is that when you address persons who are suffering in the manner described above (unconditionally, without personal interest, even without interest in relieving your own discomfort when confronted with someone in an unjust situation), you are addressing them as people who belong to your world, and who rightly break into your world with a call for justice. Thereby you recognize them as being justified in their call for you to justice. What you do to them is not only determined by *you*, it is determined by them and their calling of you.

---

11. For more on this triadic structure, which is expressed in different ways in Jesus' ministry as well as in his criticism of the theology of his contemporaries, see Henriksen, *Desire, Gift, and Recognition*.

12. For an exploration of this return, or gift-exchange outside of desert or merit, cf. the interesting treatise by Bo Kristian Holm, *Gabe und Geben bei Luther: Das Verhältnis zwischen Reziprozität und Reformatorischer Rechtfertigungslehre* (Berlin: Walter de Gruyter, 2006).

You recognize yourself as the other's neighbor, and the other as yours. That is the first step of recognition. Hence, you belong together, and your self-perception means that you are in no way justified in excluding the other from your world. The bottom line of this recognition then, is that you see the other as the image of God (be this explicit or not): he or she is reminding you of God's justice, and is calling you to be an image like him or her by being a response-able witness in action.

Second, the parable then continues to indicate that they are related to, or belong to Christ, and are among *his* family. Not only Christ is revealed, but God — as concerned with injustice and with those who are suffering under it. Moreover, by suggesting that one recognizes the other as *imago Dei* when one shows mercy to those who suffer, the consequence of this recognition is that they too have a common vocation with Christ's: to be images of God. Hence, there is a close relationship between the three parties involved, most expressively manifested in the notion of *imago Dei*. The notion of *imago Dei* thus helps us reconstruct the extensive theological dimension in the designation of the suffering ones as "the least members of my family."

The third part of the answer is the implication of the above, namely that you meet Christ in your neighbor. Because Christ is the true image of God, all of humanity is related to him, and is in some sense represented in him. As the true image of God, Christ is what all other humans are called to become. We are accordingly in a position where we can see Christ in the face of every other human — as the one who calls us to mercy, compassion, and love.

We can now return to the question raised in a Protestant context: Does all this mean that in the end, good works are what is required for a positive outcome in God's final judgment? Well, what the parable seems to suggest is that good works are important, not for the final judgment as such, but for the neighbor. However, the importance of good works for salvation seems to be undermined by the fact that what ends up as most important, is the ability to *recognize* the other as part of my world, as a person presenting me with a valid and justified call to justice. Hence, this person not only belongs to my world as such, but my world as a gift from God that I am called to share with others.

The recognition of the other, and of his or her valid claim to break into my world and call me to justice, thus implies that I *believe* my world is God's gift, and that the Other is the *imago Dei* who calls. In other words, the basic and underlying presupposition for the whole outcome of the judgment is the ability to recognize oneself, the other, and the world as all rooted in the creative act of a giving God. The theological expression for this recognition is usually faith. By living out of the faith in these gifts, one is set free from concern for oneself and is able to care for the other. This opens up to salvation in the broad sense of the word. In this sense, salvation is based on faith, not on works — but salvation is nevertheless also internally related to good works and expresses itself in restoring justice in the world.

However, the *faith* expressed in this recognition of the other as part of my world is not necessarily articulated or expressed by an explicit faith in Christ: Christ might still be unknown, but one might nevertheless be able to respond to the call of justice and to offer the gifts to others. If we reason like this it becomes theologically safeguarded how one can also act as the image of God without faith in God, by giving others the chance to experience God's world *as gift*. However, this *unthematized* witness is in need of a revelation (in Christ) in order to be acknowledged and recognized as the gift of the triune God. The parable suggests that this final revelation takes place in the final judgment.

The parable thus suggests that faith is important for the development of a full recognition of the other and of the world, but that faith in a Christian sense of the word — as belief in Jesus Christ as the savior of the world — is not required in order for humans to be able to *function* as images of God in relation to others in need. Faith nevertheless serves as an expression of the personal commitment where what is at stake is fully recognized and can be interpreted adequately. It is in faith that the link between the three parties involved (God, self, neighbor) is revealed and manifested — outside the context of reciprocity or an exchange economy. This three-party (triadic) relationship also excludes the possibility of seeing the judgment as a simplistic, one-to-one relationship between God and the individual mediated by the individual's meriting works. Rather, the judgment is mediated by the individual's recognition of the call to justice and of the neighbor as the image of God, which also implies recognition of God as the one who bestows that designation and is the ultimate source of that calling.

The element of *surprise* is, as suggested, closely related to the fact that there can be no determination of the outcome due to any kind of calculated economic concerns. One can say that the only way to express the kingdom as gift is through a surprising judgment — one in which the other is recognized first and foremost by herself and for herself —

so that we are not tempted to treat the other as a means for pleasing God. Or, to put it the other way: that we are not first and foremost asking if the other is someone representing God — because that would easily and accordingly lead us back to a situation where we meet the other by asking if he or she might represent God or belong to God — or not. Such an approach would put us in the position of asking who merits our good works or not, and thereby have us determining what is just or not. Contrary to this approach, the point emerging from the parable is that the beneficial works are to be solely for the neighbor, and with no means for negotiation about the justice of our calling. The works express our desire for the neighbor's good, well-being, and welfare, and not our desire for appearing as just before God.

The judgment is therefore the place where it will be revealed that there is more at stake than this desire and the recognition of the other, namely the desire for the reality of God manifested in human community. But this cannot be revealed beforehand, unless the non-economic logic of gift runs the risk of being compromised. Hence, the judgment reveals a new dimension in recognition of what has to be hidden for the sake of the gift to be a gift — seen from the perspective of the giver (God).

In a certain sense, one can say that the basis for the judgment is not human agency as such, but rather the *other as recognized,* directing and guiding this agency. This approach lends even more weight to an understanding that does not see the good works *per se* as what qualifies for a positive judgment, but rather *the relationship to the other as it is expressed in recognition and community.* From this angle too it becomes possible to see what those people confronted with a *negative* judgment are actually lacking:

Primarily, the parable seems to imply that those who face a negative judgment lack the ability to recognize the other as related to them. Accordingly, they are also unable see that Christ is present as the third party in these (lacking) relationships. There is thus a double problem implied in the answer they give to the judge when he confronts them with what they did not do to him. First, they ask when they have met him in situations of suffering, hunger, etc., and thereby suggest that if they had done so, they would have given him what he needed. This response reveals the ignorance or neglect of relationships between the needy, Christ, and themselves. Second, the same answer also reveals *self-righteousness.* They try to justify their lack of good works by saying they were unable to recognize Christ in any of the people they met, but in reality they disclose their own lack of faith in Christ, and in God as the one present in the Other's face, calling them to satisfy the Other's justified needs.

Put bluntly, the rejected try to justify themselves by saying they have had no chance to do good works toward Christ. They seem ignorant of the triadic structure of God's gifting. They see their own works as just another means for providing themselves with merit. But this justification does not work, because it implies that they can establish their righteousness regardless of their relation to their neighbor in need. That is what they cannot do. The one who is unable to meet the other's needs by recognizing herself as one at the same level immediately faces the challenge of being self-righteous in a way that excludes the other.

It is this type of self-righteousness that Matthew addresses throughout his Gospel, and it is related to his call for good fruits. A piety that is oriented toward doing good for the sake of the agent easily ends up as a self-centered form of seeking, where the other is only an indirect object or tool in a desire primarily aimed at securing one's own position. Such an attitude cannot produce good fruits, as it is *constitutively* not concerned for the other.

The conclusion to this way of life, in which one is basically oriented only toward oneself, is that community is ruled out, or that one excludes oneself from community and fellowship by not recognizing the other as part of one's own world. The one who is judged as not righteous is thus the one who, by excluding the other, excludes herself. She is the one who lets her own totality determine the world, instead of letting the other be a witness to the richness of *infinite* justice, to use a Levinasian pair of concepts most apt for describing this situation.

The present analysis implies that it is not God who excludes humans from relationships in the last judgment, but that humans, by excluding others from community, exclude themselves.[13] God — as Christ witnesses in Matthew — remains the welcoming host for both good and bad (cf. 22:10). Hence, the hospitality and generosity of God go unquestioned, as does God's concern for justice.

---

13. For a more elaborate treatment of this dimension in the text, cf. Kathryn Tanner, *The Politics of God: Christian Theologies and Social Justice* (Minneapolis: Fortress Press, 1992).

The interpretation presented here then also implies that it is in no way a lack of justice that leads to some humans standing outside the kingdom: it is *human injustice,* and the lack of recognition of both the other and of God's generosity toward all humans. Human injustice keeps humans shut out of the kingdom, opposed to the grace and hospitality of God that welcomes them to join it. From a modern angle, this should not be hard to understand: a God who cares for the suffering and cannot tolerate neglect of them, as well as a God who welcomes everyone that does good to them, is a God who is righteous. By revealing how he himself is subject to what humans do to other humans, Christ also indicates that he (or God) is affected by what humans do or don't do. This points back to what was said about the vulnerability of God: God is able to suffer (in terms of being subjected to) the consequences of human agency.

At this point we might also add that the similarity in the response of the different groups might suggest another possible (but admittedly speculative and provoking) reading as well: as both groups respond with the same words, this might be read as indicating that it is not different people we are facing, but that the response of the believer and the non-believer, due to its verbal similarity, might just as well be taken as the response of the same individual — acting out of faith or not. The parable may suggest a division *within* humans as well as between them, indicating that humans are simultaneously sinners and believers. When read this way, the parable cannot be so easily used for separating different groups from each other, but rather suggests that we might all find ourselves in both positions: partly acting out of faith and trust for the sake of the neighbor, and partly out of concern for ourselves and our privileges. A reading like this presents the parable as a mirror for all of us — believers or otherwise.

Against the background of this parable, we are now finally able to construct a possible framework for understanding more of the beatitudes in Matthew 5. Those who are poor in spirit, those who mourn, etc., will be rewarded. The reason for their blessedness and their hope is not determined by present conditions, but by the promise of a different future in the kingdom of God. The future is the reason for their blessedness; when people are open to this future, their very relation to it integrates them in a new reality in which they are not closed into themselves.

We might well ask then: What kind of people is Jesus addressing in the beatitudes? The same as those judged righteous in Matthew 25: those whose practice creates community and fellowship, those who seek peace and righteousness, those who show mercy and thus contribute to the emergence of a better future, without divisions between people. They might do so for different reasons, but *what* they seek is nevertheless in accordance with the vision for a better future.

I want to strengthen this argument from another angle: What happens if the hope for the future is not articulated in this manner? What takes place if one concludes that justice will not rule in the end, that there will be no peace on earth, and so forth? As indicated earlier, the very articulation of goodness is a condition for goodness to be recognized and take place. A vision of a different world is a condition for a different world that is not determined by present conditions. That is what the beatitudes point to, and what the parable about the last judgment suggests: righteousness for those who suffer will be part of the future.

Conclusion

Summing up, then, we can say that Christ, also in his parable about the judgment, testifies to God's inclusive community.[14] This is a community where everyone is perceived as mutually related to each other, and where justice is manifest in and through the recognition of this relatedness. Moreover, by revealing God as the one who has prepared the kingdom "before the foundation of the world," and implicating himself as the judge who welcomes to this kingdom, Jesus shows that justice and righteousness are integral to the world as God has created it — and as Christ, as the *logos*, he invites us to perceive and express it. Without the hope for justice and community expressed by him, hope would be less. But Christ calls humans to this community and gives witness to what it means: the triadic structure of a community based on God's gifting.

The surprise of the judgment is thus closely related to the fact that it ignores our conceptions of merit and desert, but recognizes God's gifts as something to be shared by all. Both parties are surprised

---

14. The observant reader may note that there is tension, not to say contradiction, between the position developed here on inclusiveness and the one expressed in Brent Waters's article in the present volume.

and disconcerted as the judgment breaks in, disturbs their world, and calls attention to something missing in their present understanding. The parable of the judgment uses this surprise as a call to regroup the furniture of the world, to reconsider and rearrange basic assumptions — in order to expand our perception of the world. Such surprises can be met in two ways: by being grateful for the chance to see the world in a new light — or by making our present world a fortress guarded by self-justification and lack of openness to the new and surprising. In the first position, the advent of the Other (God, the neighbor) is welcomed; in the second, we exclude ourselves from them. The parable should remind us that we are in need of this surprise, so that we might see in our neighbor the presence of him who justly passes judgment — in order to include everyone. That Christ appears as the judge in Matthew is reasonable against his backdrop: he is the one who knows and practices this justice — much to our surprise.

7. Should We Do What Jesus Did? Evolutionary Perspectives on Christology and Ethics

J. Wentzel van Huyssteen

And when Jesus had been baptized, just as he came up from the water, suddenly the heavens were opened to him and he saw the Spirit of God descending like a dove and alighting on him. And a voice from Heaven said, "This is my son, the Beloved, with whom I am well pleased."

MATTHEW 3:16-17

Introduction

The rather perplexing issue of whether, and how, Christology should relate to ethics, for me at least, can only be approached by first asking how exactly, in the case of Jesus, God's revelation can be located not just in history, as theologians as diverse as Wolfhart Pannenberg and Marjorie Suchocki have argued, but specifically in evolutionary history itself. If, as I will argue, God's revelation is indeed mediated through the realities and trajectories of evolutionary history, then not only will the question of incarnation be tied to radical embodiment, but also Jesus' embodied mind — his consciousness and moral awareness — will be crucial for an understanding of both his unique relationship to God and any possible connection between Christology and ethics. In my own most recent work on the evolutionary roots of theological anthropology,[1] I have

---

1. J. Wentzel van Huyssteen, *Alone in the World? Human Uniqueness in Science and Theology* (Grand Rapids: Eerdmans, 2006).

149

concluded that the theological notion of *imago Dei* should be revisioned to reclaim its most concrete, embodied meaning. In this sense the evolutionary history of our species, as well as those characteristics that should be seen as most defining the "uniqueness" or distinctiveness of *Homo sapiens,* particularly human consciousness, imagination, moral awareness, and religious disposition, have direct consequences for defining an embodied notion of the "image of God." When finally in the New Testament Jesus is seen as the definitive image of God, what would this mean for an understanding of Jesus' own embodied mind, his consciousness, self-awareness, maleness, and personhood? Clearly, then, this focus on the identity of Jesus will shape the question of the ethical relevance of who he was, what he did, and what he said.

If next we find in ancient doctrine a hermeneutical and metaphorical starting point for thinking about Jesus as "fully human and fully divine," then the sheer fact of his complete humanness should also be a (biblical) key to understanding his imaging of God as an embodied male who shares with us our most defining human characteristics precisely as they have evolved in evolutionary history. Furthermore, on a postfoundationalist approach to the problem of Christology and ethics, the theme of the conference out of which this volume arose now by definition emerges as an *interdisciplinary* problem: since Jesus was, as we are, deeply embedded in evolutionary history, what might the sciences tell us today about the evolution of our most uniquely human characteristics, our consciousness, self-awareness, linguistic capacities, religious propensities, embodied imagination and sexuality, and, most importantly, the evolution of our moral sensibilities? And how might the evolution of these uniquely human characteristics help us understand better who Jesus was, and therefore where his moral authority came from, and whether, and why, that should matter for our ethics?

Against this background I believe that any discussion of Christology and ethics should start with what we are learning from the sciences about the evolution of consciousness and the evolution of morality. Both methodologically and substantially these seem to be the necessary building blocks for searching, first for an *evolutionary* link, and then for a *theological* link between Christology and ethics respectively. Thanks to contemporary primatology, paleoanthropology, and also the neurosciences, we know today that the embodied human mind's capacity for moral awareness, the innate sense for "right and wrong," is embedded in deep evolutionary history. How much, in the case of Jesus of Nazareth, should we speculate about his evolved sense of right and wrong, and would a theological perception of "divine nature" add anything to why Jesus Christ (and the way we construct our Christologies) may be important today for ethics?

Ultimately I will argue for the kind of Christological implications for ethics that will minimize doctrinal abstractions and focus on the pragmatic impetus of Christology for ethics. Viewing our Christologies less as foundationalist frameworks and more as epistemic pointers creates a space for the awareness of mystery in Christology even as it opens up our theological and interdisciplinary reflections to a Christomorphic future.

Ethics and Evolution

Evolutionary Epistemology

In this section I want to raise two questions: *First,* what do we learn from evolutionary history about the evolution of morality and moral awareness in humans? And *second,* what do we learn from evolutionary history about the way we perceive moral laws or construct our moral codes and our ethical rules and systems? However, in trying to answer these questions I want to broaden the evolutionary scope of my argument by first taking a cue from evolutionary epistemology. Generally speaking, evolutionary epistemology, with its explicit focus on the evolution of cognition, helps evolutionary biology understand the steps in which a succession of organisms have acquired nervous systems and brains whereby they obtain, store, retrieve, and utilize information about their environments in a way that furthers their survival.

This information has been so successful over time because it has proven to be so reliable for survival. This kind of explicit awareness and exploration of the external world reached a peak in *Homo sapiens,* who through conscious self-awareness, language, imagination, and later mathematics were able to formulate concepts and theories for the interpretation of this environment.[2] And this is what almost all evolutionary epistemologists would call *hypothetical realism,* that is, our falli-

2. Arthur Peacocke, *Theology for a Scientific Age: Being and Becoming, Natural, Divine, and Human* (Minneapolis: Fortress Press, 1993), p. 73.

ble knowledge is reliable enough to facilitate prediction and control of our environment. In this specific sense both our sense impressions and our evolved cognitive structures must be broadly trustworthy or we would not have survived as a species. We do indeed owe our highly developed powers of cognition to evolution and its age-long process of coming to terms with, or adapting to, external reality. This evolutionary process is not just narrowly biological but is quite explicitly one of *knowledge,* for any adaptation to a particular circumstance of external reality presupposes that a measure of information about this context has already been absorbed. In fact, as a species we seem to have survived our general vulnerability only by the exercise of cognitive abilities that in our species have reached a rather unique peak of development.[3]

If, therefore, we take the evolution of human consciousness and cognition seriously, we quickly realize that even a conscious activity such as theological reflection/cognition is not only radically shaped by the enduring influence of its own traditions, and therefore by its social, historical, and cultural embeddedness. It would also imply that theology, and theological reflection and knowledge, is not only shaped by cultural evolution, but is also definitively shaped by the deeper biological roots of human rationality. This is precisely the point made by evolutionary epistemology: like all living beings we humans have resulted from evolutionary processes, and consequently our mental capacities are constrained and shaped by the mechanisms of biological evolution.

All evolutionary epistemologists agree that the theory of evolution in essence is a theory of knowledge precisely because the process of evolution is the principal provider of the organization of all living things and their adaptations. Evolution thus turns out to be about much more than the "origin of species," as it is a much richer, holistic process that has shaped the way our minds work and how we know the world. As such, evolutionary epistemology highlights both the deeply embodied and the fallibilist nature of all human knowledge and explains that there are advances and growth in human knowledge, but that this "progress" is not necessarily an increase in the accuracy of depiction or an increase in the certainty of what we know. This view is strengthened by the conviction that self-conscious human cognition is a bridge between biology and culture, between biological evolution and cultural evolution.

3. Peacocke, *Theology for a Scientific Age,* p. 79.

The hypothetical realist approach of evolutionary epistemology thus implies that our embodied cognitive apparatus is adaptive, and that our knowledge of the world around us consists of proposals made to this environment. On this evolutionary epistemological view, knowledge is thus revealed as an interactive relationship between an embodied knower and something/someone that is known. Moreover, I would argue that, from an epistemological view, human cognition or knowledge is revealed as a complex interactive process of expectation, interpretation, and explanation. This is why, at a cultural and philosophical level, evolutionary epistemologists would want to reveal extreme forms of non-foundationalism or anti-realism as *epistemic narcissism,* because these ideologies would have us believe that knowledge is not a relation between a knower and what is known, but a narcissistic, inward reflection disconnected from those aspects of the world we are claiming knowledge of.[4]

From an evolutionary epistemological point of view, the interactionist nature of all human knowledge, precisely because of its deep biological history, emerges as a deeply embodied knowledge. And through our language abilities we have created cultures, vast bodies of knowledge and moral codes, which can all be seen as evolutionary artifacts that enable us to benefit from the trials and errors of our ances-

---

4. From a philosophy of science perspective scholars often, and correctly I would argue, see evolutionary epistemology as an important but somewhat neglected reaction to the failure of logical positivism. Positivism is widely seen today as failing to account for the growth of human knowledge, for major shifts in the history of science (like the shift from Newtonian physics to Einstein's general relativity) and in the history of theology (like the dramatic shift from medieval Scholastics to the Reformation), or for general paradigm shifts in cultural history (for instance, from modernity to postmodernity, etc.). What is often ignored, however, is the fact that there occurred two very different and competing moves away from positivistic philosophy of science: one move was toward Wittgenstein's philosophy of language games and Thomas Kuhn's now-famous theory of paradigms; the other was toward Karl Popper's evolutionary epistemology and the all-important injection of Darwinism into philosophy/philosophy of science. Thus, in addition to the acknowledgment of the theory-ladenness and paradigm dependency of knowledge in the first instance, evolutionary epistemology seeks to explain the knowledge we have as an extension of the adaptive evolutionary process that began millions of years ago. I would argue that *both* of these very important reactions to positivist views of human knowledge, in very different ways, opened our eyes to the interpretative, hermeneutical dimension of all knowledge. It should therefore not be surprising that in contemporary postfoundationalist views of knowledge, hermeneutics and epistemology would powerfully merge.

tors. Or, as some evolutionary epistemologists would put it: with the arrival of *Homo sapiens* human evolution became the evolution of this embodied knowledge. On this more embodied, holistic view of human knowledge, not only are more narrowly conceived notions of reason or rationality included, but human consciousness too becomes more richly redefined in terms of feelings, emotions, instinct, and intelligence. Thus one of evolutionary epistemology's most valuable contributions to notions of biological and cultural evolution becomes clear: once embodied intelligence evolved in our species, our self-conscious brains achieved a causal force that in many ways now equals that of our genes.

What evolutionary epistemology shows us, finally, is that we humans can indeed take on cognitive goals and moral ideals that cannot be explained or justified in terms of survival-promotion or reproductive advantage only. Therefore, once the capacities for rational knowledge, moral sensibility, the aesthetic appreciation of beauty, and the propensity for religious belief have emerged in our biological history, they cannot be explained only in biological/evolutionary terms anymore. In this sense we clearly transcend our biological origins and do have the ability to transcend what is given to us both in biology and in culture. As British philosopher Anthony O'Hear strikingly puts it: we are prisoners neither of our genes, nor of the ideas we encounter as we make our way through the world.[5]

Evolutionary epistemology now provocatively reveals what happens as, both epistemically and morally, we make our way through our contextualized worlds. It is especially interesting to look at this through a Kantian perspective. Immanuel Kant argued that it is our minds that order our sensations and that we possess some knowledge *a priori* independent of these perceptions. But Kant did not tell us why our sensations are ordered by our minds as they are and not otherwise; nor did he tell us anything about the *origins* of this mental power. From an evolutionary point of view any *a priori* knowledge is the result of evolutionary experiences, of evolutionary learning. And in this sense what is seen as an individual's *a priori* appears as in fact an evolutionary *a posteriori,* that is, that which has been previously and interactively learned from experience. In this way evolutionary epistemology offers a

5. Anthony O'Hear, *Beyond Evolution: Human Nature and the Limits of Evolutionary Explanation* (Oxford: Oxford University Press, 2002), p. vii.

dynamization and a historization of the Kantian categories and as such goes far beyond Kant's philosophy. Clearly, once we realize the impact of evolutionary origins of humans, it should be quite natural to ask about the biological grounding of pure reason.[6]

From this directly follows that, for evolutionary epistemologists, religious belief and moral convictions could not be imposed on us by God, but take shape naturally from the long evolutionary history of our very nature, our existential needs, our hopes and desires, our fear and awareness of death. But this is no sociobiological argument: there certainly is substance to the argument that humans are genetically disposed to moral awareness, to religious and, in a wider sense, metaphysical beliefs.[7] Wuketits thus wants to explain metaphysics and religion as "natural phenomena." This is not to say, however, that we are able to explain *everything* by means of biological evolution — which is precisely what an evolutionary epistemologist, who focuses so strongly on cultural evolution and its embeddedness in biological evolution, should say. It also means that through evolutionary epistemology we can gain some understanding of our own metaphysical beliefs and their causes as part of our very nature.

Evolutionary Epistemology and Ethics

If our mental capacities result from evolution and if our mind should be seen as a particular biofunction,[8] then we should realize that our morality, or more accurately, our typical human moral awareness, can also be explained in terms of evolution. This implies a quite specific relationship between evolutionary epistemology and evolutionary ethics: evolutionary epistemology — as some primatologists and moral philosophers would also argue — clearly shows the biological reasons for the evolution of moral awareness, but this does not lead to an evolutionary explanation for the formulation of specific moral codes or norms. Evolutionary ethics can help us reconstruct the preconditions for moral behavior but says nothing about the validity of certain norms that have

6. Franz M. Wuketits, *Evolutionary Epistemology and Its Implications for Humankind* (Albany: SUNY Press, 1990), p. 185.

7. Wuketits, *Evolutionary Epistemology,* p. 199.

8. Wuketits, *Evolutionary Epistemology,* p. 200.

been developed by cultural evolution and are thus constrained by sociocultural conventions. This is the reason why there may be different *rationales* inherent in different sociocultural systems, and why different cultural contexts may lead to different moral codes.[9]

Evolutionary epistemologists would, therefore, want to avoid the *naturalistic fallacy,* that is, the idea that any *ought* follows from what *is,* that is, that the fact that we are "wired" for moral awareness might necessarily lead to insight in, or the preference for, certain moral laws. For non-sociobiologists the theory of evolution, then, is a purely scientific theory and cannot by itself entail any normative or prescriptive ethical conclusions. In this sense no moral norms *(ought)* for either moral or immoral behavior can be supported on the basis of purely biological premises *(is)*. For instance, no evolutionary epistemologist or evolutionary ethicist would argue that because there *is* a struggle for existence in nature there *ought* to be such a struggle in human societies, or because there is a struggle for survival on a biological level all human behavior, even altruistic or seemingly selfless behavior, would always mask deeply selfish behavior.

Evolutionary ethicists are, therefore, interested in why humans behave the way they do, how the evolutionary origins of human behavior are to be explained, and in which way our behavior has been constrained by biological factors. In this sense one could say that the starting point of evolutionary ethics is the insight that morality has a biological basis, and that it has developed as a systems property of the brain. Ethical behavior is indeed a product of our biological evolution, but this fact by itself does not entail any normative assertions: from the fact that morality has developed we cannot conclude that any particular trait of human behavior is good or bad (right or wrong) in an ethical sense. Put differently, an evolutionary account of ethics does not support any moral code, but it may help us understand why such codes have developed.[10] We should therefore be careful to always distinguish between the *evolution of morality* in a neutral sense, and the *evolutionary justification of moral codes*. Evolutionary ethics in this second sense has a bad history and has resulted in ideologies like Social Darwinism.

When I use the term "evolutionary ethics" I use it to characterize the view that morality has indeed evolved and there have been biologi-

9. Wuketits, *Evolutionary Epistemology,* p. 201.
10. Wuketits, *Evolutionary Epistemology,* p. 202.

cal roots of moral behavior, as we will see in an example from the work of primatologist Frans de Waal. However, from the evolutionary gene- sis of our moral awareness we cannot derive right or wrong.[11] Ac- cepting that our moral awareness has evolved also means accepting that our moral codes may not be fixed forever as unchangeable entities.

As humans we are therefore free to find our own moral goals in this world, and an evolutionary approach to ethics and morality helps us understand under which circumstances humans have created what kinds of values and moral codes. Certainly, some traits of our moral be- havior may be derived from archaic behavioral patterns and from the intense drive to survive. If moral codes should regulate the interactions among individuals in a society, then these codes must also have been useful for survival. In fact, to our phylogenetic ancestors it must have been of a certain survival value to believe that moral codes are simply given, and therefore objective — as is often found today where certain groups believe that ethical norms are unchangeable and can be derived from some set of eternal "divine" principles.[12]

In an evolutionary approach to ethics these kinds of beliefs will rightly be dismissed, and the creation of moral norms, in an *a posteriori* sense, will be found to lie on a constructive, cultural level. This of course means that humans in principle are free to change their moral codes, but this also means that we humans carry great responsibility for ourselves and that this responsibility cannot and should not easily be delegated to "objective divine moral codes" (in this sense even the Ten Commandments and Jesus' love command, over time, are revealed as *a posteriori* moral laws). This also frees us from the foundationalist need for an idea of absolute moral truth: our idea of truth is relative to our historical and social contexts and their histories, and only a coherentist, postfoundationalist approach can sufficiently explain this.

What evolutionary epistemology finally gives us is the open view of evolution: basic patterns of our behavior depend on, and have been developed through, our evolutionary past. But this is *not* a determinist view. As higher organisms we are capable of learning so that even evolu- tionary programs may be modified.[13] Appreciating this ethological fact and appreciating the human brain's plasticity leads us to a non-

11. Wuketits, *Evolutionary Epistemology,* p. 202.
12. Wuketits, *Evolutionary Epistemology,* p. 203.
13. Wuketits, *Evolutionary Epistemology,* p. 207.

deterministic view of human nature: we humans have the responsibility to make our own decisions on the norms and limits to our own behavior. Only we ourselves are responsible for our actions in the world. We are, therefore, constrained but not determined by our evolutionary past.

Ultimately, a fragile balance is revealed between the way we are bound to the laws of nature and the limited freedom we have to significantly shape our moral destiny. We humans indeed have enough freedom to do good, or evil, or both, and in this sense we are, after all, responsible for much of what happens to us. To be able to act freely thus implies that we are morally responsible for our actions and choices even as we learn to cope with limiting constraints. On the one hand, we are bound to the laws of nature through biological, genetic, and hormonal constraints, while also to our cultural contexts and personal histories. On the other hand, we have a remarkable freedom to choose who we want to be and how we want to find ultimate meaning in spite of these constraints. In this sense we are significantly free to choose and act even if our physical and psychological natures are deeply shaped by constraints for which we can never be held responsible.

Morality and Evolutionary Ethics

Primatologists like Frans de Waal have long argued that the roots of human morality can be clearly discerned in social animals like apes and monkeys. In fact, these animals' feelings of empathy and their expectations of reciprocity are essential behaviors for mammalian group living, and, from an evolutionary viewpoint, the *building blocks* of human morality are indeed evolutionarily ancient.[14] The background of this argument is the fact that all social animals have had to constrain or alter their behavior in various ways for group living to be worthwhile. Exactly these constraints, evident in monkeys and even more so in chimpanzees and bonobos, are part of the human inheritance, too, and in de Waal's view form the sets of behavior from which human morality has been shaped. Importantly, de Waal is not asking us to think of animals as moral beings, and he does not claim that even chimpanzees possess morality. But he does argue that human morality would be im-

---

14. Frans de Waal, *Primates and Philosophers: How Morality Evolved* (Princeton: Princeton University Press, 2006), pp. 7ff.

possible without certain proto-moral emotional building blocks that are clearly at work in chimpanzee and monkey societies.

For his notion of proto-morality de Waal points especially to the presence of consolation and empathy in primates and humans. Social living requires empathy, which is especially evident in chimpanzees, as well as ways of peacemaking and bringing hostilities to an end. De Waal has found that every species of monkey has its own protocol for reconciliation after fights and believes these actions are undertaken for the greater good of the community and as such are a significant precursor of morality in human societies. In addition primates also have a sense of reciprocity and fairness. For de Waal, then, four kinds of behavior can be seen as the basis of sociality: empathy, the ability to learn and follow social rules, reciprocity, and peacemaking. Human morality in this sense has grown out of primate sociality, but with two extra levels of sophistication: humans create and enforce their society's moral codes much more rigorously with rewards, punishment, and reputation building. They also apply a degree of judgment and reason for which there are no parallels in animals.[15]

In his argument that our human morality grows out of the social instincts we share with bonobos, chimpanzees, and apes, de Waal also criticizes what he calls the "veneer theory," which holds that human ethics is simply an overlay on our selfish and brutish nature. De Waal draws on his extensive work with primates to illustrate the evolutionary origins of morality. For humans as well as for the great apes, morality is not a veneer masking self-interest. It is intrinsic to our embodied evolutionary natures that the evolutionary outcome of altruism is conducive to species survival, and thus to understanding that humans are not only amoral, selfish, and savage, but also moral by nature. On this view not just sympathy and empathy but also right and wrong are feelings that we share with other animals: even our feelings for ethics and justice are also part of nature. On this truly holistic and embodied view, goodness, generosity, and genuine kindness come just as naturally to us as meaner and more aggressive feelings.[16]

15. De Waal, *Primates and Philosophers*, pp. 13-17; cf. Nicholas Wade, "An Evolutionary Theory of Right and Wrong," in *The New York Times: Books on Science*, October 31, 2006, pp. 2-3.

16. In a slightly different interdisciplinary approach Marc Hauser has recently built on this idea to propose that humans are born with a "moral grammar" wired into the neural circuits of their brains by evolution. See Marc D. Hauser, *Moral Minds: How Na-*

In this way Frans de Waal sets out to understand morality in terms of its deep evolutionary history. De Waal next argues that "evolution rarely throws out anything": in the slow process of evolution by natural selection structures are transformed, modified, co-opted for other functions, or "tweaked" in another direction — precisely what Charles Darwin meant by "descent with modification."[17] De Waal now argues that the same is true for biological traits: the old always remains present in the new. Exactly this point is important for the debate about the origins of *empathy:* although human cognitive, aesthetic, and moral capacities have reached "dizzying heights," it remains true that both developmentally *and* evolutionarily, advanced forms of empathy are

------

ture Designed Our Universal Sense of Right and Wrong (New York: HarperCollins, 2006). Hauser argues that this "moral grammar" generates instant moral judgments that are often inaccessible to the conscious mind. This viewpoint has far-reaching consequences: it implies, first, that our moral codes and education can at best give shape to an already-innate behavior; and, second, that religions are not the exclusive source of moral codes but, rather, are the social enforcers of instinctive moral behavior (cf. Wade). Thus Hauser argues that this moral grammar operates in much the same way as the "universal grammar" proposed by linguist Noam Chomsky as the innate neural machinery for language. Like this universal grammar for language, moral grammar is also first of all a system for generating moral behavior and not a list of specific ethical rules. It does, however, constrain human behavior so tightly that many moral codes turn out to be the same or fairly similar in various societies (do unto others . . . ; care for children and the weak; don't kill; avoid adultery and incest; don't cheat, don't steal, etc.). This innate moral grammar, therefore, also allows for many variations that are often deeply culture-bound, since cultures can assign different weights to different moral or ethical rules. Hauser's proposal is a quite deliberate attempt to claim "matters of right and wrong" from philosophers and ethicists and to open up this conversation for science, particularly evolutionary biology. He believes that this moral grammar evolved because restraints on behavior are required for social living and have been favored by natural selection because of their survival value (cf. Wade, pp. 2-3). Hauser thus challenges the general belief that moral behavior is only learned, which is exactly Frans de Waal's point. On Hauser's specific view social animals possess the rudiments of a moral system in that they can recognize cheating or deviations from expected behavior. Generally, however, they lack the psychological mechanisms on which the pervasive reciprocity of human society is based. Hauser also argues that the kind of moral grammar now universal among humans presumably evolved to its final shape during the hunter-gatherer phase of the human past. For Hauser this moral grammar may have evolved through what is known today as "group selection": a group bound by altruism toward its own members and rigorous discouragement of cheaters would be more likely to prevail over a less cohesive society, and in this way genes for moral grammar would have become more common.

17. De Waal, *Primates and Philosophers,* pp. 21-22.

preceded by and grow out of more elementary ones.[18] On this view empathic understanding acquires a fundamental role in the evolution of human communication and interpersonal discernment.

What de Waal now argues is that in the end culture and language in a "top-down" sense shape embodied expressions of empathy. Crucial to this argument is the distinction between *being the origin of* and *shaping.* What de Waal ultimately wants to argue is that empathy is the original, pre-linguistic form of interindividual linkage that only secondarily has come under the influence of language and culture. Interpersonal signaling and empathetic communication in human infants are excellent examples of how infants signal their states of mind to their caregivers through smiling and crying.[19] This obviously has survival value for the infant, evoking in caregivers (mothers and fathers) immediate empathetic responses. This is true for all mammals, but especially obvious in primates and humans. For a human characteristic such as empathy to be so pervasive and to develop so early in life, there is clearly a direct evolutionary continuity with other mammals.[20]

Two crucial, distinct questions that I wanted to deal with in this paper can now be rephrased as follows. Taking into account the deep history of the evolution of hominids and humans, does the theory of (human) evolution help us answer the following two questions: (1) *Can* we be morally good? and (2) Why *should* we be morally good? Philosopher John Hare has argued that we do *not* get answers to these ques-

---

18. De Waal, *Primates and Philosophers,* p. 23.

19. De Waal, *Primates and Philosophers,* p. 24.

20. This opens up the exciting possibility, in terms of a hermeneutics of the body, of actually discovering the creative evolutionary links in hominid history between the evolution of morality, language, sexuality, and music. Not only do all of these reach back to the rather spectacular change to bipedalism in deep prehistory; they also allow us to recognize the integrated, embodied nature of *rhythmicity, semanticity* (Maxine Sheets-Johnstone, *The Roots of Thinking* [Philadelphia: Temple University Press, 1990], pp. 21, 123), and *empathy,* naturally extending Sheets-Johnstone's apt statement: "Semanticity is a built-in of bodily life, literally a built-in of being a body" (p. 128). If, in addition, Steven Mithen is correct about music and melody predating language in hominid evolution, then we can add to the empathy (De Waal, *Primates and Philosophers*) and sexual-signaling (Sheets-Johnstone) framework also a pre-linguistic sense of mood, melody, harmony, and rhythm that served a very clear communicative purpose (Steven Mithen, *The Singing Neanderthals: The Origins of Music, Language, Mind, and Body* [Cambridge, MA: Harvard University Press, 2006]). And in the same way as with empathy and sexuality, this innate musical ability in humans would also have been deeply shaped by language and culture.

tions from the theory of evolution.[21] I will argue, however, that the theory of evolution does indeed help us answer the first question, but not the second question. Dealing with these two distinct questions will help us answer broader questions such as whether we can indeed find an evolutionary basis for human morality, and, if so, whether evolutionary ethics might enable us to find an interdisciplinary, transversal connection to theology, and ultimately even to Christology.

John Hare has argued that the first question, "Can we be morally good?" is the question raised by the moral gap between the demands of morality and our natural capacities.[22] But what exactly does this mean and how should we think about the nature of human morality? In trying to answer this question Hare reaches back to the work of John Duns Scotus, a late medieval thinker who represents a long tradition of Christian reflection on morality. Building on Scotus, Hare distinguishes between "two affections of the human will": the *affection for advantage* (as an inclination toward one's own happiness and perfection) *and the affection for justice* (which can be seen as an inclination toward the "good" in itself; as will become clear, this affection for justice can also be tied to God and to some divine command theory where we obey the moral law because it is what God commands us to obey). On this account there is nothing intrinsically wrong with seeking one's own advantage; what counts morally is that the affection for justice is ranked over that for advantage. From this perspective the motivation behind our ethical opinions and actions may be mixed, but the "moral law" demands that we rank the inclination for justice over whatever natural or innate inclinations for advantage we might have. And whatever freedom we may have is precisely because we humans have the capacity for an affection for justice in addition to the affection for advantage.[23] In fact, nonhuman animals only have the affection for advantage and can only pursue their own advantage by necessity.

The power of the way in which the issue of morality has been constructed in the history of the Christian faith is that the freedom to choose for the "affection for justice" is enabled only by a notion of a God whose goodness so far transcends us that our ability to respond in

21. John Hare, "Is There an Evolutionary Foundation for Human Morality?" in *Evolution and Ethics: Human Morality in Biological and Religious Perspective,* ed. Philip Clayton and Jeffrey Schloss (Grand Rapids: Eerdmans, 2004), pp. 187-203, at 187.

22. Hare, "Is There an Evolutionary Foundation?" p. 187.

23. Hare, "Is There an Evolutionary Foundation?" p. 188.

faith results in the power to reduce our self-love, our affection for advantage.[24] As far as John Hare is concerned, he is not merely "building God into our account of morality"; rather, he is arguing that an account of some form of theism gives one a more coherent background for dealing with the gap between the moral demand and the capacities we are naturally born with. If this "gap picture" of human morality is correct, then we in fact have to recognize two kinds of "gaps": first, the *affection gap* between animals who only seem to have an affection for advantage and humans who also have an added affection for justice; second, the *performance gap*, which exists in our lives between the demand to be moral and our actual performance in response to that demand. This second gap draws our attention to the fact that what we identify as the moral law demands a revolution of the human will, a fundamental reordering away from one's own advantage toward what is good. Hare makes it clear, following Scotus and Kant, that we are born with a faulty ranking of the two affections, and we cannot change this without assistance.[25]

Against the background to these two "gaps," Hare now wants to respond to what he sees as "two different arguments that can be found in evolutionary ethics": the first argument is that we can understand how humans can be morally good by looking at the source of this goodness in evolutionary capacities that nonhuman animals already have. For Hare "this makes human goodness nonmysterious and forestalls the need to appeal to anything spooky, like the assistance of God."[26] Hare, however, wants to claim that there is an affection gap, that is, there is something crucial about human morality that is not found in nonhuman animals. According to Hare evolutionary ethicists also make a second argument concerning the performance gap: by appealing to evolutionary pressure during early periods of human history, human morality is just like every other part of human life, and the fundamental explanation is in terms of natural selection or adaptation. I think Hare correctly wants to move beyond all sociobiological and related explanations for morality and rightly claims that there is indeed something crucial. Human morality is unique in that it cannot be explained by locating its source in natural selection alone. But if de

---

24. Hare, "Is There an Evolutionary Foundation?" p. 189.
25. Hare, "Is There an Evolutionary Foundation?" p. 190.
26. Hare, "Is There an Evolutionary Foundation?" p. 191.

Waal is correct in that we have precursors for human morality in primates, especially chimpanzees, in terms of Scotus's distinction there still is no "affection for justice."[27] On this view, sociality and social control are indeed building blocks for human morality, but are not morality in the sense of an affection for justice.

In his argument, which points to an important distinction between biological and cultural evolution, Hare is correct in asking: Why should we think that because evolution (I would say, *biological* evolution) explains some of the most important features of life, it therefore has to explain *all* of them?[28] We should therefore move away from the kind of genetic self-promotion that claims to explain religion and morality and realize that this is not only a reductionist view, but also already a metaphysical view that is no longer part of the theory of evolution, and in itself cannot be justified biologically. But is Hare correct in concluding that what we can learn about the origins of morality through the theory of evolution is something about the "raw material," so to speak, on which God's assistance works? I will argue that any "assistance" from God as "working on" our affection for advantage will not be achieved by giving us any "objective moral code," but rather by enabling our innate capacities for right and wrong to be taken up in the freedom of human consciousness and creativity in making discerned choices for good over bad, right over wrong, as we construct our ethical choices.

Christology, Ethics, and Evolution

Jesus: Embedded in Evolutionary History?

We now turn to the question of Christology and ethics. What I would like to do in this second and final section is to ask what kind of (or model of) Christology might converge with an interdisciplinary dialogue with the sciences and philosophy, that is, what epistemic pointers do we find in the interdisciplinary conversation on the evolution of consciousness and moral awareness that might help us unveil important links between Christology and ethics?

27. Hare, "Is There an Evolutionary Foundation?" p. 193.
28. Hare, "Is There an Evolutionary Foundation?" p. 196.

To base one's faith in God on the conviction that the character and nature of God are revealed in Jesus Christ is already to say that what we can know of God is necessarily mediated through history. But if it is mediated through history, then what we are calling "revelation," and what we are interpreting as God's revelation, shares in the ambiguities of history and is therefore of necessity in the limited, fallibilist form of all our knowledge. Moreover, if God is revealed to us through the remote history of Jesus, then our perceptions of that revelation are themselves conditioned by our own time and place. And if God is revealed to us as Christians through that "foundational" history, then we read that specific history not only through the lens of our own personal and cultural spectacles but also through the multiple lenses provided for us through the many successive interpretations of the gospel in the long history of ideas of Christian history.

If the revelation of God given in Jesus Christ is thus deeply *incarnational,* that is, embodied in Jesus and embedded in the history of Jesus, then no single interpretation of Christ can claim to be final knowledge of God, or even final knowledge of what God has done for us in Christion.[29] It is precisely in this sense that I would argue against dehistoricizing the contents of faith (and thus of Christology) as if it were possible to have a perception of God untouched by the epistemic, hermeneutical, and pragmatic ambiguities of history. A more embodied theology that takes seriously our own evolution as well as the evolution of our ideas about God and Christ will be able to embrace fully, and in this broader sense, the incarnational nature not only of Christ but of the Christian faith itself.[30]

Against this background I briefly want to turn to the thought of Friedrich Schleiermacher. I believe that, in spite of the weight of history and historical controversies, Schleiermacher still gives us significant, if not surprising epistemological pointers to deal with these issues, even for a very contemporary issue like Christology and evolution. In *The Christian Faith* Schleiermacher already argued in a remarkably contemporary and evolutionary way that the physical aspects of our human existence not only preceded but also provided the basis for what later evolved as our capacity for spirituality and faith in God. In

---

29. Marjorie Hewitt Suchocki, *The Fall to Violence: Original Sin in Relational Theology* (New York: Continuum, 1994), pp. 52-53.

30. Suchocki, *The Fall to Violence,* p. 88.

this sense he posits that in the long evolution of humanity, our physicality involved a necessary self-preservation instinct that led to a protection of one's own self and kind over against that which was defined as other. This mode of self-centeredness served well to ensure the survival of the human species, but Schleiermacher clearly sees our "physical beginnings" as existing and necessary for the sake of that which would later emerge from physical existence, that is, the God-consciousness of human spirituality.

It is fascinating to remember, especially in light of the sharp focus today on consciousness in the neurosciences, that Schleiermacher already famously distinguished among three grades or levels of self-consciousness: *first,* the confused animal grade of consciousness; *second,* what he called "the sensible consciousness"; and *third,* the feeling of absolute dependence. These three grades are structured developmentally, with the second arising from the first, and the third from the second. As finite human beings we primarily experience the second grade, which is structured as a tension between feelings of freedom and dependence. For Schleiermacher the "actual occurrence" of human self-consciousness is never separated from the lower grade of animal consciousness, and as such it always "participates in the antithesis of the pleasant and the unpleasant."[31] Schleiermacher does say "that the animal state is to us really entirely strange and unknown. But there is general agreement that, on the one hand, the lower animals have no knowledge, properly so called, nor any full self-consciousness which combines the different moments into a stable unity, and that, on the other hand, they are nevertheless not entirely devoid of consciousness."[32] The origins of typically human, second-grade "sensible self-consciousness" can, therefore, clearly be found in the earliest humans: "If we go back to the first obscure period of the life of man, we find there, all over, the animal life almost solely predominating, and the spiritual life as yet entirely in the background; and so we must regard the state of his consciousness as closely akin to that of the lower animals."[33]

When the sensible self-consciousness has "expelled" the animal confusion, then there is disclosed a higher tendency, and the expres-

---

31. Friedrich Schleiermacher, *The Christian Faith* (Edinburgh: T. & T. Clark, 1976), p. 18.

32. Schleiermacher, *The Christian Faith,* p. 18.

33. Schleiermacher, *The Christian Faith,* p. 18.

sion of this tendency in this level of self-consciousness is the "feeling of absolute dependence."[34] And this feeling of absolute dependence, so characteristic of the third level of consciousness, is equivalent to our being conscious of being in relation to God. Here self-consciousness becomes God-consciousness, in which our finitude is not transcended but put into proper perspective. In this sense to feel oneself absolutely dependent and to be conscious of being in relation to God are one and the same thing. In this sense, too, self-consciousness cannot be separated from God-consciousness, and the feeling of absolute dependence becomes a clear self-consciousness in such a way that the two cannot be separated from one another. In this sense the feeling of absolute dependence becomes a clear self-consciousness only as this idea simultaneously comes into being. Further, it can be said that God is given to us in feeling in an original way. And "if we speak of an original revelation of God to man or in man, the meaning will always be just this, that, along with the absolute dependence which characterizes man . . . and all temporal existence, there is given to man also the immediate self-consciousness of it, which becomes a consciousness of God."[35]

Furthermore, in a clear move beyond any form of pantheism, Schleiermacher always makes it clear that an awareness of God should not be confused with an awareness of the world and the unity of the world. The feeling of absolute dependence, accordingly, is not to be explained as an awareness of the world's existence, but as an awareness of the existence of God, as an absolute undivided unity.[36] Moreover, the very fact that this God-consciousness can emerge follows from the effectiveness of the preceding self-centeredness of physicality. In Suchocki's words: self-centeredness has yielded the survival and growth of the species into a complexity that can now support its own transcendence.[37] In order to achieve this transcendence, however, self-centeredness must be released, replaced by the God-consciousness of recognizing interdependence. Thus our emergent spirituality struggles against the basis of its very existence and is called upon to reverse the very orientation that allowed its emergence. The tension that is implied by this transition is exactly what Schleiermacher has called the basis for sin and evil.

---

34. Schleiermacher, *The Christian Faith*, p. 22.
35. Schleiermacher, *The Christian Faith*, pp. 17-18.
36. Schleiermacher, *The Christian Faith*, p. 132.
37. Suchocki, *The Fall to Violence*, p. 89.

Schleiermacher also points quite specifically to what we today would call a "biological basis" for sin, and the human predicament is precisely that our nascent spirituality is much weaker than our long-established selfishness. For Schleiermacher this problem of sin and original sin is resolved by God's own interjections into creation through incarnation in the form of the Redeemer. This Redeemer, being of God, is capable of that which the rest of humanity so sorely fails at. But also being human, the Redeemer fits into the interconnectedness of all finite existence, so that what the Redeemer accomplishes becomes a fact of existence that affects us all.[38] And the Redeemer, who is God incarnate in Jesus of Nazareth, lives in perfect God-consciousness, proclaims that consciousness, and passes it on to the rest of humanity. In this Redeemer, the world achieves its completion and humanity achieves its release from its imprisoning sin.

The question, of course, is whether Schleiermacher's Christology, especially because of its remarkable compatibility with evolutionary thought, necessarily leads to a "low Christology." In an intriguing recent essay, Kevin Hector has argued the exact opposite.[39] Hector argues that any attempt to define Schleiermacher's Christology as "low" would be seriously inadequate because it would neglect the important role that *actualism* plays in his theology. Actualism here is a strong move away from substance metaphysics to a deeply relational way of thinking that focuses on the dynamics of events and relationships.[40] Through correctly understanding Schleiermacher's dynamic relationality of Jesus' relationship to God, it becomes possible to see Christ as the one who reproduces God's pure act of love through his own God-consciousness. Here Christ exists as pure relational activity and so, for Schleiermacher, is God incarnate. On this view, therefore, Schleiermacher's Christology is not "low" at all, but in fact quite "high" — in some respects even higher than traditional Chalcedonianism,[41] if we mean by "high" the unequivocal recognition that Christ is God incarnate and that he is uniquely so.

Hector thus very much argues against a fairly customary reading of Schleiermacher as denying Christ's full divinity, compromising his

38. Suchocki, *The Fall to Violence*, p. 89.
39. Kevin Hector, "Actualism and Incarnation: The High Christology of Friedrich Schleiermacher," *International Journal of Systematic Theology* 8, no. 3 (2006): 307-22.
40. Hector, "Actualism and Incarnation," pp. 307-8.
41. Hector, "Actualism and Incarnation," p. 308.

humanity, and thus seeing Christ as the most exalted of humans but not as truly divine. Moreover, we know Jesus through our fellowship with him, and in this fellowship we are drawn out of our previous sinfulness and into blessedness. However, this drawing-out cannot be explained in terms of normal human history, because everyone in that history participates in corporate sinfulness. The possibility of this happening must then come from "outside" history, and it must come in such a way that its activity depends solely on its outside impulse. This possibility does not *remain* outside of history, however, as we know from the fact that it has become our possibility too: in Jesus Christ, this possibility enters into history and thereby becomes ours. Hence, when we examine our experience of Christ, we see that we cannot explain Christ merely in terms of normal human history. And this is what Schleiermacher meant when he concluded that Christ must be God incarnate, because this alone explains the fact that his life is the pure, relational act that establishes fellowship between us and God.[42]

The very identity of Jesus Christ's person is thus tied up in the spiritual function of the God-consciousness that is one with his self-consciousness. And again, to ascribe to Christ an absolutely powerful God-consciousness and to attribute to him an existence of God in him are exactly the same thing. Jesus is the only "other" in which there is an existence of God in the proper sense.[43] But as a person of this kind he needs to have the whole of human development in common with us, so that even this existence of God must in him have had a development in time. And if God is a God of love, and if God's relational activity can only be described as pure love, then Christ too is the pure act of love, of unifying God's love with us. For Hector this is exactly what Schleiermacher asserts: Christ is the One who reproduces God's pure, loving act in human history and is therefore God incarnate. And the key to this divinity of Christ is his God-consciousness, which functions as the relational medium by which God's love is apprehended and turned into Christ's own activity.[44] Christ's God-consciousness is, on this view, that which makes it possible for God to become incarnate in a human. This is not the same as our general, human, "innate" God-consciousness, which of course is presupposed in our faith in God and

---

42. Hector, "Actualism and Incarnation," p. 310.
43. Schleiermacher, *The Christian Faith*, pp. 387-88.
44. Hector, "Actualism and Incarnation," p. 311.

Jesus Christ. But Christ is the only creature in whom the God-consciousness was absolutely clear and determined each moment, to the exclusion of all else, so that it must be regarded as a continual living presence and a real existence of God in him.[45]

Hector is, therefore, correct in arguing that "perfect God-consciousness" in Jesus Christ can be equated with "divinity" precisely because Christ's God-consciousness is the human "organ," what today we will call the embodied mind, through which God's activity becomes incarnate. The important thing about Christ, then, is not his God-consciousness *per se,* but the fact that this consciousness is the means through which God's being is incarnated. In this way it is clear that Schleiermacher offers us a non-substantialist and post-essentialist picture of God as the pure activity of love, of Christ as the historical repetition of this activity, and of Christ's work as a repetition of his person.[46]

Moral Direction Through Ongoing Critical Discernment?

These conclusions are greatly enhanced if we return briefly to the issue of the evolution of morality and ultimately ask why for theologians Jesus' person and work may contain a moral imperative for Christians today. In his provocative recent book, *The Evolution of Morality,*[47] Richard Joyce directly deals with the important question: If we human beings are the product of biological evolution, what exactly does that imply about our moral sense? In what sense may we then argue that the moral sense is evolved, and would that imply that morality as such is evolved in a way that would explain, vindicate, or undermine our moral judgments as well as the moral codes and moral laws we construct?

The argument in the book develops along two distinct stages: in the first Joyce asks the question, "Is the human capacity to make moral judgments the result of biological evolution?" And his conclusion is, yes, the moral sense is indeed an innate, evolved faculty.[48] This innate "human moral sense," however, does not imply belief in any particular set of moral judgments, but is, rather, a capacity to make

---

45. Schleiermacher, *The Christian Faith,* p. 397.
46. Hector, "Actualism and Incarnation," pp. 312, 322.
47. Richard Joyce, *The Evolution of Morality* (Cambridge, MA: MIT Press, 2006).
48. Joyce, *The Evolution of Morality,* p. 142.

moral judgments as such, a natural tendency to think about things in moral terms — an argument, as we saw, also made by scientists Frans de Waal and Marc D. Hauser. Initially, of course, natural selection might seem an unlikely way by which to arrive at human moral awareness. Does the process of evolution by natural selection not, by definition, favor those organisms that are best able to outproduce others by competitive advantage? How could this selfish process, then, promote the kind of cooperative and altruistic behavior that we normally associate with moral goodness? As counterintuitive as it might seem, Joyce proceeds to argue five ways in which natural selection might very well have favored those organisms that were most inclined to altruistic or pro-social behavior.[49]

The first is kin selection, a process in which a survival advantage is conferred on organisms that sacrifice some of their own fitness on behalf of those who are genetically similar. Joyce's further point is that altruistic behaviors directed toward kin might eventually have helped bring about similar behaviors toward non-kin. The next four mechanisms are then all examples of such non–kin-based helping: mutualism (when various or multiple creatures cooperate to achieve a single, beneficial end); direct reciprocity (in which one creature sacrifices its fitness in order to advance the fitness of another); and indirect reciprocity (indirect reciprocal exchanges involve an animal being "repaid" for its kindness by an animal other than the one that it initially helped). Joyce links this kind of behavior in a very interesting way to the notion of "reputation" or "fame," where an animal acquires the reputation of being strong and helpful and thus attracts a greater number of mates in the future.[50] The final mechanism is group selection, in which a fitness advantage is conferred on an entire group of organisms due to the presence of altruistically minded individuals among them.

Richard Joyce makes the argument that these five pro-social mechanisms all occur in the animal kingdom, but he is also quick to point out that pro-social behavior does not yet constitute human morality. In this sense there would be a clear difference between an evolutionarily developed moral sense, including pro-social behavior and emotions like empathy and altruism, and the actual making of moral judgments. This does not necessarily place Joyce at odds with

49. Joyce, *The Evolution of Morality*, pp. 29-44.
50. Joyce, *The Evolution of Morality*, pp. 31ff.

Frans de Waal's notion that evolution has provided us with the psychological makeup, tendencies, and abilities to develop a compass for life's choices and to live in communities, because pro-social emotions are the "essence of human morality." Joyce is indeed correct, I believe, to find the "essence of human morality" in discernment, prohibitions, and evaluative judgments, that is, in the human capacity to think in moral, normative terms, not just some notion of empathy or trans-kin concern. While Joyce does see a substantial gap between the moral sense and the making of moral judgments, Frans de Waal has convincingly argued for identifying proto-morality precisely in pro-social behavior and seeing those as "building blocks" toward human morality. In this sense the difference between de Waal and Joyce on the role of pro-social, proto-moral behavior in animals is one of nuance and degree, with de Waal providing a more detailed biological substratum for Joyce's philosophical argument.

For Joyce the argument that our human moral sense is innate does not mean that everyone, everywhere, agrees on some basic set of shared moral beliefs. In fact, for Joyce no moral beliefs are "epistemically justified," that is, the natural, inborn tendency to think normatively never leads to an evolutionary explanation for why any specific set of moral codes or moral laws is universally correct or given in any strong sense of the word. Clear moral judgments, however, have "practical clout" in terms of the formal, social, conventional ways we come to make moral judgments and decisions, and as such they make inescapable and authoritative demands on us.[51] But, in an interesting convergence with evolutionary epistemology, whatever authoritative demand or practical clout moral judgments, codes, or laws may have on us, they do not find their source in external/eternal or internal/evolutionary sanctions, but in ongoing human discernment and convention. I will not follow Joyce to the end of his "moral skepticism" and his conviction that no moral judgments are ever epistemically justified. On the contrary, exactly the fact that through discernment and moral judgments, pragmatically embedded in concrete cultural contexts, we come to agreed-upon moral codes and the *a posteriori* affirmation of our seasoned "moral laws" provides the pragmatic "clout" and postfoundationalist justification for our moral convictions.

I believe Joyce's very helpful distinctions between an innate, evo-

---

51. Joyce, *The Evolution of Morality*, pp. 57-64.

lutionary moral awareness and the evaluative discernment needed for making intelligent moral judgments does not have to lead to moral skepticism. On the contrary, each and every one of our beliefs does indeed have a complex causal history; but it would be absurd to conclude from evolutionary, neurological capacities, and from historical, philosophical, or broader cultural reasons behind the history of our beliefs and belief-systems, that all our beliefs are unjustified, including also our religious and moral convictions. On a postfoundationalist view some of our religious beliefs are more plausible and credible than others. This goes for our tendency to moralize and for the strong moral convictions we often hold: on a postfoundationalist view we not only get to argue for some of the enduring moral codes and laws within the context of the Christian faith, but also for why it may be plausible to think that at least some of those moral beliefs are more reasonable than others.

We have now seen that on de Waal's, Hare's, and Joyce's views, in spite of a powerful focus on the evolutionary origins of moral awareness, ethics as such emerges on a culturally autonomous level, which means that the epistemic standing of the particular moral judgments we make is independent of whatever the natural sciences can tell us about their genesis. Joyce's problem is that he simply does not consider the possibility that our moral beliefs can be shown to be epistemically justified, or unjustified, without reference to natural scientific accounts of the origin of our capacity to come to these beliefs.[52] The evolutionary origins of the human moral sense indeed tells us nothing about how we get to construct moral decisions, codes, and laws. That, however, does not mean that we cannot give a philosophical, postfoundationalist account of how we arrive at these informed judgments, codes, and laws without having to fall back on supranaturalist or sociobiological "rules" for moral behavior.

A Moral Imperative to Follow Jesus?

If we now take into account what we have learned so far about so-called *a priori* accounts of knowledge or morality, our moral codes or "laws" in

---

52. Cf. Zed Adams, review of *The Evolution of Morality,* by Richard Joyce, *Ethics* 117, no. 2 (January 2007): 368-69.

the fullest sense of the word are indeed, in an evolutionary epistemological sense of the word, *a posteriori*. For Christian theology the choice will not be between a moral vision that is inherent in revelation and is, therefore, "received" and one that is "invented" or "constructed." Instead, on a postfoundationalist view our moral codes and ethical convictions of what is "received" are themselves an interpretative enterprise, shaped experientially through our embeddedness in communities and cultures.

But where does this leave us on the question why Jesus' person or work might be normative for our behavior? In another intriguing and constructive rereading of Schleiermacher, Kevin Hector has made a theological argument for why Jesus might be normative for our moral behavior, an argument that closely converges with my own post-foundationalist reading of the grounding of moral behavior in responsible discernment and evaluative judgment.[53] In this constructive pneumatology Hector is looking for creative, and what I would call "bottom-up" ways to talk about how the Holy Spirit works in our daily lives. Via a creative reading of Schleiermacher's pneumatology, Hector now wants to answer questions about how the Spirit "indwells" us and "writes God's laws on our hearts," and how that bears witness to Jesus Christ.[54] For Hector it is clear that Schleiermacher sees the Spirit as mediating Christ's new humanity to us, thereby extending Christ's redemptive work to us. If God is the pure activity of love, then in every instant of his life Jesus perfectly reproduces this activity as his own. And since Christ is perfectly receptive to God's activity and spontaneously reproduces it as his own, Christ is God incarnate, as we saw earlier. But what this now further implies is that we as believers must reproduce Christ's activity *as* our own, but we cannot do so on our own. Our reproduction of Christ's activity is wholly dependent upon Christ, as is redemption, which can never be based on our initiative but only on that of God in Christ.

The problem, according to Schleiermacher, is that we do not have the direct personal connection that the disciples had with Jesus. In fact, we are connected to Jesus through his followers — our redemption is still through Jesus Christ alone, but we now have that not through

---

53. Kevin Hector, "The Mediation of Christ's Normative Spirit: A Constructive Reading of Schleiermacher's Pneumatology," *Modern Theology* 24, no. 1 (2008): 1-22.

54. Hector, "The Mediation of Christ's Normative Spirit," pp. 2ff.

Christ's physical presence but only through fellowship with him, through his followers, through the church.[55] But how can the power of Jesus' influence ever be equated to that of believers through the centuries? That can only happen if the faith community's activity in some sense represents Christ's own activity so that the self-revelation of Christ is now mediated by those who preach him,[56] and in such a way that the activity that proceeds from him is essentially still his own.[57] And this presence of Jesus Christ in the community of believers, in the church, is the Holy Spirit. Another way of putting this: God mediates Christ's activity to us through the Spirit's presence in the church, and as such the Spirit mediates what Jesus said and did through the community, through which it then becomes *ours*.[58]

Schleiermacher's profound claim, then, is that we begin to understand Jesus' presence in our lives by understanding the Spirit's work when taking Jesus' disciples as a model. In the disciples we see the transformation we are trying to make sense of, the transformation through which Jesus' words and deeds became their own.[59] Moreover, Jesus recognized the disciples' significant transition and as such validated them as competent judges of the beliefs and actions of others, and as thereby having internalized Jesus' instructions. As such not only could the disciples now reproduce Jesus' normative judgments, but in the ongoing history of the Christian faith their judgments would now be accepted by others *as* normative, and in that sense restating not only Jesus' influence on the disciples and all believers since, but also why we today should "do as Jesus did."

Because Schleiermacher has focused on the *normative* dimension of Christ's words and deeds, he is able to also account for our doing the same things as Christ in ever-changing circumstances.[60] What we have here, then, are again socially mediated, experientially interpreted norms filtered through the history of the church and mediating to us *a posteriori* moral codes and normative judgments. For Schleiermacher God *is* present in Jesus who *is* present in the Spirit, and therefore he could make sense of the Spirit's work by talking about Jesus' normative

55. Hector, "The Mediation of Christ's Normative Spirit," p. 3.
56. Schleiermacher, *The Christian Faith,* pp. 363-64.
57. Schleiermacher, *The Christian Faith,* pp. 490-91.
58. Hector, "The Mediation of Christ's Normative Spirit," p. 4.
59. Schleiermacher, *The Christian Faith,* p. 529.
60. Hector, "The Mediation of Christ's Normative Spirit," p. 8.

judgments becoming our own as we learn them from those whose judgments have been recognized and critically evaluated as going on in the same way as his. This critical (postfoundationalist) evaluation of the tradition as we stand in the tradition is our only fallible way of judging whether or not certain beliefs and actions count as really following him, as qualifying as "doing what Jesus did." In this way belief and interpretation fuse in the ongoing task of theology and Christian ethics, or, if you will, Christology and ethics.

In this way Schleiermacher opens up a way of understanding the Spirit's work in terms of the way that Jesus' norms are mediated through an ongoing process of mutual, critical recognition and evaluation. This "non-objective" grounding of the moral authority of Jesus through social and historical interpretation does not imply relativism and the idea that Jesus' words could mean whatever we take them to mean. On the contrary, a postfoundationalist position on Christ's normative sayings means exactly that in order to judge our own theological evaluations of these normative statements as plausibly correct, our current beliefs, actions, judgments, and so forth must also be constrained, but not finally determined, by previous interpretations. Learning to follow Jesus, learning "to do what Jesus did," is to learn to find the trajectory on which others preceded us in interpretation and action by internalizing what we interpretatively recognize as normative for our current contexts.[61] This ongoing, never-ending interpretative task of relating Christology to ethics can inspire us with moral direction even as it fills us with epistemic humility.

This interpretation of Schleiermacher's views on the social and cultural mediation of Jesus' normative statements might get another unexpected "boost" from evolutionary theory. In a recent essay, David Lahti, in dealing with the evolution of morality and its adaptive significance, has found an intriguing and creative example for the adaptive role of moral evolution through cultural transmission in Jesus' Sermon on the Mount (Matt. 5–7).[62] Lahti argues that Jesus used his Sermon on the Mount as a way of challenging the traditional Hebrew understanding of "culture," ancestry, and "in-group" by turning away

61. Hector, "The Mediation of Christ's Normative Spirit," pp. 14, 17.
62. David C. Lahti, "'You Have Heard . . . but I Tell You . . .': A Test of the Adaptive Significance of Moral Evolution," in Clayton and Schloss, eds., *Evolution and Ethics*, pp. 132-50.

from notions of kin-relatedness to a new notion of relatedness based on shared values instead.[63]

Lahti claims to have found 105 moral statements in the Sermon in the Mount that refer to actions and/or attitudes that are good or bad, none of which encourage kin-relatedness, tribal affiliation, or ethnicity.[64] The remarkable fact that Lahti now points to is how perfectly this fits with Darwin's own observations about the evolution of human culture. These teachings encourage this very change of attitude that Charles Darwin observed in human cultures, that is, a move away from a more primitive state of morality toward moral consideration for all persons regardless of relatedness.[65] The question, of course, is what normally are the causes of change in a culture's typical moral attitudes? Morality originated, according to Darwin, as within-group cooperation arising in the context of between-group competition. Various evolutionary biologists are now stressing the point that Darwin also made, that is, that social selection tends to be the overwhelming determinant that makes human behaviors adaptive. Social selection, then, as a subset of natural selection, along with the cultural influence of social environments, implies that certain changes in a society can lead to shifts in the kinds of behaviors that tend to be adaptive. And here moral norms may provide a valuable mechanism for tracking the social environment.[66]

It is precisely against this background that a comparison of two social environments, Hebrew culture and the Palestine of Jesus' time, provides an explanation of how a particular moral, ethical reform (that of Jesus) may have been an adaptive attitude adjustment. In this sense the moral teachings of Jesus realigned and modified earlier Jewish moral prescriptions, encouraging attitudes and actions that would be novel for their time. Strikingly, Jesus does create a division between groups in the Sermon on the Mount, but they may now be seen as *moral* differences rather than kinship, political, or ethical differences.[67] This fits completely with the evolutionary view that the spreading of values in human communities can enlarge the group: the moral reform

63. Lahti, "'You Have Heard . . . but I Tell You,'" pp. 140-43.

64. Lahti, "'You Have Heard . . . but I Tell You,'" p. 140.

65. Charles Darwin, *The Descent of Man, and Selection in Relation to Sex* (Princeton: Princeton University Press, 1981), pp. 107-84.

66. Lahti, "'You Have Heard . . . but I Tell You,'" pp. 133-34.

67. Lahti, "'You Have Heard . . . but I Tell You,'" p. 142.

of Jesus as portrayed in the Sermon on the Mount thus reflects an adaptive adjustment to a new social environment and lifts up a deliberate contrast between new norms being presented and the norms that would have been familiar to the Jewish people. But, as the repeated phrase "You have heard . . . but I say to you" implies, for Jesus the law itself is still to be obeyed (Matt. 5:19) even as traditionalism and innovation are now in tension.

Lahti is thus suggesting that these changes in moral emphasis allow us to see Jesus through the eyes of faith and through the eyes of evolutionary biology: such a view not only is in line with Darwin's understanding of the evolution of morality but also reveals that Jesus' life and teachings existed at a time when they would find maximal societal impact — first passed on by the in-group consisting of Jesus' disciples, later passed on by a vast history of ongoing critical evaluation and theological/ethical reinterpretation. I believe it is precisely this ongoing social mediation and cultural reinterpretation that would become the hallmark of what it means to follow Jesus, to "do as Jesus did." This argument is also consistent with the idea that "perfect God-consciousness" in Jesus Christ is equal to his divinity precisely because Jesus' God-consciousness is the human "organ," the embodied mind through which God's activity becomes incarnate. The important thing about Jesus, then, is not his God-consciousness as such, but the fact that this consciousness is the means through which God's being becomes present in incarnation. In this way it is clear that Schleiermacher offers us a non-substantialist and post-essentialist picture of God as the pure activity of love, of Jesus as the unique historical repetition of this activity, and of his words and deeds as a reflection of the moral authority of his person.

8. The Philosophical Turn to Alterity in Christology and Ethics

F. LeRon Shults

The contemporary conceptual field within which scholars interested in Christian ethics and Christology meet and participate in interdisciplinary dialogue has been shaped by a growing philosophical tendency to celebrate the *different* and suspect the *same*. Not everyone shares an enthusiasm for this shift, but few would deny the importance of understanding the significant and complex effects it has registered on conversations across the academy, society, and the church.

Fascination with — and fear of — "the other" are dominant characteristics of our current cultural and intellectual milieu.[1] This preference for *alter* over *idem*, the exaltation of *heteron* over *tauton*, has certainly posed challenges for Christian theology, but it has also served as a generative force in many of the most influential philosophical and theological proposals of our late modern context and now provides new opportunities for the inner development of and mutual engagement between Christology and ethics.

---

1. Several examples of primary sources contributing to this "turn to alterity" will be offered below. For introductions to the role of the concept of difference across various disciplines cf., e.g., Alan Bass, *Interpretation and Difference: The Strangeness of Care* (Stanford, CA: Stanford University Press, 2006); Nathan Widder, *Genealogies of Difference* (Chicago: University of Illinois Press, 2002); Philip Goodchild, ed., *Difference in Philosophy of Religion* (Aldershot, UK: Ashgate, 2003); Antony Easthope, *Privileging Difference* (New York: Palgrave, 2002); Mark Currie, *Difference* (London: Routledge, 2004); and Richard Kearney, *Strangers, Gods and Monsters: Interpreting Otherness* (London: Routledge, 2003).

Why Attend to Philosophies of Difference?

Paying attention to the depth and breadth of this "turn to alterity" is important for the task of this book for several reasons. Insofar as the discourse of Christology and ethics is embedded within and seeks to engage our late modern context(s) it is important for students of these subjects to understand the philosophical reasons for and implications of this categorical alteration. Most scholars of Christology and ethics are aware of this shift, but it is not always explicitly thematized. For Christian theology the ultimate goal of tending to others is redemptive fellowship — welcoming persons into the community of believers or facilitating more intimate communion among those who explicitly strive to follow the way of Christ in the world. This includes formulating claims about Jesus Christ and normative human agency, which requires the use of particular linguistic and conceptual forms.

Philosophical categories function as conceptual mediators between Christology and ethics, and the way we "hold onto" such mediating concepts also influences our capacity for intentional interdisciplinary engagement. A theologian or ethicist might pretend not to rely on philosophical categories, but such pretense simply veils their functioning. By critically tending to our own categorizing tendencies we can — humbly and hopefully — make our theological intentions more explicit. The mediation involved here is not unilateral. Yes, philosophy shapes our disciplines, but reflection on the good life and on the way of Jesus Christ in turn shapes our use of language and our forms of life in the world. Attending to philosophical categories may be a necessary moment within this ongoing interdisciplinary task, but it is not sufficient. We must learn to tend not only to the role of the concept of "the other" within our constructions but also to the ways in which our conceptual constructing is itself always and already shaped by our interpreted experience of existentially relevant "others."

Unless and until we deeply engage philosophies of difference our efforts will be superficial and fail to participate in the redemptive transformation of human imagination in contemporary culture. The bulk of this chapter is an attempt to make explicit the way in which the late modern affirmation of alterity has shaped the interdisciplinary conceptual space shared by our disciplines. By underlining and tracing the breadth and depth of this turn to alterity, we can more readily respond to its challenges and take advantage of its opportunities. My ultimate goal here is to point to the shared interest among theologians and ethicists in transforming moral desire for and with the Other and others (God and neighbor), which takes shape as participating in the way of Jesus Christ. Both disciplines are (or ought to be) concerned about the practical space of social interaction and the liturgical space of ecclesial engagement, both of which are entwined within the conceptual space of christological doctrine and moral reasoning. This means that the dominance of plurality, the ubiquity of otherness, and the excess of difference that increasingly characterize global discourse are pastorally and existentially relevant as well.

Of course we also have reasons to be suspicious of the notion of a philosophical "turn to alterity." The concept of a turn to alterity could be taken to suggest that we can trace a linear progression from sameness to difference. I am not suggesting a simple evolutionary scheme in which later is better. Although these categories are always present together and mutually define one another, we can still observe a shift of emphasis, a leaning toward or privileging of the different over the same in late modern philosophy. As we will see, this is in fact a reversal of the dominant tendency to value sameness in most Western thought. Nevertheless, this is not a simple progression but in many ways a recovery of resources in the tradition that did emphasize otherness in discussions of God and creation. I will argue in my fourth section, "Tending to the Other(s) in Late Modern Ethics and Modernity," that we can even speak of a theological *re*-turn to alterity — not a naïve regurgitation of ancient formulae, but a re-figuration of often-ignored intuitions about the regulative and constitutive function of the category of difference.

We might also have material concerns about the implications of a turn to difference as a generative category for our disciplines. Both Christian ethics and Christology want to accommodate and reinforce the Christian belief that we are called to be conformed to the likeness of Christ (Rom. 8:29), to be of the same mind as our lives become like his (Phil. 2:1-3; 3:10). We should be suspicious of attempts to jettison the category of the same from our fields of discourse; concepts like identity and union cannot be simply eradicated from Christology and ethics. Theological articulation cannot be satisfied with a discourse in which the play of difference wanders aimlessly into nihilistic incoherence; systematic theology in particular must remain attentive to the role of similitude in the ongoing search for a unifying, cohesive presentation of the gospel.

Moreover, simply replacing the problematic dominance of the same with a new hegemony of the different would ignore the way in which these categories are dialectically defined and interdependent. Nevertheless, our attitude toward sameness can never be the same after the turn to alterity. As we will see, the renewed philosophical insistence on giving otherness its due has contributed to the theological development of more communal and other-oriented construals of (for example) atonement theory and moral formation, developments applauded by all of the contributors to this book.

Another reason to engage philosophies of difference has to do with the interdisciplinary reciprocity of Christology and ethics, which is the overarching theme of our book. Attending to otherness has implications not only for particular formulations within the disciplines, but also for the challenges and possibilities of mutual engagement with disciplinary "others." We need more nuanced ways of tending to otherness, to the differentiated space within which our disciplinary efforts operate. One of the main functions of this chapter, therefore, is to outline the conceptual space within which the too-often and erstwhile alien disciplines of Christology and ethics may now be reciprocally related (and differentiated) in healthy, creative interdisciplinary dialogue.

The next two major sections of this chapter provide a summary of the philosophical turn toward privileging alterity (or difference) from Plato to Kant, and from Hegel to Deleuze. The reason for this division and the rationale for my limited selection of examples in this shift will hopefully become clear as we go along. In my brief exposition of all of these thinkers, my main concern is not engaging in the debates over the value of their proposals or their relation to each other, but simply observing the way in which these philosophers' own valuation of the concept of difference played a role in the shift toward attending to alterity that characterizes so much late modern hermeneutical discourse.

Then in the fourth section I will demonstrate some of the ways in which late modern theologians and Christian ethicists have tended to difference and what difference this has made in their approaches, both within and across the fields. The conclusion summarizes the argument that this turn to alterity creates a new conceptual, practical, and liturgical space(time) in which both Christology and ethics can work together by participating in the transformation of moral desire — precisely by attending to the differentiating functions of our discourse about goods with others.

As Paul Ricoeur observes, the complex history of the relation between the categories of the Same and the Other is "at the very least, intimidating."[2] In this short chapter all I can hope to do is offer an overview of the tension between these (and related) categories and their hermeneutical influence on some of the great philosophers and theologians whose work most deeply impacts Christology and ethics. A second limitation of this overview is that I will not focus on some of the important distinctions within the writings of some of these philosophers between kinds of difference. A discussion of the nuances and functions of different terms like *heteron* and *diaphora*, or between *alius* and *oppositio*, would distract us from my overall concern, which is to outline the general trajectory of the shift away from the privileging of sameness (over difference) as a regulative concept in Western philosophy and theology, which in turn has shaped both ethics and Christology and the complex relation between them.

Alterity from Plato to Kant

In order to understand the late modern turn *to* (or the return of) alterity we must recognize that it is in some sense a turn *from* the dominance of identity — or sameness — as a philosophical category.[3] The relations among the five genera or "kinds" outlined by the stranger in Plato's *Sophist* are notoriously ambiguous. These five generic categories are "being," "rest," "change," "the same," and "the different" (254^d-259^d). On the one hand, this final category of the different (*heteron*) requires the most argumentation for its inclusion. It initially seems to be forced into the list simply because the other kinds are different from (and in relation to) one another. However, the stranger also suggests that the different *pervades* all of the other generic forms. The different "shares" in being or "that which is" and conversely, that which is shares in the different. Precisely in this differentiation from being, the different *is*, which means it can be *what is not*.

2. Paul Ricoeur, *Oneself as Another*, trans. Kathleen Blamey (Chicago: University of Chicago Press, 1992), p. 299.

3. Some of the material that follows also appears (in a different context and for a different purpose) in my *Christology and Science* (Aldershot: Ashgate; Grand Rapids: Eerdmans, 2008), chap. 2. There I explore in more detail the material implications of the turn to alterity for Christology, especially the doctrine of the Incarnation.

In Plato's *Timaeus* the metaphysical implications of the privileging of sameness over difference becomes more evident. The demiurge created the world soul by mixing intermediate forms of being, the same and the different, that is, a mixture of their changeless and corporeal counterparts. He then mixed these three mixtures together to make a uniform mixture. This required "forcing the Different, which was hard to mix, into conformity with the Same" (35ᵇ). The different is linked to the unequal movement of the wandering stars (planets) and the soul's accounting of perceptible things, while the same is linked to the uniform movement of the outer fixed stars and makes knowledge of rational things possible. In the discussion of the One and the Many in *Parmenides* it is clear that the category of difference is not easily applied to the One, while the same is more explicitly connected to being, in which the different can never be (146ᵈ).

Aristotle also privileged sameness over difference in his ontology and epistemology, both of which were dominated by the category of substance. In the *Metaphysics,* he insists that the same and the different are predicated not of substances, but of the relation between things on the basis of quality or quantity (V.9). He acknowledges that "same" and "other" can be predicated of all existent things with regard to all other existent things. But he makes a distinction between this kind of otherness *(heteron)* and an other "otherness" *(diaphora),* which he reserves for the predication of things that differ in substance or by accidental properties (X.3). This latter mode of difference is most important for Aristotle because it is the basis of his approach to logic and his theory of being. For example, his understanding of God as the best substance, the unmoved mover, or thought thinking itself (the same), is explicitly compared to the less valuable thinking of human substances, which think the good as something different from themselves (XII.9). All of this flows from his overarching epistemological claim that the like — rather than unlike — is the key to knowledge. Knowledge is *of the like by the like* (1000ᵇ5).

The principle of similarity also guides Aristotle's ethics. The ideal form of friendship in the *Nicomachean Ethics* is between those who are "alike in excellence" (1156ᵇ7). The most constant friendships are among those who get the same thing from each other, and "from the same source, as happens between ready-witted people, not as happens between lover and beloved." Lovers stay constant in their friendship only if they learn to love each other's character, "these being alike" (1157ᵃ).

We might well wonder about Aristotle's love life, but the point here is that his ethics is guided by the principle of sameness or identity, which is grounded in the interiority of the individual, not the relation of exteriority vis-à-vis those who are different.

This moral philosophy is structured by a particular understanding of the *individual's* pursuit of happiness. Aristotle observes that we often find different ends among human activities, but the goal of ethics is to find that which is the highest good, which is the same for all — happiness. Different people may pursue happiness in different ways, but the goal is the same: the eudaimonic fulfillment of the individual soul. Aristotle notes that while some goods are external, others have to do with the body, and still others with the soul: "and we call those that relate to soul most properly and truly goods." Thus the ends *(teloi)* with which ethics ultimately deals are those goods toward which the inner faculties of the soul are oriented — not "external goods" (1098^b15).

The approach to ethics among most of the Stoics was also focused on the inner struggle of the individual soul. A virtuous life is one in which the individual achieves a "natural" life of right reason. It is beyond our current project to clarify the distinctions among the ancient Greek ethical approaches, but we may point to the way in which they tended to center around the debate over the nature and relation of *eudaimonia* (happiness) and *aretē* (virtue). The Peripatetics and the Stoics argued over the valuation of these ideals, some insisting that virtue is sufficient for happiness, others claiming that a happy person will naturally be virtuous.

For our purposes the important point is to note that underlying these disagreements is a shared Hellenistic assumption that ethics is first and foremost about the inner states of individuals. This is true for Plato as well. In the *Republic,* he depicts the just soul as ordered in the same way as the just city; the rational part of the soul rules the appetitive and spirited parts of the soul, as the deliberative class rules the money-making and auxiliary classes. Justice is about putting oneself in order. Justice "isn't concerned with someone's doing his own externally, but with what is inside him, with what is truly himself and his own" (443^d). In other words, interiority and sameness precede exteriority and difference in ancient Greek ethics.

The category of difference was further demoted in the work of the philosopher Plotinus, perhaps the most influential of the (neo)Platonists, in the third century CE. He accepted Plato's five kinds

(*Enneads* VI.2), including his insistence that sameness and difference must be included among the primary genera. However, he was less enthusiastic about this inclusion, and tends here and elsewhere to speak of the principle of differentiation primarily in relation to quantity, relation, and matter, which is the lack of quality and form (cf. *Enneads* II.4). Explicit concerns about justice and politics fade into the background in the work of Plotinus, and inner contemplation comes to the fore. For him the category of *heteron* applies to the material world of existents and even to the operation of the intellectual principle but not to the transcendent One, which contains "no otherness" (*Enneads* VI.9.8). Plotinian salvation involves putting away the otherness of the material body and reaching out for communion with the Supreme, which is beyond differentiation.

The Christian doctrine of the incarnation was initially articulated during the centuries in which this Neoplatonic philosophy, alongside a mixture of Aristotelian and Stoic voices, came to dominate Western intellectual discourse. It is not surprising that the privileging of sameness over difference registered its effect on Christology. The single (albeit complex) sentence that is the Chalcedonian Definition (451 CE) uses the term *ton auton* (the same) eight times. This repetition is so burdensome that most English translations render only a few of them.[4] The christological debate was focused materially on how Jesus Christ could be of the *same* divine substance as the Father, the *same* human substance as the rest of us, all in the *same* identical person. Formally, the goal was forcing all believers to formulate their understanding of Christ in exactly *the same* way under threat of anathema.

This logic of sameness (and substance) provided the context within which the apparently irresolvable tension between Nestorianism and Eutychianism came to structure the debate. The obsession with sameness in Christology was reinforced by the Greek understanding of the fixity (sameness) of the human species and a doctrine of God that emphasized simplicity and impassibility (sameness), which problematized the *differentiation* of the trinitarian persons, especially in the West. The philosophical (re)turn to alterity may challenge some of

---

4. For example, Philip Schaff's translation, which is set next to the Greek, translates only four occurrences of *ton auton*. Schaff, ed., *The Creeds of Christendom: With a History and Critical Notes*, 6 vols., vol. 2: *The Greek and Latin Creeds with Translations* (Grand Rapids: Baker, 1931), pp. 62-63.

these formulations, but it also provides conceptual space for articulating the doctrine of the incarnation in a way that tends to the significance of Jesus' differentiation from the Father and the Spirit, as well as human "others." Insofar as much of the Christian tradition followed versions of natural law that focused on the interior virtue of individuals, a similar claim may be made about the late modern ethical turn to the other.

The great syntheses of the Middle Ages relied more heavily on Aristotle. We can take Thomas Aquinas as our primary example in both Christology and ethics. For the purposes of the theme of this chapter, two Thomistic tendencies are particularly relevant. First, it is important to note that his comprehensive treatment of the virtues in *Summa Theologiae* has to do with the perfection of natural virtues, and not immediately and primarily with following the way of Jesus Christ (although *imitatio Christi* plays a secondary role). His resistance to the philosophical category of difference shaped not only this formal separation of ethics from Christology, but also material decisions within these fields.

The second point is that, for Thomas, difference is a *problem*. In *ST* I.47.I, the distinction between (and plurality of) creaturely things in general is problematic for his doctrine of creation, for it seems that God — understood as a simple unitary substance — could not (or ought not) create a variety of different things. If one begins with this idea of God it seems to follow logically that secondary agents must have created the diversity (as in Plato's *Timaeus*). Thomas resists this conclusion and appeals to the individualistic notion of God as a single subject with diverse objects of "his" intellect and will.

Difference is also a problem in his doctrine of God, which naturally ramifies into his Christology. In Thomas's discussion of the relation between the Father and the Son, he builds on Augustine's argument in *De Trinitate* that they are identical in essence but distinct as persons *(hypostaseis)*. Later this is applied to the Spirit as well. The three are not different things *(aliud)*, but they are different persons *(alius)*. In *ST* I.31.2, Thomas clarifies the use of the terms "difference," "alien," and "other" in God. Only the term "other" *(alius)* should be used of the relation between the Son and the Father, insofar as it is understood to refer to a distinction *(distinctio)* of personal subsistence. This should not be taken as a "formal" difference, however, in the sense of *differentia,* for there is one form only in God. Therefore, the term difference does not properly apply to God *(Et ideo nomen differentis non proprie competit in divinis).* The Son is *alius* than the Father, but not *alienum.* For our purposes here, the point is that these Scholastic mental gymnastics were required in part because of the prior privileging of the category of identity and sameness over alterity and difference.

The conceptual struggle with the problem of "distinctions" and "differences" in philosophy and theology continued throughout the medieval period. In his nominalist privileging of particular (or absolute) things, William of Ockham treats a series of questions on relations and distinctions in the Sixth Quodlibet. Question 8: Is similarity or dissimilarity a "little thing" distinct from absolute things? Question 11: Is diversity, distinctness, or identity a thing distinct from absolute things? To such questions, Ockham answers with a resounding no. What matters is that the particular *suppositum,* the thing, and its similitude to or distinction from other things are only names, and should not be given ontological status; they are not even "little things." Question 26 applies this to God: Are identity, similarity, and equality real relations in the divine nature? Ockham answers that these do not refer to anything distinct from the divine persons. Terms such as "similarity" and "dissimilarity" are not "little things" in creatures, and so *a fortiori,* he argues, they are not "little things" in God.

The focus on particular things (rather than universal ideas) contributed significantly to the rise of early modern science. However, the natural philosophers of that era increasingly came to take the category of difference seriously, even in mathematics itself. For example, the use of derivatives in differential calculus required attending to the function of differentiation itself within mathematical equations. Although infinitesimals were used by Archimedes and developed in more detail by later Indian philosophers, the modern approaches and notations of calculus developed by Newton and Leibniz opened up new possibilities for measuring derivatives (changes of functions in mathematics). In other words, attending to the difference between two points and the differences in their changing functions provided a way of dividing differences themselves, which in turn made possible further developments in theoretical mathematics, from Euler's use of the differential operator to solve linear differential equations to nonlinear applications in physics such as Schrödinger's wave equations for quantum systems.

The dominance of the category of sameness over difference in philosophy also began to be increasingly challenged during the early modern period. When Locke dealt with the question of identity and diversity in his 1689 *Essay concerning Human Understanding*, he challenged the notion that personal identity requires the "same Identical Substance" (Book II.27.11). It is not the "same immaterial Substance" but continuity of consciousness that makes a person the same self. This is intrinsically linked to ethical questions, because as Locke observes, it is the postulation of such a personal identity that is the basis of legal and moral responsibility. Sameness is clearly still the dominant concern here, but Locke made a chink in the armor of substance metaphysics that would make an enormous difference in later theories of human nature.

Throughout David Hume's *A Treatise of Human Nature* (1739) Locke is an implicit or explicit opponent, both in terms of philosophical categories and moral subjectivity.[5] Hume initially does not even want to include the term "difference" among the categories of relations, but sees it more as "a negation of relation, than as anything real or positive" (p. 15). In Part IV of Book I, however, he treats it in more detail. The human imagination "confounds the succession [of related objects] with the identity" (p. 135). Hume is critical of both ancient and modern philosophy for failing to realize that the mind is too easily deceived into ascribing "an identity to the changeable succession of connected qualities" (p. 145). For Hume the mind is constituted by the successive perceptions, and there is properly no identity in the different perceptions that successively appear. We have these ideas of identity or sameness, and we develop notions of soul, self, and substance to disguise the variation, because of our propensity to attribute identity. "For as such a succession answers evidently to our notion of diversity, it can only be by mistake we ascribe to it an identity" (p. 167).

During the "dogmatic slumber" from which Hume awakened him, perhaps Immanuel Kant was dreaming (among other things) of the power of human reason to comprehend all things — God, humanity, and the cosmos — under the category of sameness. In part, his *Critique of Pure Reason* (1781) was a chastening of this hubris of knowledge, linked often to the Cartesian *cogito ergo sum*. For Descartes, the determi-

---

5. David Hume, *A Treatise of Human Nature*, ed. D. F. Norton and M. J. Norton (Oxford: Oxford University Press, 2002). The subtitle indicates Hume's awareness of the link to ethics: "being an attempt to introduce the experimental method of reasoning into moral subjects." Page numbers given parenthetically in the text refer to this edition.

nation "I think" logically implies undetermined existence, "I am" presupposing that existence is required for thinking, that all thinking things exist. In the paralogisms of pure reason, however, Kant argues that Descartes claimed too much. All we can say is "I exist thinking," which itself determines the existence of the ego in time. Insofar as "I think," the "I" that thinks is no mere appearance: "in the consciousness of myself in mere thought I am the being itself, although nothing in myself is thereby given for thought. . . . 'I exist thinking' is no mere logical function but determines the subject (which then is at the same time object) in respect of existence."[6]

Gilles Deleuze argues that Kant's form of the *cogito* (I exist thinking) represents the "discovery of Difference." Kant introduces what Deleuze calls a third logical value: "the determinable, or rather the form in which the undetermined is determinable (by the determination)." Here we are dealing with Difference "no longer in the form of empirical difference between two determinations, but in the form of a transcendental Difference between the Determination as such and what it determines: no longer in the form of an external difference which separates, but in the form of an internal Difference which establishes a prior relation between thought and being."[7] This interpretation challenges the common reading of Kant as a hopeless dualist or constructivist and undergirds the argument of those who would appeal to him as a resource for maintaining the infinite qualitative distinction between God and the world as that which makes possible human thought itself. The main point for our purposes here, however, is that Kant's critique of reason (contra Descartes) opened wider the conceptual space within which Difference could be thought on (at least) equal terms with Sameness.

When Kant addresses explicitly ethical issues in the *Critique of Practical Reason* (1788), the role of the concept of difference is ambiguous. On the one hand, he seems to be focusing on universality and individuality in line with ancient Greek moral philosophy. Theorem II asserts: "All material practical principles are, as such, of one and the same kind and belong under the general principle of self-love or one's own happiness."[8]

6. Immanuel Kant, *Critique of Pure Reason,* trans. N. K. Smith (New York: St. Martin's Press, 1965), p. 382.

7. Gilles Deleuze, *Difference and Repetition,* trans. P. Patton (New York: Columbia University Press, 1994), p. 86.

8. Immanuel Kant, *Critique of Practical Reason,* trans. L. W. Beck (New York: Macmillan, 1993), p. 20. Page numbers given parenthetically in the text refer to this edition.

The fundamental law of pure practical reason is: "so act that the maxim of your will could always hold at the same time as the principle for giving universal law" (p. 30).

On the other hand, when Kant engages the ancient schools of ethics, his reservations with the category of identity are evident. He notes that both the Stoics and the Epicureans, in their debates over the concepts of happiness and virtue, both "followed one and the same method, since neither held virtue and happiness to be two different elements of the highest good, but both sought the unity of principle under the rule of identity" (p. 117). This unfortunate attempt at "digging up an identity between such extremely heterogeneous concepts" was shared, but they differed in the way in which they "tried to ferret out the sameness of the practical principles of virtue and happiness," though they disagreed on how to "force out this identity" (p. 118). For Kant the antinomy of practical reason is that it seems impossible either that happiness could cause virtue or that virtue could cause happiness; the ancient Greek schools failed because they tried to hold them together analytically.

Kant's own proposed solution was to think them synthetically, using the distinction he had already developed between phenomenon and noumenon. Later he makes clear that he is using a similar table of categories derived from his critique of pure reason: quantity, quality, relation, and modality. The subcategories "of relation" are: relation to personality, relation to the condition [*Zustand*] of the person, and reciprocally, that is, the relation of one person to the condition of others (p. 69). So we can see that Kant brings "the other" (reciprocity, etc.) more deeply into the heart of philosophical categorization, but he does not *begin* there, or at least not explicitly. Nevertheless, unlike the Greek focus on the inner substance of the individual soul, Kant gives relationality a more central and generative role in ethics. The main point here is not the adequacy or even clarity of his solution, but the way in which he introduced difference into the very concept of the "highest good." This was an important moment in the philosophical turn to alterity.

Before we move on, let us take stock of the impact of all this on Christology and ethics. In much of early modern theology, at least in Protestant Scholasticism, these modes of inquiry had been increasingly separated. Few would deny that they were connected in some sense, but the connection was typically understood as external, one of logical implication rather than intrinsic participation. As moral reflection increasingly came to be divorced from theology in the seventeenth and eighteenth centuries, it naturally drifted even further from Christology. Christian ethicists were tempted to defend their positions on allegedly universal grounds, without immediate appeal to any ontological participation in the way of Christ in the world. Kant's critiques played a significant role in the philosophical turn to alterity but, ironically, the way in which they reinforced this "Enlightenment" lure toward universality (linked to sameness) led many theologians in the nineteenth century to resist particular formulations that attended to differentiation within God.

Alterity from Hegel to Deleuze

It was precisely Hegel's rigorous and explicit (re)introduction of differentiation into the nature of the Absolute that marks him off from Kant and represents a radical challenge to the tradition of substance metaphysics that had so deeply shaped Christian theology. Moreover, his incorporation of differentiated concepts of goodness and justice into the basic logical and ontological categories of thought and being had implications for both moral and christological reflection. Later nineteenth- and twentieth-century theologians found lots of reasons to criticize Hegel, but this should not lead us to miss the significance of his contribution to the shape of contemporary discourse in which tending to the other(s) takes place, a contribution that made possible a variety of developments in and between Christology and ethics.

The categories of otherness and difference are central to Hegel's argument throughout *Phenomenology of Spirit* (1807).[9] In the preface he argues that "Spirit becomes object because it is just this movement of becoming an other to itself, i.e., becoming an object to itself, and of suspending this otherness" (p. 21). These concepts are intrinsic to his understanding of the Spirit at every moment in the dialectic of its becoming. For Hegel, "things" are determinate in conscious perception only "in so far as they *differentiate* themselves from one another, and *relate* themselves to *others* as to their opposites" (p. 69).

9. G. W. F. Hegel, *Phenomenology of Spirit*, trans. A. V. Miller (Oxford: Oxford University Press, 1977). Page numbers in the text refer to this edition. Emphases are in the original, unless otherwise noted.

The absolute flux of the play of Forces appears in the Understanding as a *universal difference* that essentially mediates that very appearance and renders it determinate. When the Understanding becomes "other" to itself in self-consciousness, this involves a self-identification that is also essentially a self-differentiating or self-sundering, which is the unity of its becoming. Self-consciousness is qualified as Reason precisely as its "hitherto negative relation to otherness turns round into a positive relation" (p. 139). Hegel argues that the simple unity "of self-consciousness and being possesses difference *in itself,* for its essence is just this, to be immediately one and selfsame in *otherness,* or in absolute difference" (p. 142).

As the dialectical movement of the Spirit unfolds in Hegel's *Phenomenology* the role of the concept of difference becomes more complex. In his treatment of culture, he insists that "*pure consciousness* of absolute Being is an *alienated* consciousness," but its "other" is not simply opposed. Consciousness of spiritual essentialities, reflected out of the world of culture, is simple consciousness, but this is "the simplicity of *absolute difference* which is at once no difference" (p. 323). Pure insight is "immanently differentiated *essence*" which calls consciousness toward Enlightenment.

When he deals explicitly with morality, he argues that the moral consciousness resolves the "difference which lies at its base," becoming a self which is no longer "a nature alien to the essence," yet without denying its *being-for-another.* The "pure negativity" of the self "is the *difference* within pure essence, a content, and one, too, which is valid in and for itself" (p. 387). Hegel continues to argue for the incorporation of differentiation and otherness within the unity of the movement of the Spirit in his analysis of natural and revealed religion in the remainder of the *Phenomenology.* This project is carried out in even more detail in his *Lectures on the Philosophy of Religion* where he explicitly spells out his own differentiated version of the Christian doctrine of the Trinity.

Because our main focus in this context is pointing out his logical and methodological use of these categories, we will simply make a few comments about his appreciation of difference in his *Science of Logic* (1811-1816). The Notion, which is the realm of subjectivity or freedom, is identified as three totalities that are "one and the same reflection, which as *negative self-relation,* differentiates itself into these two [universality and particularity], but into a *perfectly transparent difference,* namely, into a *determinate simplicity or simple determinateness* within their one and the same identity."[10] For Hegel, in other words, difference is introduced into being itself; difference itself is posited in the becoming of essence (p. 383). Absolute essence "*differentiates* the determinations which are *implicit [in sich]* in it. Because it is self-repelling or indifferent to itself, *negative* self-relation, it sets itself over against itself and is infinite being-for-self only in so far as it is at one with itself in this its own *difference* [emphasis added] from itself" (p. 390).

The category of difference also plays a key role in Hegel's critique of the dominance of "substance" in the philosophy of Spinoza. For the latter, difference was understood primarily as a moment within the mode of the intellect, which was "external" to substance. For Hegel, on the other hand, substantiality is substantial identity as posited, but this positedness "is a *determinate being* and *differentiation*." He argues that this positedness, which is itself being-in-and-for-itself, "constitutes the difference of the Notion within itself; because the positedness is immediately being-in-and-for-itself, the *different moments* of the Notion are themselves the *whole Notion, universal in their determinateness and identical with their negation*" (p. 596). In the final section on the "Absolute Idea," Hegel outlines all three moments by tending to their modes of differentiation in the unity of the Notion, which "has realized itself by means of its otherness and by the sublation of this reality has become united with itself" (p. 837).

Now we can see why many late modern philosophers worried that Hegel took back what he seemed to give, finally privileging sameness over difference once again in a final unity. But our goal here has simply been to point out the significance of his transitional role in emphasizing difference more than most other philosophers before him. Christian theologians and ethicists had good reason to worry about the *way* in which Hegel utilized difference within his philosophy, but this did not keep many of them from reaping the conceptual and existential fruit of the turn to alterity.

Søren Kierkegaard, often considered the "father" of postmodernity, illustrates this better than perhaps any other nineteenth-century thinker. His critique of Hegel in *Philosophical Fragments* is thinly veiled. Human understanding is not sublated and united with the Absolute through consciousness; rather, it is confronted by the "absolute para-

10. G. W. F. Hegel, *Science of Logic,* trans. A. V. Miller (Amherst, NY: Humanity Books, 1999), p. 571. Pages given parenthetically in the text refer to this edition.

dox" of the unknown. The unknown is "the frontier that is continually arrived at . . . it is the absolutely different in which there is no distinguishing mark."[11] The understanding cannot think the "absolutely different," argues Kierkegaard, but neither can it escape it, for it confronts the individual in each moment as the Eternal. He insists that the difference cannot be grasped, although the understanding is always tempted to confuse itself with the difference. In relation to the task of our book it is important to note that this analysis occurs in the context of Kierkegaard's treatment of the doctrine of the incarnation.

In *The Sickness unto Death*, he focused (like Hegel) on the importance of relationality for understanding the self. "The human self is such a derived, established relation, a relation that relates itself to itself and in relating itself to itself relates itself to another."[12] For Kierkegaard the self exists only in (or as) a relation relating itself to an other, and that which establishes the relationality itself is a Power beyond it, an infinitely qualitative Other.

In Kierkegaard's non-pseudonymous edifying discourses, especially *Works of Love*, the relation between the God-relation and the relation to the neighbor is emphasized even more strongly. He acknowledges that similarity and difference play a role both in Christian and pagan love. However, Christian love is not based on similarity or dissimilarity between the self and others (as in Aristotle), but on the confrontation with Eternity, the infinite qualitative difference that is indifferent to worldly differences. "Dissimilarity is like an enormous net in which temporality is held; there are in turn variations in the meshes of this net — one person seems more trapped and bound in existence than another."[13] But the dissimilarity between this and that finite difference does not occupy Christian love.

Kierkegaard argues that Christianity "allows all the dissimilarities of earthly life to stand, but this equality in lifting oneself up above the dissimilarities of earthly life is contained in the love commandment, in loving the neighbor" (p. 72). The Christian "like for like" is based not on the analysis of worldly differences, but on the infinite

11. Søren Kierkegaard, *Philosophical Fragments*, ed. and trans. Howard V. and Edna H. Hong (Princeton: Princeton University Press, 1985), p. 44.

12. Søren Kierkegaard, *Sickness unto Death*, ed. and trans. Howard V. and Edna H. Hong (Princeton: Princeton University Press, 1983), pp. 13-14.

13. Søren Kierkegaard, *Works of Love*, ed. and trans. Howard V. and Edna H. Hong (Princeton: Princeton University Press, 1995), p. 71.

qualitative difference, the unknown, the Good, which commands love of the other, and must be sought as the one thing in purity of heart. Eternity's "equality" is to will to love the neighbor, which does not ignore the dissimilarity but recognizes that it is a disguise that hangs loosely on the individual, so that "in each individual there continually glimmers that essential other, which is common to all, the eternal resemblance, the likeness" (p. 88). This "indifference" of Christian love presupposes the absolute or infinite qualitative difference between the individual and the Eternal.

If Kierkegaard's use of alterity was intended to serve the cause of facilitating Christian faith, Nietzsche's was intended to abolish it (or what he understood it to be). For example, attention to difference is a key component of his critique of slave morality (Christianity being the prime example) in *Genealogy of Morals*. Slave morality "from the outset says No to what is 'outside,' what is 'different,' what is 'not itself'; and this No is its creative deed."[14] In *Beyond Good and Evil*, Nietzsche calls for an appreciation of otherness, a celebration of the pathos of difference that emerges out of the differences in social relations. "Without this pathos, that other, more mysterious pathos could not have grown at all, that demand for new expansions of distance within the soul itself."[15]

Other late-nineteenth- and early-twentieth-century philosophers also contributed to the turn to alterity. For example, Charles S. Peirce's pragmatic attention to the "overagainstness" of conscious engagement in the world, which led him to articulate the basic philosophical categories as "classes of relations" (firstness, secondness, and thirdness), acknowledges the immediate function of difference in human thought (and practice). The phenomenological approach of Edmund Husserl and his followers focused on intentionally discerning the differences in appearances that condition interpretation.

Martin Heidegger stands out as one of the most significant twentieth-century contributors to the philosophical turn to alterity. In *Being and Time* his depiction of *Dasein* (being-there) as being-in the world, being-with and being-for others, is spelled out through an analysis of themes like resoluteness, anticipation, and care. The differentia-

---

14. Friedrich Nietzsche, *Genealogy of Morals,* trans. Walter Kaufmann (New York: Vintage, 1976), p. 36.

15. Friedrich Nietzsche, *Beyond Good and Evil,* trans. J. Norman (Cambridge: Cambridge University Press, 2002), p. 151.

tion of (and within) Dasein as authentic human existence emerges within the inherently relational and differentiated space of temporal experience.

But the classical locus of Heidegger's treatment of alterity is his *Identity and Difference*.[16] In that context he interprets Parmenides' fragment "for the Same are thinking as well as Being" as meaning that "thinking and Being belong together in the Same by virtue of this Same." This way of speaking of the "identical," which has so deeply shaped Western metaphysics, is "almost too powerful." For Heidegger the "matter of thinking" is the difference between Being and beings — it is this difference *as* difference. He calls for a "step back" in relation to this difference, which "goes from what is unthought, from the difference as such, into what gives us thought" (p. 50), which sets "the matter of thinking, Being as difference, free to enter a position face to face" (p. 64). Difference is the key concept in dealing with the Being of beings and with the beings of Being. For Heidegger, "we think of Being rigorously only when we think of it in its difference with beings, and of beings in their difference with Being" (p. 62), which allows the difference itself to come into view.

He observes that we encounter "this thing that is called difference . . . everywhere and always in the matter of thinking, in beings as such — encounter it so unquestioningly that we do not even notice this encounter itself." Both Being and beings "appear by virtue of the difference, each in its own way." The difference, Heidegger argues, is that Being appears as an "unconcealing overwhelming," while beings appear as an "arrival that keeps itself concealed." Being and beings are "present, and thus differentiated, by virtue of the Same, the differentiation." This differentiation grants and holds apart the "between," in which the overwhelming and the arrival are "held" and "borne away from and toward each other." Thinking the perdurance of overwhelming and arrival (Being and beings) brings thought closer to rigorous thinking, "closer by the distance of one step back: Being thought in terms of the difference" (pp. 63-65). This understanding of difference was central to his influential critique of "ontotheology," which he viewed as an inappropriate subsumption of God and world under the category of the same in human thought.

---

16. Martin Heidegger, *Identity and Difference,* trans. J. Stambaugh (Chicago: Chicago University Press, 1969).

The category of "the other" played a crucial role in the philosophy of Emmanuel Levinas, whose influence on the so-called "turn to ethics" as well as the "theological turn" in French phenomenology makes him particularly relevant for the overall concern of this book. Western philosophy, he argues, has focused too strongly on sameness and substance, and too quickly accepted the question of "being" as the appropriate starting point. Ontology, however, can too easily become a "reduction of the other to the same by interposition of a middle and neutral term that ensures the comprehension of being."[17] Instead Levinas insists that ethics should be "first" philosophy, beginning with the face-to-face relation with the other (and the Other). "The statement of being's *other*, of the otherwise than being, claims to state a difference over and beyond that which separates being from nothingness — the very difference of the *beyond*, the difference of transcendence."[18] Ethics, theology, and otherness are intertwined for Levinas.

In *Totality and Infinity* Levinas argues that the relation between "the same and the other, metaphysics, is primordially enacted as conversation." He rejects the idea that the same can establish its identity by simple opposition to the other, for then it would be part of a totality encompassing the same and the other. For Levinas the metaphysical other is other "with an alterity that is not formal, is not the simple reverse of identity, and is not formed out of resistance to the same, but is prior to every initiative, to all imperialism of the same." This Other has an alterity "that does not limit the same, for in limiting the same the other would not be rigorously other: by virtue of the common frontier the other, within the system, would yet be the same." Levinas does not hesitate to call this absolute Other "God," and refers to religion as "the bond that is established between the same and the other without constituting a totality."[19]

According to Levinas, the "presence of the Other" calls into question the exercise of same. When one places being before the existent, ontology before metaphysics, freedom is placed before justice. Such a model "is a movement within the same before the obligation to

17. Emmanuel Levinas, *Totality and Infinity: An Essay on Exteriority*, trans. A. Lingis (Pittsburgh: Duquesne University Press), p. 43.

18. Emmanuel Levinas, *Otherwise Than Being*, trans. A. Lingis (Pittsburgh: Duquesne University Press, 1998), p. 3.

19. Levinas, *Totality and Infinity*, pp. 38-40.

the other." Levinas aims to reverse the terms; the effort of *Totality and Infinity* "is directed toward apperceiving in discourse a non-allergic relation with alterity . . . in maintaining, with anonymous community, the society of the I with the Other — language and goodness" (p. 47). Given his emphasis on linking ethics and theology, as well as his openness to including the power of messianic expectation of the Face in philosophy, it is no surprise that many theologians have engaged Levinas in their reconstructive efforts.

Jacques Derrida did not think that Levinas (or Heidegger or Hegel) went far enough in their support of the categories of otherness or difference. He insisted that "Tout autre est tout autre" (Every other [one] is every [bit] other).[20] In *Writing and Difference,* he criticized Levinas in particular for relying too heavily on spoken discourse (language). Derrida argued that although Levinas attempted to break with tradition, he ultimately allowed the categories of the Same and the Other to force an "adequation of Ego to the Same, and of Others to the Other."[21] Any "logocentric" privileging of conversation is not able to escape the violence of metaphysics, insists Derrida; instead, he proposed that we attend to the "trace" left by writing or inscription. This trace is "the ungraspable and invisible difference" between breaching forces, i.e., "psychic life" as "the difference within the exertion of forces." Derrida introduces the term *différance* to indicate this differing that defers, which "originates" consciousness.[22]

The neologism *différance* is meant to signify both differing and deferring, but Derrida intended for it to be understood as neither a concept nor even as a word, but as the possibility of conceptuality, of linguistic signification itself. One can never get or expose or grasp difference; one can only experience its traces. He explicates the term more carefully in the first chapter of *Margins of Philosophy.* Derrida writes of *différance* as "older" than being. It is not a name but "unceasingly dislocates itself in a chain of differing and deferring substitutions."[23]

---

20. Cf. Jacques Derrida, "Tout autre est tout autre" [Every other (one) is every (bit) other] in *The Gift of Death,* trans. D. Wills (Chicago: University of Chicago Press, 1992).

21. Jacques Derrida, *Writing and Difference,* trans. A. Bass (Chicago: University of Chicago Press, 1978), p. 109.

22. Derrida, *Writing and Difference,* pp. 201-3.

23. Jacques Derrida, *Margins of Philosophy,* trans. A. Bass (Chicago: University of Chicago Press, 1982), p. 26.

Différance refers to the "interval" that separates "the present from what it is not in order for the present to be itself" while also dividing "the present in and of itself, thereby also dividing, along with the present, everything that is thought on the basis of the present." This interval constitutes itself, dividing itself dynamically; it is "the becoming-space of time or the becoming-time of space (temporalization)." What has come to be called "deconstruction" does its work in the context of the traces of retentions and protentions left behind by *différance*, "which (is) (simultaneously) spacing (and) temporalization."[24]

Gilles Deleuze is another well-known example of a late modern philosopher who privileges alterity. His most extensive treatment of the theme occurs in *Difference and Repetition*. According to Deleuze the problem with most previous philosophical treatments of difference has been the tendency to confuse "the concept of difference" with a "merely conceptual difference." Simply inscribing difference in the "concept in general" does not provide a "singular Idea of difference," because it is already mediated through (conceptual) representation. For Deleuze this means that we should think of the Different not simply as one "category" among many, i.e., not as a universal concept that represents being. Rather, what he calls Disparity (or difference-in-itself, or pure difference) is the "condition of that which appears," that which makes representation (and categorization) possible as the identification of the similar. The sufficient reason of all phenomena is "the Unequal in itself, disparateness as it is determined and comprised in difference of intensity, in intensity as difference."[25]

Deleuze accepted Heidegger's point that difference is not mediated through the same, but argued further that: "There must be a differenciation of difference, an in-itself which is like a *differenciator*, a *Sich-unterscheidende*, by virtue of which the different is gathered all at once rather than represented on condition of a prior resemblance, identity, analogy or opposition" (p. 117). The Disparate, according to Deleuze, is the dark precursor that "differenciates" differences, operating constitutively "between" repetition; it is "the in-itself of difference of the differently different . . . the self-different which relates different

---

24. Derrida, *Margins of Philosophy,* p. 13.
25. Gilles Deleuze, *Difference and Repetition,* trans. P. Patton (New York: Columbia University Press, 1995), pp. 222-23.

to different by itself" (p. 119). His understanding of "repetition" need not detain us here; for our current purposes the more significant point is Deleuze's novel interpretation of Nietzsche's idea of the "eternal return" as an affirmation of difference.[26]

According to Deleuze it is not the Same that eternally returns (overcoming or negating all difference). On the contrary, the Same does not preexist the Different but is only that which is said *of* differents. Nevertheless, only as the Same comes to be can "differents resemble one another." It is always differences that "resemble" one another or are represented as opposed, analogous, or even "identical." In other words, one cannot get behind difference, but "difference is behind everything . . . behind difference there is nothing" (p. 57). For Deleuze, therefore, the Same is not that which returns but the "returning" of "that which returns — *in other words, of the Different*" (p. 300). Here Deleuze makes a conscious decision to reject the common reading of the world (in Western philosophy) that begins with the assumption "only that which resembles differs" and to embrace the claim that "only differences can resemble each other."[27]

It is important to conclude this brief overview of the renewed attention to difference in late modernity with the observation that many philosophers, even those who appreciate and emphasize alterity, have warned that some formulations in this shift have swung the pendulum too far. It is certainly possible to overemphasize, or to emphasize wrongly, the category of difference in such a way that the significance of the categories of sameness and identity is ignored. Paul Ricoeur, for example, has been critical of the way in which the other is privileged in Levinas. Ricoeur is concerned that the encounter with the other, the alterity of the face, not be allowed to overwhelm the need for the self to maintain its own ipseity.[28] Another example is Alain Badiou. On the one hand, he acknowledges in his book *Ethics* that "infinite alterity is quite simply what there is." Against the tide of some forms of deconstruction, on the other hand, Badiou insists that celebrating otherness is not by itself a sufficient basis for ethics (or philosophy as a whole).

26. Cf. Gilles Deleuze, *Nietzsche and Philosophy*, trans. H. Tomlinson (New York: Columbia University Press, 2006).

27. Cf. Gilles Deleuze, *The Logic of Sense*, trans. M. Lester (New York: Continuum, 2004), p. 300.

28. Paul Ricoeur, *Oneself as Another*, trans. K. Blamey (Chicago: University of Chicago Press, 1992).

We must also recognize the "advent of the Same," the "event of a truth" that is the "same for all."[29]

This ongoing debate about the role of the categories of difference and sameness in late modern philosophy is part of the contemporary context within which scholars in Christian ethics and Christology carry out their work. While this categorical alteration exposes the reliance of some traditional formulations (and practices) on an ancient and early modern valorizing of sameness, it has also provided a fresh opportunity to reattach moral discourse to Christology. As we will see, several of the most significant late modern proposals in our fields have allowed otherness to play a generative role in their conceptual (as well as practical, and even liturgical) engagement with and articulation of the way of Jesus Christ and the transformation of moral desire.

Tending to the Other(s) in Late Modern Ethics and Christology

Although the category of sameness has often dominated discourse in the Christian tradition, especially under the influence of Greek metaphysical and ethical intuitions, attention to difference has ever been present. The ancient Hebrew testimony to the holiness of Yhwh and Jesus' proclamation of a reign that is "not of this world" are examples of the centrality of the affirmation of the difference between God and creation in the biblical witness. Moreover, the call to care for those who have been alienated, to love not only one's neighbors but also one's enemies, is central to New Testament moral teaching. The emergence of feminist and liberationist voices within late modern theology has played a particularly significant role in reminding us that tending to oppressed "others" was central to the ministry of Jesus and ought to be a major focus of the Christian church.

In other words, scholars in Christian theology (and so in ethics and Christology), have a *responsibility to* tend more carefully to alterity in their formulations as we engage the categories of our contemporary context(s). However, in another sense Christian theology also shares *re-*

---

29. Alain Badiou, *Ethics,* trans. P. Hallward (London: Verso, 2001), pp. 25-27. However, for Badiou the Same is not linked to being but to becoming: "The Same, in effect, is not what is (i.e., the infinite multiplicity of differences) but what *comes to be.*"

sponsibility for the late modern shift toward an appreciation of the concept of difference. Our disciplines have participated in and contributed to this categorical alteration in a number of ways, but I will limit myself here to pointing out three major developments in late modern formulations of the doctrine of God. In the last century or so, we can trace a growing tendency among theologians to tend to the (infinite qualitative) difference between God and the world, to the differentiation within the life of the trinitarian persons, and to the constitutive differential relation of Eternity to time.

We can refer to these general developments as the retrieval of divine infinity, the revival of trinitarian doctrine, and the renewal of eschatological ontology. Here we are not dealing with a simple regurgitation of past formulations, but a recovery and refiguration of resources in the biblical tradition that have privileged the heuristic value of difference. For this reason, we might even speak of a theological *re*-turn to (and *re*-figuration of) the significance of alterity. These three (interwoven) trajectories are connected to a focus on difference (or otherness) in our theological subdisciplines. A full description of these trajectories is beyond the scope of this chapter,[30] but we can introduce them briefly and provide some examples in order to illustrate how tending to difference philosophically has played a role in these major late modern theological developments, which have both shaped and been shaped by ethics and Christology.

The first trajectory is the retrieval of divine *infinity,* or the recognition of the implications of the infinite difference between God and creation for finite cognition. As we saw above, thinkers like Kierkegaard and Levinas were particularly influential at the philosophical level of this shift. Many contemporary Christian ethicists have built on the work of these and other similar authors, but it is important to note that this trajectory from a theological point of view is a retrieval (and refiguring) of resources in the Christian tradition. The link between the late modern fascination with otherness and the apophatic tradition in Christianity has often been observed. In other words, the so-called "negative" way is a positive resource for acknowledging the experience of an infinite presence that conditions all human conceiving and differentiating.

---

30. These trajectories are outlined in more detail in my *Reforming the Doctrine of God* (Grand Rapids: Eerdmans, 2005).

Walter Lowe's *Theology and Difference: The Wound of Reason*[31] provides a clear illustration of and contribution to the linking of this aspect of the philosophical (re)turn to alterity to ethics. Lowe's overall
goal is to show the connection between what he calls "an analogy of
difference" apparent in the theology of Karl Barth and the deconstruc-
tive attention to *différance* in Jacques Derrida. Perhaps his most important contribution for the purposes of our project, however, is pointing
to resources in the work of Kant, especially in his moral philosophy.
Lowe outlines this claim by treating the second critique under the
heading "the otherness of the ethical," attempting to show that for
Kant values are irreducibly heterogeneous.

For Lowe, ethics is not grounded or secured by the operation of
reason that works up a "chain of Being." It is a problem — an imperative — that always confronts us as other, qualitatively infinite other, as
Kierkegaard (and Barth) would later say. In his final chapter, "The
Ethics of Otherness," Lowe emphasizes that this "strong" difference is
not simply an opposition (among many), but a qualitative difference
between finite and infinite that fosters rather than negates the richness
of finite difference(s). He is critical of deconstructionists like Mark C.
Taylor whose approach ends in a dissolution of the subject, structure,
and God. Lowe observes that ironically this move presupposes a fundamental sameness between God and the world (both are susceptible to
deconstruction). Although Lowe's work here does not engage the specific concerns of Christology, it does open up space for new forms of
christological imagination that do not begin with a privileging of
sameness.

The revival of trinitarian doctrine is a second trajectory that illustrates a growing tendency to rely more heavily on the concept of
differentiation, as in some sense constitutive of rather than contradic-
tory to the unity of God. The most important trinitarian proposals in
the last century have little interest in defending abstract language
about a three-in-one substance. They have drawn attention to the concrete experience of a lively divine presence that calls creatures to share
in a peacefully differentiated life of loving and being loved. As long as
trinitarian doctrine was dominated by the demand that one start with
the categories of substance and sameness, it made very little sense, re-

---

31. Walter Lowe, *Theology and Difference: The Wound of Reason* (Bloomington: Indiana University Press, 1993).

quiring a late-arriving appeal to "mystery." But allowing categories of relationality and difference a constitutive and regulative role in our interpretation can provide an understanding of God that can help us make sense of our experience of ourselves and others in the world. This does not mean that the language of difference should be uncritically applied to God, in the way sameness sometimes has been, which would go against the first trajectory, but that linguistic tending to difference and otherness has opened up new ways to imagine the trinitarian relationality of God as the ground of human differentiation and identification.

Oliver Davies's *A Theology of Compassion: Metaphysics of Difference and the Renewal of Tradition* illustrates this trajectory. He engages a variety of late modern philosophers, including many of the usual suspects treated in the preceding section, proposing a relational (trinitarian) ontology of compassion that links being and love. For Davies, compassion is "the recognition of the otherness of the other, as an otherness which stands beyond our own world, beyond our own constructions of otherness even."[32] Rather than give up wholly on metaphysics, he wants to speak about being as the "medium of the relation between self and other" (p. 138). On this model, compassion stands at the heart of empirical reality, as the encounter with the presence of the real, personal other.

When Davies turns to an explicit treatment of the doctrine of the Trinity, he is careful to affirm the formula *mia ousia — treis hypostaseis*. However, he notes that "the radical mystery of the Christian Trinity comes into view in a particular way when we set beside it the primary ontological formula [i.e., being as the medium of relation between self and other, which] . . . preserves the distinctness of the self and other and guarantees their relation" (p. 258). Recognizing the inadequacy of all human language for God, Davies nevertheless suggests that trading ontotheological and "spatial" imagery for the language of "infinite relationality" or "infinity of relation" opens up opportunities for reflection that are more capable of affirming the mystery of the difference within the unity of the triune persons, as well as "the constitution of personhood through the dialectical embrace of the other" (p. 266).

A third trajectory that can be traced in late modern theology is the

---

32. Oliver Davies, *A Theology of Compassion: Metaphysics of Difference and the Renewal of Tradition* (Grand Rapids: Eerdmans, 2001), p. 17.

renewal of eschatological ontology, which also impacts both Christology and ethics. In addition to Infinity and Trinity, recent theology has also paid more attention to divine Futurity, to the constitutive differentiating presence of the eschatological advent of Eternity in relation to the creaturely experience of time. Each of our subdisciplines is shaped by our understanding of the arrival of the reign of divine peace, which is already among us and yet is to come. In the case of ethics, this has meant focusing on how temporal hope is constituted by the advent of God. One of the earliest to link ethics and eschatology was Helmut Thielicke, for whom "theological ethics is eschatological or it is nothing."[33] Not surprisingly, however, it has been primarily systematic theologians who have explored the metaphysical implications of eschatology.

One of the most well-known examples of this trajectory, who also explicitly engages the question of otherness and difference, linking Christology to ethics, is Jürgen Moltmann. For him the paradigm of transcendence is not unchangeable being, but the future. Not just "the future" as one mode of time, however, but the coming and arrival of God that calls (in)to life as it comes to meet (and so creates) human becoming. Temporality in all its modes is constituted by this arrival of Eternity. However, Eternity here is not defined over against time, as one side of the same reality (composed of changeable and unchangeable being). If we understand Eternity not as the "mere negation of temporality" but as the "fullness of creative life — then it is possible to conceive an opening for time in eternity."[34]

In *Experiences in Theology*, the final of his systematic "contributions" to Christian theology, Moltmann returns to this theme, which had already guided his first contribution *(Theology of Hope)*. The promise *(pro-missio)* of God is "an advance-sending into the present of what is to come, which awakens hope by bringing God's future into the present."[35] However, Moltmann's interest in alterity is more explicit in *Experiences,* where he spells out the hermeneutics of hope in terms of an

33. Helmut Thielecke, *Theological Ethics,* vol. 1, ed. William H. Lazareth (Grand Rapids: Eerdmans, 1966), p. 47. Ethics "lives under the law of the 'not yet' but within the peace of the 'I am coming soon' (Rev. 22:20)." Cf. Oliver O'Donovan's linking of resurrection and ethics in *Resurrection and the Moral Order* (Grand Rapids: Eerdmans, 1994).

34. Jürgen Moltmann, *The Coming of God,* trans. M. Kohl (Minneapolis: Fortress Press, 1996), p. 281.

35. Jürgen Moltmann, *Experiences in Theology,* trans. M. Kohl (Minneapolis: Augsburg Press, 2000), p. 55.

encounter with the other, stressing the category of difference. "It is in our encounter with the difference of others that we experience the character of our own selves" (p. 171). God is known in the different, and so the major constructive part of this book provides an introduction to black theology for whites, liberation theology for the first world, minjung theology for the ruling classes, and feminist theology for men. Pushing the reader to come to perceive something new, Moltmann observes how "cognition of the same and the similar leads to the recognition of what we already know, and to endorsement, whereas knowledge of what is different and alien evokes pain over the alteration in our own selves" (p. 334).

Tending to the other(s) in late modern theology has had an influence not only on the trajectories that have shaped Christian ethics in these ways, but also on *formal* and *material* developments in the major doctrines of Christology. Formally, we find a growing willingness to transgress the boundaries between the classical loci in Christology, especially incarnation and atonement. The early modern dichotomy between substance and function led to a hardening of the well-known distinction between the person and the work of Christ, between the identity (sameness) of the incarnate Son and his agency (function) in relation to others. Moreover, the doctrine of the *parousia,* which was often excluded from Christology proper and exiled to the end of dogmatic presentations, has been increasingly brought back into the heart of the doctrine. So the (re)turn to alterity has contributed to a more holistic, integrated presentation of faith in and fidelity to the way of Jesus Christ.

We can also see that attending to the category of difference has also shaped several of the influential *material* christological proposals of the late twentieth century. I will give one example of each of these classical loci (incarnation, atonement, *parousia*) in turn. Wolfhart Pannenberg, no fan of "postmodernity," argued in his *Jesus — God and Man* for a refiguring of Logos Christology. He saw the latter as aiming to maintain the distinction within the unity of Jesus and God, but proposes the use of the concept of revelation instead of Logos, which in its patristic formulations relied too heavily on a two-natures (substance) doctrine of the *incarnation.* As the revelation of God, Jesus' identity with the eternal Son of God is "dialectical."[36] This requires an under-

---

36. W. Pannenberg, *Jesus — God and Man,* 2nd ed., trans. L. Wilkins and D. Priebe (Minneapolis: Fortress Press, 1977), p. 342.

standing of human personhood as inherently differentiated and open to the other. On this model, increasing differentiation "is a condition for increasingly intensive community and unity" (p. 348). In his *Systematic Theology,* Pannenberg argues that the self-distinction of Jesus from the Father is the inner basis for his divine sonship. Jesus is the incarnate Son only in his self-distinction from the Father by subordination to his royal rule; this *differentiation* is vindicated and confirmed by the resurrection, which reveals the self-actualization of the trinitarian God in the world.[37]

Atonement theory has also been affected by attention to difference. For example, we can trace a shift from an early modern focus on the *ordo salutis,* the causal order of the states of the individual, to an emphasis on salvation as a *salutary ordering* of communities, a real dynamic transformation of the way we live with others.[38] One of the most significant factors in this shift has been the engagement of Western theology with the Eastern idea of salvation as *theosis* or deification. Freed from the categories of sameness and substance, participating in the divine (trinitarian) nature can be construed and experienced not as a fusion of substances but as a sharing in communion. In his *Communion and Otherness,* Eastern Orthodox theologian John Zizioulas argued that the Cappadocians made otherness a primary ontological category. He pointed out that Maximus the Confessor, for example, considered otherness as *constitutive* of the whole universe. This ontology of otherness allows an understanding of union with God as communion in which the otherness of the other "does not dissolve in sameness" because persons desiring union are defined in their mode of being in relation to others.[39]

The doctrine of the *parousia* of Jesus Christ (and the consummation of the world) has also been materially impacted by the turn to alterity. As might be expected, this is related to the renewal of eschatological ontology, in which the temporal being of creation is understood as constituted by the arrival of divine Eternity. This is well illustrated

37. W. Pannenberg, *Systematic Theology,* vol. 2, trans. G. Bromiley (Grand Rapids: Eerdmans, 1994), chap. 10.

38. For a treatment of this shift in soteriology, cf. F. LeRon Shults and Steven J. Sandage, *The Faces of Forgiveness: Searching for Wholeness and Salvation* (Grand Rapids: Baker Academic, 2003), pp. 148-61.

39. J. Zizioulas, *Communion and Otherness,* ed. P. McPartlan (London: T. & T. Clark, 2006), pp. 31, 34, 54.

in the work of Eberhard Jüngel. He, too, has insisted that the revelation of God in the resurrection of the Crucified discloses differentiation in and as God, both differentiation of the trinitarian persons and the differentiation of God from nothingness, which he spelled out in terms of an "analogy of advent." Moreover, for Jüngel, the advent of God — mediated through the Spirit of Christ — is understood as the truly infinite eschatological difference that constitutes the world by making it new. Christian hope is created and upheld by an "eschatological outdistancing," by the divine address which provides an experience of "a newness which makes the entire world old." God's "coming" to the creation *makes* the world relationship new.[40]

Finally, tending to the Other and the other(s) in late modern theology has also contributed to the interdisciplinary integration of the sometimes alienated fields of Christology and ethics. I will limit myself to one important example, Karl Barth. Whether or not one agrees with Barth's methodological or material decisions, he illustrates well the connection between attending to alterity and the integral linking of ethics and Christology. In his early *Römerbrief*, Barth affirmed Kierkegaard's "infinite qualitative difference" as methodologically significant for his approach. The material implications for ethics were spelled out in several places; for Barth, the "ethical problem" appears precisely where the existence of "others" itself emerges as a problem. Fellowship in "one body" requires "an encountering of the OTHER in the full existentiality of his utter OTHERNESS."[41]

In his posthumously published lectures on *Ethics* (given between 1928 and 1930), Barth argued for an approach to "theological ethics" guided by and focused on the "Word of God." Already at this early stage, he proposed a treatment of ethical themes structured by the command of God the Creator, God the Reconciler, and God the Redeemer.[42] These three loci later structured the outline of his *Church Dogmatics*. In *CD* I/2 (§22.3), he insisted that dogmatics, insofar as it deals with the Word of God (which is first and foremost Jesus Christ), has to be ethics as well. This is the ground of his decision for a unified

40. E. Jüngel, *God as the Mystery of the World*, trans. D. Guder (Grand Rapids: Eerdmans, 1983), pp. 174, 224, 285, 329.

41. Karl Barth, *Epistle to the Romans*, trans. E. Hoskyns (Oxford: Oxford University Press, 1968), pp. 10, 443.

42. Karl Barth, *Ethics*, trans. G. Bromiley (New York: Seabury Press, 1981), pp. 52, 61.

treatment of the disciplines, which continues throughout the other volumes. What is important in connection to our project is that Barth's interpretation of Jesus Christ and his understanding of the command of the triune God are wrapped up within his insistence on God as "wholly other." It is not without reason that so many of the examples above, and several of the proposals in the current book, engage Barth so heavily.

The main point of this section has been to show that these significant developments in Christology and ethics are connected to a philosophical shift toward tending to difference in late modernity. Attending to this shift will become increasingly crucial in the ongoing dialogue. My purpose has not been to commend this or that particular example, but to suggest that what they hold in common is a fresh attention to alterity, which has opened up conceptual space for creative work within each discipline as well as creative reciprocal engagement and mutuality between the fields.

As we have seen, simply reversing the privileging of sameness over difference is problematic for many reasons, not only philosophically but also theologically and ethically. If everything is dissolved into otherness, there is no basis for similarity; the latter is in some sense required to make sense of the call to become *like* Christ. However, we have also seen how the fresh attention to and use of the category of difference have provided new opportunities for Christology and ethics. By way of summary and conclusion, let me point briefly to several ways in which continuing to tend to otherness within and among our disciplines can facilitate the dialogue and support our attempts to move toward appropriately differentiated integration.

- First, this exercise reminds us of the importance of humbly acknowledging the role of philosophical categories in our ongoing theological reconstruction.
- Second, it can help us better understand the broader theological trajectories of late modernity, especially those streams within which many of the most significant developments in Christology and ethics have been forged.
- Third, continued attention to the categories of difference and relationality can facilitate the integration of the traditional loci of Christology, which tended to be separated when theologians relied primarily on the categories of sameness and substance.

- Fourth, one of the overarching goals of this book — bringing Christology and ethics into a more explicitly mutual relationship — can be facilitated by paying attention to the way in which we treat (and name) the "other" in our ongoing conversations.
- Fifth, reflecting on the role of alterity in our theological and ethical discourse can also open up new opportunities for engaging late modern voices outside the Christian tradition.
- Sixth, the turn to alterity can provide resources for articulating key concepts in our fields such as reciprocity and community, a concern shared by all of our contributors.
- Finally, developing the courage to confront our own tendency to alienate "others" who terrify us is an important moment within the ongoing transformation of our own moral desire.

Epilogue

Brent Waters

This collection of essays does not offer the definitive guide for charting, much less explicating, the relation between Christology and ethics, nor was it intended to be such a map. Rather, collectively these essays identify some landmarks along an expansive horizon that may suggest some areas for future exploration. Consequently, the preceding chapters mark a modest step in promoting critical and constructive inquiry into the relation between Christology and ethics, for even a cursory reading of these essays discloses a vast terrain to be mapped and developed. Future forays into this terrain will prove fruitless if, for example, Christology is isolated from a broader range of doctrines, and thereby from how it should inform Christian moral discourse and practice.

In this respect, this diverse collection of authors shared the common task of moving theological and moral deliberation beyond the simple attempt of emulating Jesus' life and teaching. They share the tacit recognition that Jesus is more than an exemplary figure, and that the moral significance of Jesus Christ is derived from a framework of theological or dogmatic formulations in general, and christological claims in particular. As indicated above, the task at hand is to refine the role of Christology within a broader range of doctrines, and how christological themes in turn inform Christian moral discourse and practice. How, for instance, are such christological themes as incarnation and atonement related to such doctrines as creation, Trinity, and eschatology, and how in turn does such a Christology shape Christian discourse and action on such questions as moral ontology, virtue, and love of neighbor? Furthermore, in pursuing such inquiry and explication, the authors again shared the tacit recognition that systematic or dogmatic theology, and ethics or moral theology, are not discrete and divisible disciplines. Rather, they are mutually informing and reinforcing. The challenge is to find appropriate modes of thought and vocabulary that strengthen this bond between Christology and ethics, thereby to play a significant role in forming the vision and deeds of the Christian moral life.

The essays also reflect a number of tensions among the authors on how these tasks should be undertaken. These tensions, however, offer potentially the most promising avenues for future inquiry, for the ensuing arguments may help to clarify the principal issues at stake, and what is required for their resolution. An exhaustive survey would require revisiting the preceding chapters, a repetitive and painstaking process that would presumably not be welcomed by the reader. Noting briefly three instances will suffice to illustrate some of these tensions.

First, what is the proper starting point and end of theological inquiry and doctrinal explication? All of the essays, either implicitly or explicitly, assume that theological inquiry and exposition begin in the present. (Where else could they begin?) There is, however, a fundamental division regarding how the present should be related to past inquiries and expositions, and how in turn this relationship shapes a theological and moral orientation toward the future. To generalize: on the one hand, tradition, both in terms of doctrine and practice, is seen as a resource to be critically reinterpreted and appropriated in light of contemporary circumstances and purposes, resulting in a progressivist eschatology. The kingdom of God, or other suitable metaphor, is both an emergent goal and consequence of prior thought and action. On the other hand, tradition, especially Scripture and the creeds, is seen as a repository of revealed truth that should serve to shape the content and future orientation of subsequent doctrinal formulations and moral practice. The future has already been disclosed in the destiny of Jesus Christ, and the task of theology is to offer normative and teleological accounts that align Christian thought and action with this end. In short, there is a disagreement on how Christian doctrine and practice should engage late modern historicism. Is history an artifact of the human will, or is it the providential unfolding of created order over time? Addressing this question in greater detail could, perhaps, clarify what is at stake in this division, thereby forcing a more explicit discussion of the various eschatologies that are represented in the essays, and how these eschatologies inspire differing accounts of social and political ordering.

Second, what are the principal and proper contexts of moral formation and action? Again, there is agreement among the authors that theological formulations and moral action do not occur in a vacuum. As the essays make clear, there are various evolutionary, historical, ecclesial, social, and political contexts that both promote and delimit theological exposition and the performance of moral acts and deeds. Moreover, these contexts are not static but subject to changing circumstances and interpretations over time. The formation, normative content, and practice of various virtues, for instance, are subject to cultural variation, as are the enactment and enforcement of civil laws, and what constitutes freedom and its proper exercise within political communities. Consequently, there is a corresponding variation of what constitutes the proper content and execution of social and political practices entailing justice, judgment, and forgiveness.

Here too the essays reflect some underlying tensions, and again to generalize: on the one hand, the contexts are not so much givens as constructs that promote fluid and highly revisable accounts of doctrine and practice. Consequently, the contextual limits are themselves subject to reconstruction in light of new developments, for instance, in science and technology. On the other hand, the contexts are seen as givens that delimit and guide theological discourse and moral action. Although interpretations of these contexts are subject to revision, they nonetheless serve as signposts that simultaneously limit and guide inquiry along a teleological path. In brief, what is at stake in this disagreement is whether or not there is a respective "nature" to these various contexts that imposes limits upon and directs theological inquiry and moral discourse. How this issue is addressed goes a long way in shaping subsequent accounts of moral, social, and political ordering. More work is needed to gain a precise understanding of what is at stake in this division, and how it might be bridged or at least gain greater clarity about the tensions it creates for systematic and moral theology in general, and Christology and ethics in particular.

This conversation, however, should not be undertaken in isolation from the final, and closely related, tension, namely: What is the human creature that is being formed and acts within these contexts? Each of the essays incorporates an implicit theological anthropology in developing their subsequent arguments. Greater attention needs to be directed toward clarifying what these anthropological assumptions entail, particularly in light of Christology and its implications for ethics.

In this instance, the issue in question is not a fundamental divide but a series of questions that cut across the essays in varying directions. For example: the various formative contexts do not create level playing fields in respect to individuals and communities. Responses to these contexts necessarily produce people of differing propensities, abilities, and capabilities; in other words, evolution — in both its natural and cultural manifestations — does not bequeath equality to each subsequent generation.

This condition is especially problematic in regard to the christological claim that in Christ there is a fundamental equality. Yet if some individuals, as the natural and social sciences suggest, have an inherent propensity toward virtue while others are drawn toward vice, to what extent, if at all, is a fundamental reformulation of such traditional doctrines as sin, grace, forgiveness, and sanctification required? More broadly, can civil communities conduct their affairs in the absence of normative hierarchies or functional inequalities? The problem becomes more acute in respect to the alterity that late modernity wishes to welcome. To what extent can difference be celebrated and embraced, for is not at least some residue of similarity required to undertake the cooperative tasks of ordering the civil community? Addressing this issue is, of course, revisiting the old philosophical and theological question of the relationship between the one and the many, albeit in a new set of circumstances. Should Christians take on the late modern venture of making the many one, however tentative and temporary such unions might be? If so, how do they avoid negating the particularities of the many that they wish to affirm? Or is the task at hand to affirm the Augustinian adage — out of the one many; to affirm that there is an underlying unity among all humans as part of a created order? If so, how should human affairs be ordered that our unity might be redeemed and restored? How do the many become one again without negating the particularity of the other in the process? In short, formulating a more explicit theological anthropology is a crucial and inescapable task if an ethic that is christologically informed is to be propounded.

As noted above, this collection of essays was never intended to offer a definitive word on the relation between Christology and ethics. Rather, the intent is to initiate inquiry and conversation. It is hoped that the authors will continue what they have started with these contributions through subsequent work, and perhaps more importantly, this book will also serve as an invitation to others to join the conversation.

Contributors

JAN-OLAV HENRIKSEN is Professor of Philosophy and Religion at the Norwegian Lutheran School of Theology in Oslo, Norway.

LOIS MALCOLM is Associate Professor of Systematic Theology at Luther Seminary in St. Paul, Minnesota.

F. LERON SHULTS is Professor of Theology and Philosophy in the Institute for Religion, Philosophy, and History at the University of Agder in Kristiansand, Norway.

KATHRYN TANNER is the Dorothy Grant Maclear Professor of Theology at the University of Chicago Divinity School.

J. WENTZEL VAN HUYSSTEEN is the James I. McCord Professor of Theology and Science at Princeton Theological Seminary.

BERND WANNENWETSCH is University Lecturer in Ethics at Harris Manchester College at Oxford University.

BRENT WATERS is Jerre and Mary Joy Stead Professor of Christian Social Ethics and Director of the Stead Center for Ethics and Values at Garrett-Evangelical Theological Seminary.

JOHN WEBSTER is Professor of Systematic Theology at King's College, University of Aberdeen, Scotland.

Index of Subjects and Names

Index of Scripture References

Index of Scripture References